LOST & FOUND

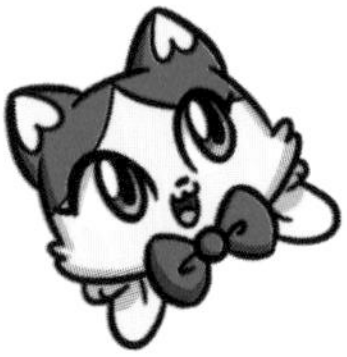

For Baba, Mama, Shawn, my teachers, and my local librarians

Lost & Found is based on the author's true story, though certain characters and places have been modified.

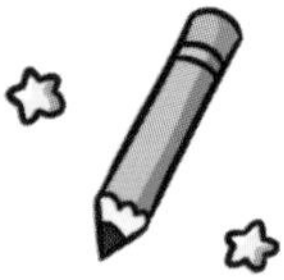

union square kids

NEW YORK

UNION SQUARE KIDS and the distinctive Union Square Kids logo are trademarks of Union Square & Co., LLC.

Union Square & Co., LLC, is a subsidiary of Sterling Publishing Co., Inc.

ISBN 978-1-4549-4547-5 (hardcover)
ISBN 978-1-4549-5264-0 (paperback)
ISBN 978-1-4549-4548-2 (e-book)

Library of Congress Cataloging-in-Publication Data

Names: Yu, Mei (Graphic novelist), author, artist.
Title: Lost & found : a memoir / story and art by Mei Yu.
Other titles: Lost and found
Description: New York : Union Square Kids, 2024. | Audience: Ages 6 to 8 | Audience: Grades 2-3 | Summary: "A little girl moves with her family from China to Canada and must find a way to learn English in order to make friends"-- Provided by publisher.
Identifiers: LCCN 2023016962 (print) | LCCN 2023016963 (ebook) | ISBN 9781454945475 (hardcover) | ISBN 9781454952640 (trade paperback) | ISBN 9781454945482 (epub)
Subjects: LCSH: Cartoonists--Canada--Biography--Comic books, strips, etc. | Immigrants--Canada--Biography--Comic books, strips, etc. | Chinese--Canada--Biography--Comic books, strips, etc. | School children--Canada--Biography--Comic books, strips, etc. | LCGFT: Autobiographical comics. | Graphic novels.
Classification: LCC PN6733.M45 Z46 2024 (print) | LCC PN6733.M45 (ebook) | DDC 741.5/971 [B]--dc23/eng/20230613
LC record available at https://lccn.loc.gov/2023016962
LC ebook record available at https://lccn.loc.gov/2023016963

For information about custom editions, special sales, and premium purchases, please contact specialsales@unionsquareandco.com.

Printed in Malaysia

Lot #:
2 4 6 8 10 9 7 5 3 1

12/23

unionsquareandco.com

Cover and interior design by Liam Donnelly

The art is 100 percent hand-drawn by Mei Yu. No A.I. was used in the making of this book.

LOST & FOUND

☹ Based on a True Story ☺

Mei Yu

union
square
kids

NEW YORK

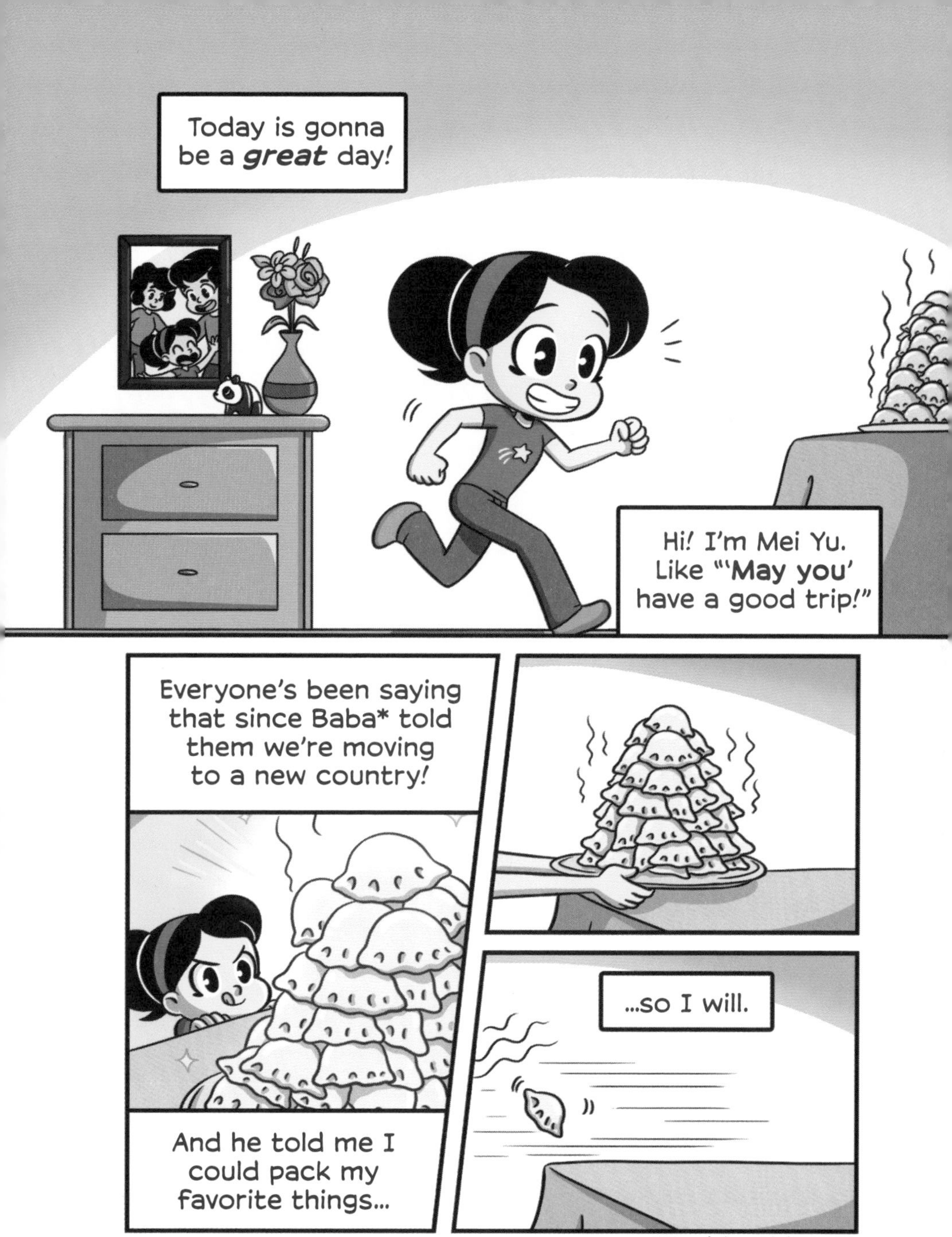
Today is gonna be a *great* day!
Hi! I'm Mei Yu. Like "'**May you**' have a good trip!"
Everyone's been saying that since Baba* told them we're moving to a new country!
And he told me I could pack my favorite things...
...so I will.

*Dad in Chinese

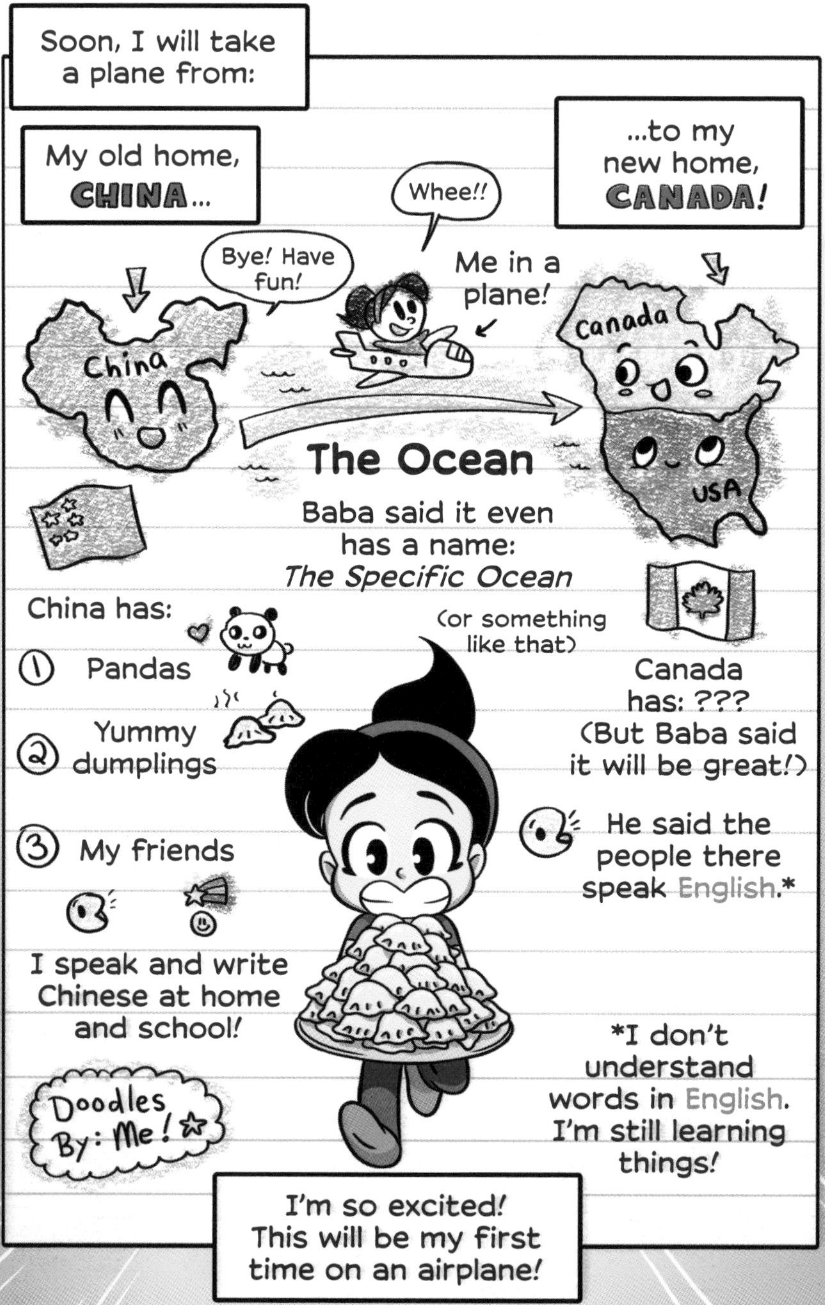

Soon, I will take a plane from:
My old home, CHINA...
...to my new home, CANADA!
Whee!!
Bye! Have fun!
Me in a plane!
China
Canada
USA
The Ocean
Baba said it even has a name: *The Specific Ocean*
(or something like that)
China has:
1 Pandas
2 Yummy dumplings
3 My friends
Canada has: ???
(But Baba said it will be great!)
He said the people there speak English.*
I speak and write Chinese at home and school!
Doodles By: Me!
*I don't understand words in English. I'm still learning things!
I'm so excited! This will be my first time on an airplane!

Green text = Words Mei doesn't understand
Black text = Words Mei understands

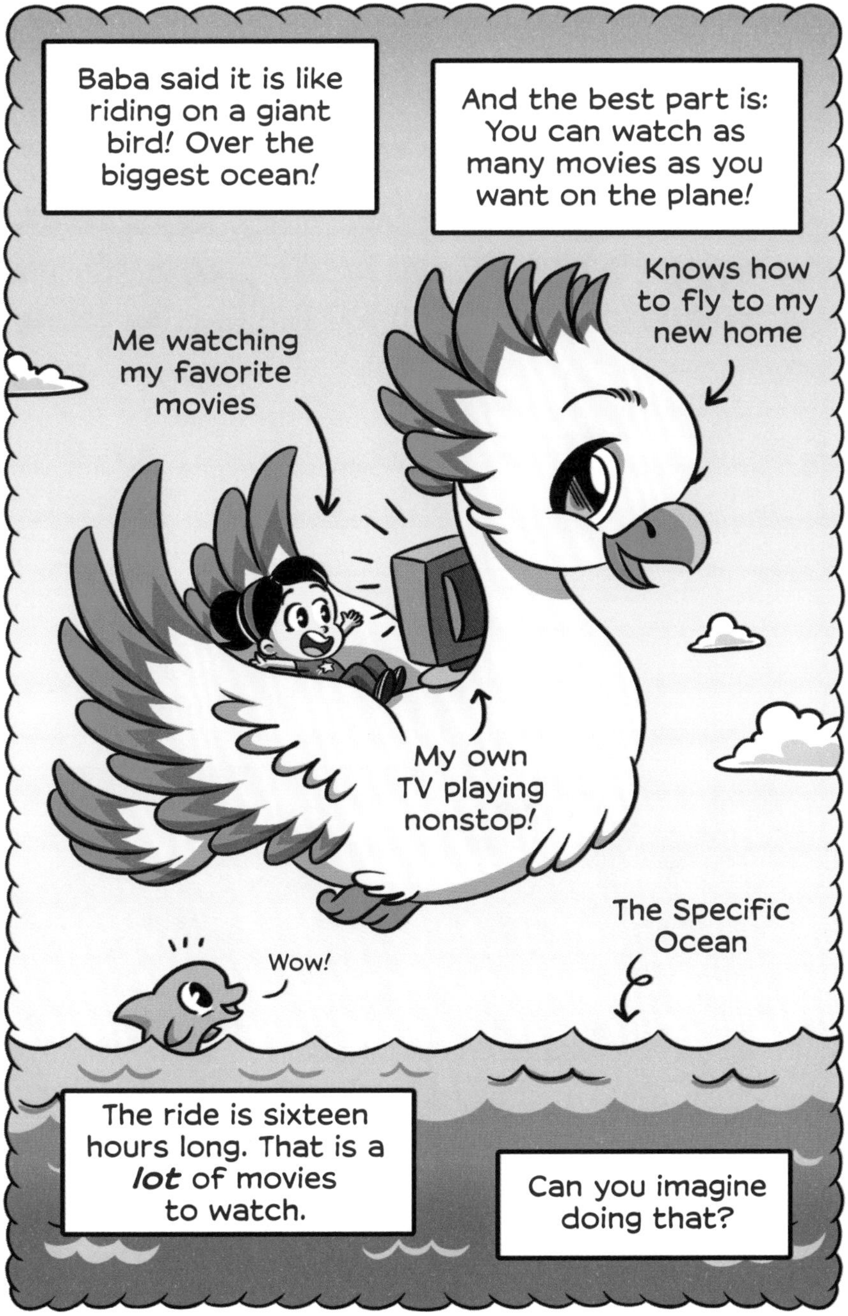

Baba said it is like riding on a giant bird! Over the biggest ocean!
And the best part is: You can watch as many movies as you want on the plane!
Me watching my favorite movies
Knows how to fly to my new home
My own TV playing nonstop!
The Specific Ocean
Wow!
The ride is sixteen hours long. That is a *lot* of movies to watch.
Can you imagine doing that?

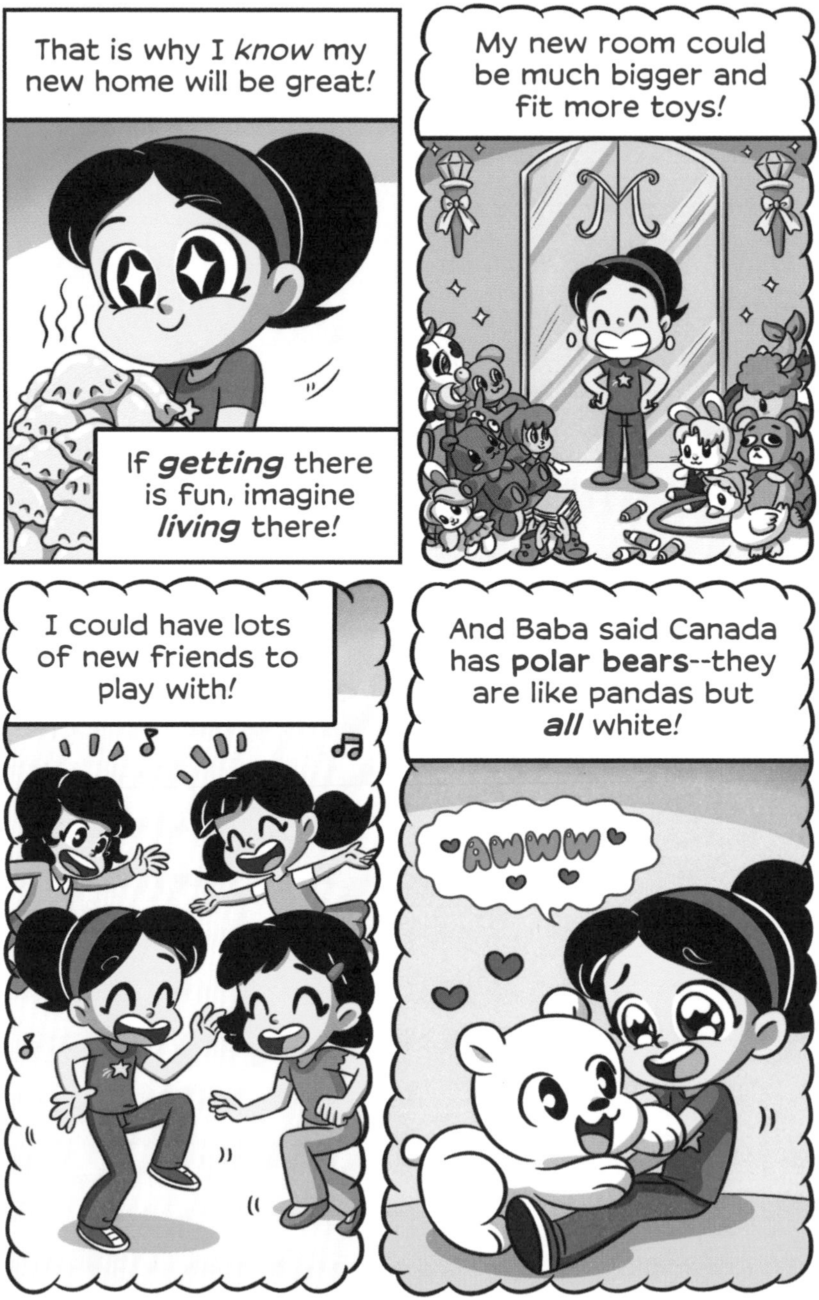
That is why I *know* my new home will be great!
If ***getting*** there is fun, imagine ***living*** there!
My new room could be much bigger and fit more toys!
I could have lots of new friends to play with!
And Baba said Canada has **polar bears**--they are like pandas but ***all*** white!
AWWW

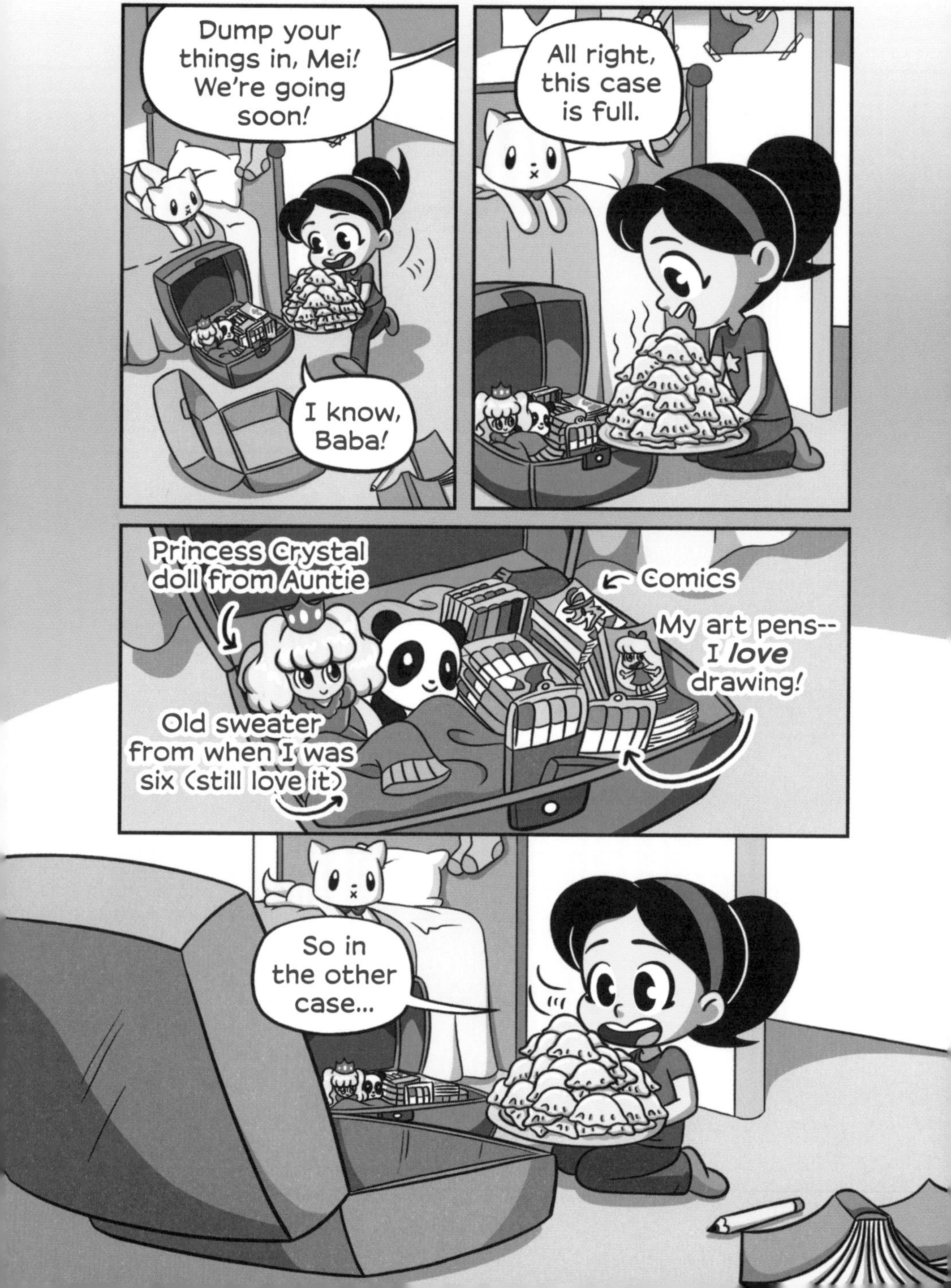

Dump your things in, Mei! We're going soon!
I know, Baba!
All right, this case is full.
Princess Crystal doll from Auntie
Comics
My art pens-- I *love* drawing!
Old sweater from when I was six (still love it)
So in the other case...

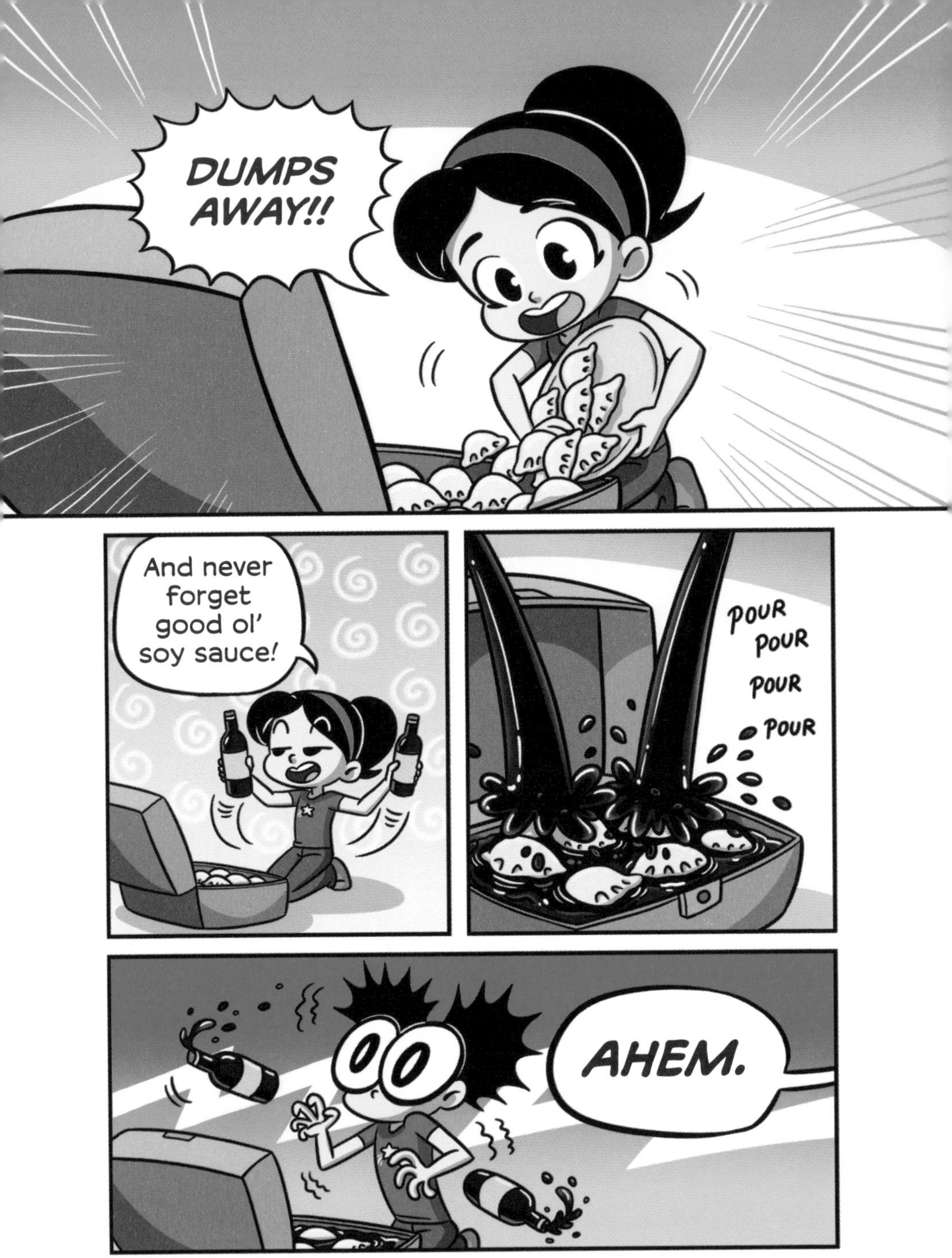
DUMPS AWAY!!
And never forget good ol' soy sauce!
POUR POUR POUR POUR
AHEM.

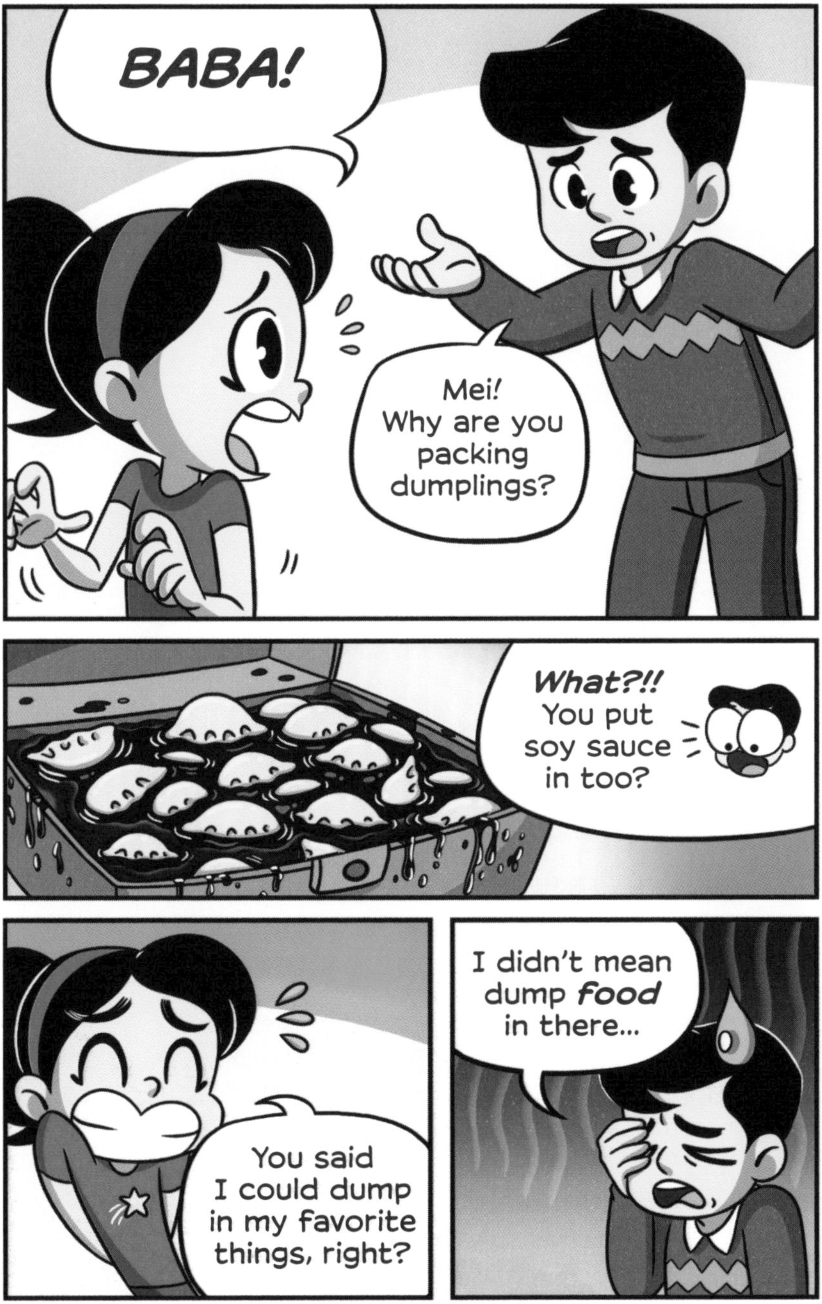
BABA!
Mei! Why are you packing dumplings?
What?!! You put soy sauce in too?
You said I could dump in my favorite things, right?
I didn't mean dump *food* in there...

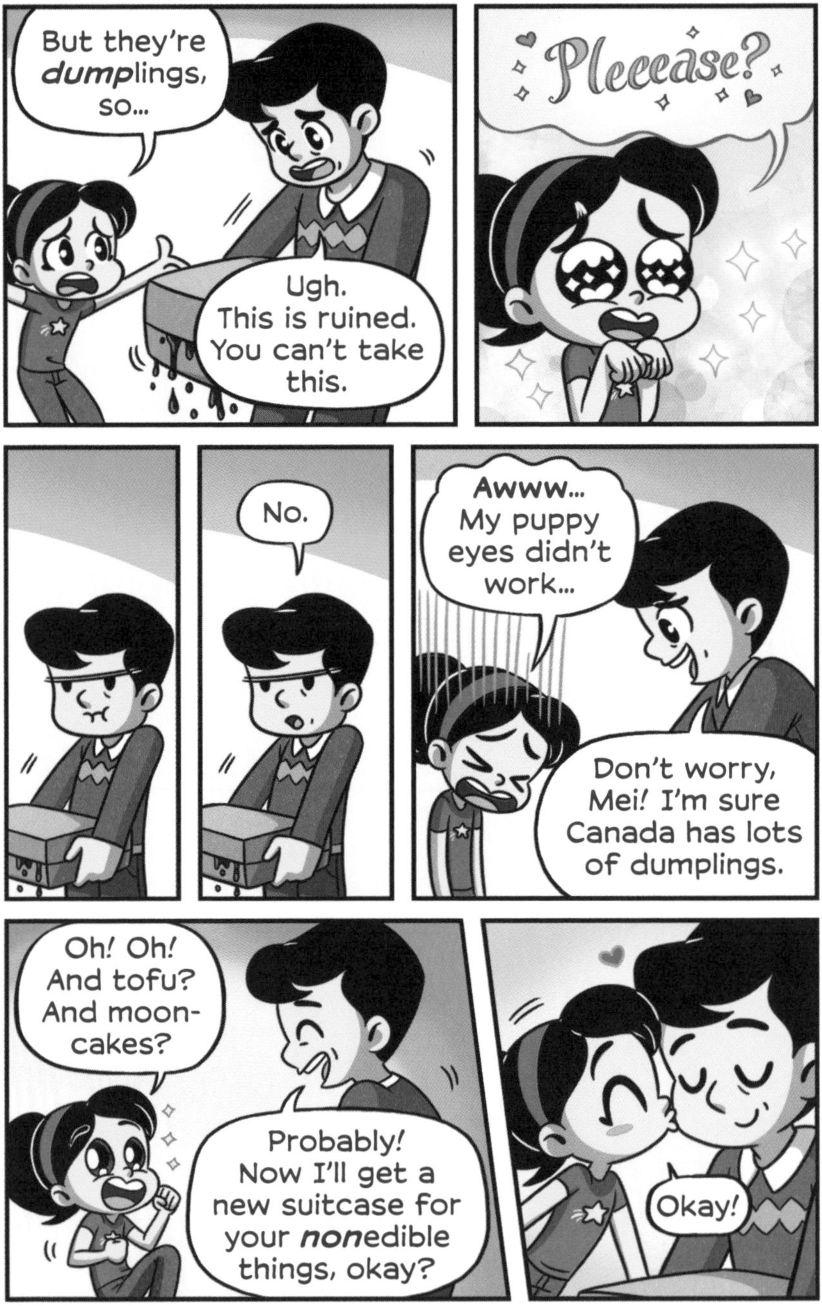
But they're ***dump***lings, so...
Ugh. This is ruined. You can't take this.
Pleeease?
No.
Awww... My puppy eyes didn't work...
Don't worry, Mei! I'm sure Canada has lots of dumplings.
Oh! Oh! And tofu? And moon-cakes?
Probably! Now I'll get a new suitcase for your ***non***edible things, okay?
Okay!

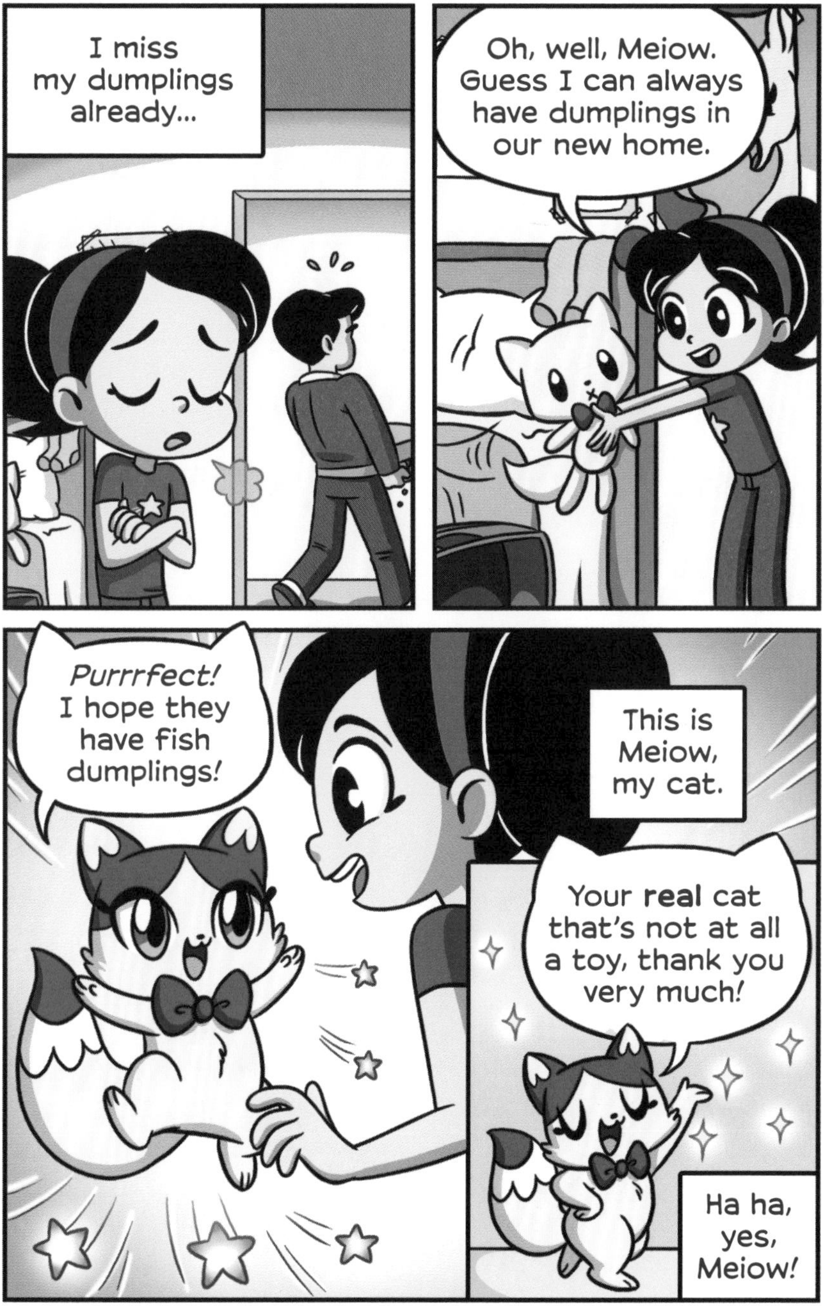
I miss my dumplings already...
Oh, well, Meiow. Guess I can always have dumplings in our new home.
Purrrfect! I hope they have fish dumplings!
This is Meiow, my cat.
Your **real** cat that's not at all a toy, thank you very much!
Ha ha, yes, Meiow!

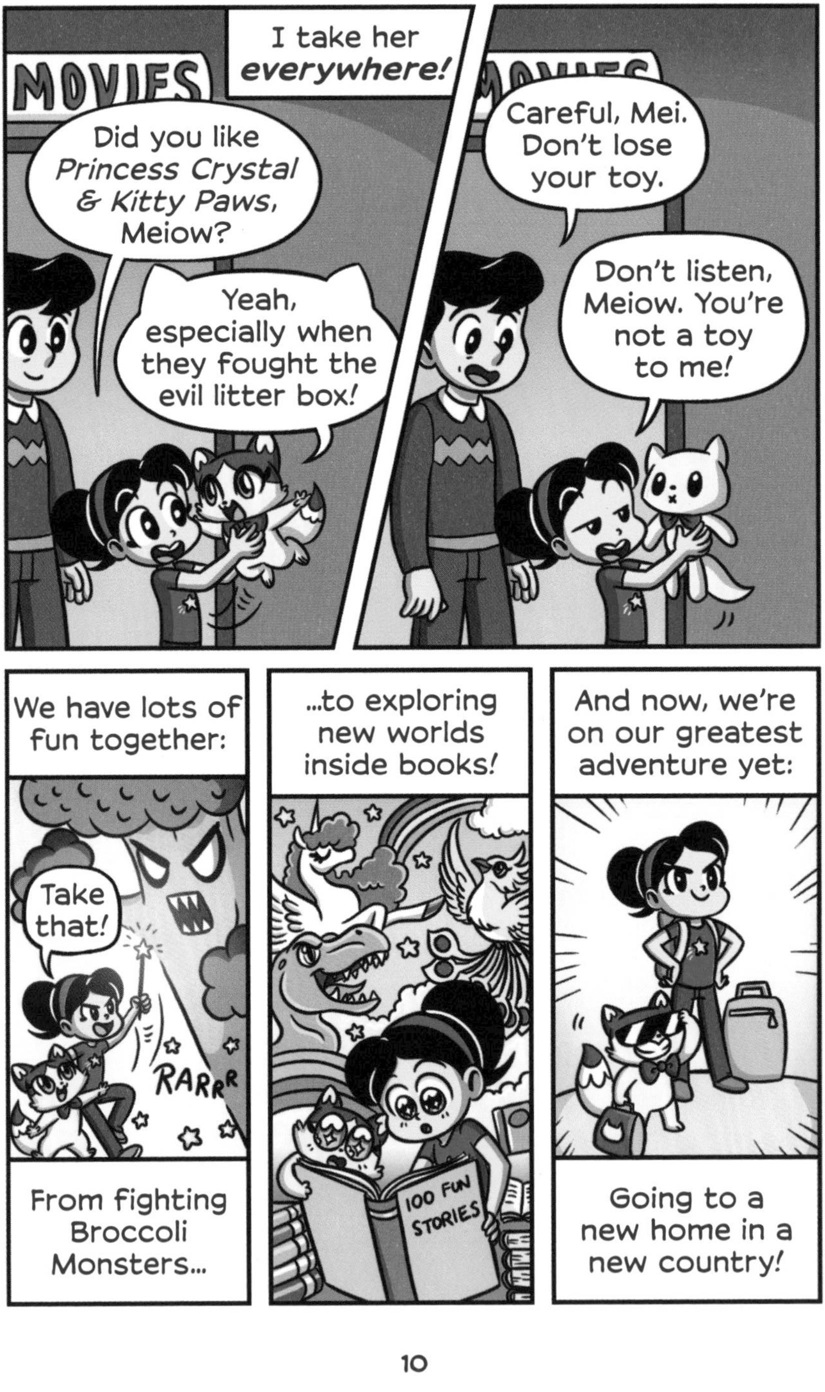
MOVIES
I take her *everywhere!*
Did you like *Princess Crystal & Kitty Paws*, Meiow?
Yeah, especially when they fought the evil litter box!
Careful, Mei. Don't lose your toy.
Don't listen, Meiow. You're not a toy to me!
We have lots of fun together:
Take that!
RARRR
From fighting Broccoli Monsters...
...to exploring new worlds inside books!
100 FUN STORIES
And now, we're on our greatest adventure yet:
Going to a new home in a new country!

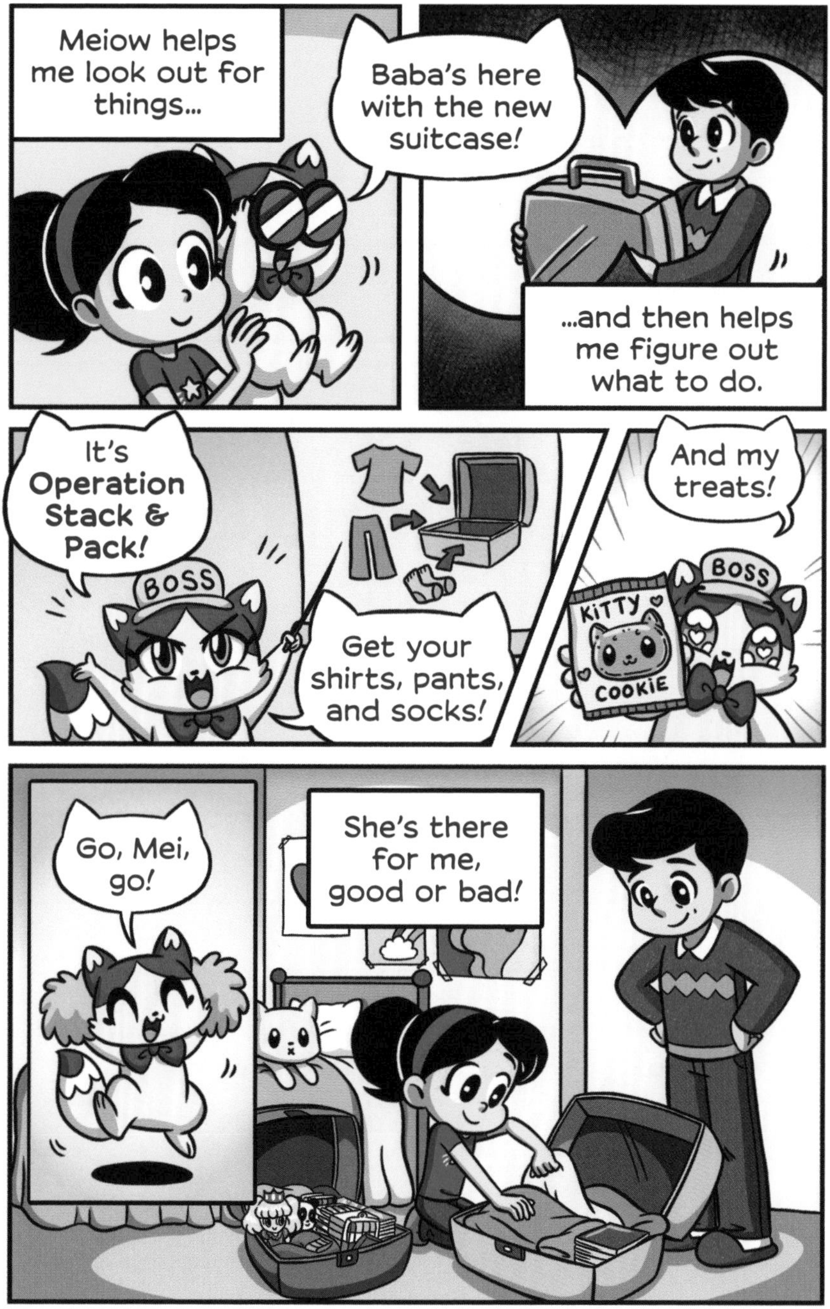

Meiow helps me look out for things...
Baba's here with the new suitcase!
...and then helps me figure out what to do.
It's Operation Stack & Pack!
BOSS
Get your shirts, pants, and socks!
And my treats!
BOSS
KITTY COOKIE
She's there for me, good or bad!
Go, Mei, go!

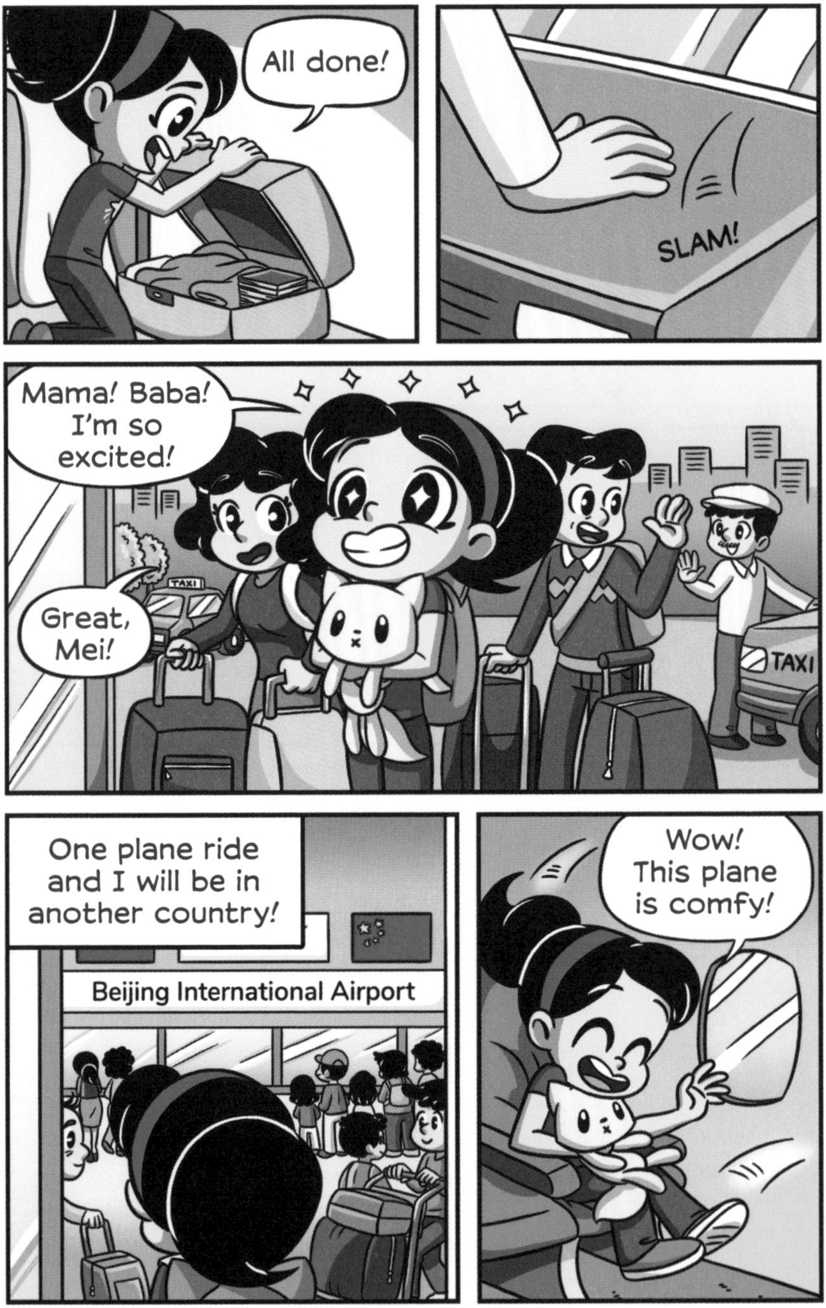
All done!
SLAM!
Mama! Baba! I'm so excited!
Great, Mei!
TAXI
TAXI
One plane ride and I will be in another country!
Beijing International Airport
Wow! This plane is comfy!

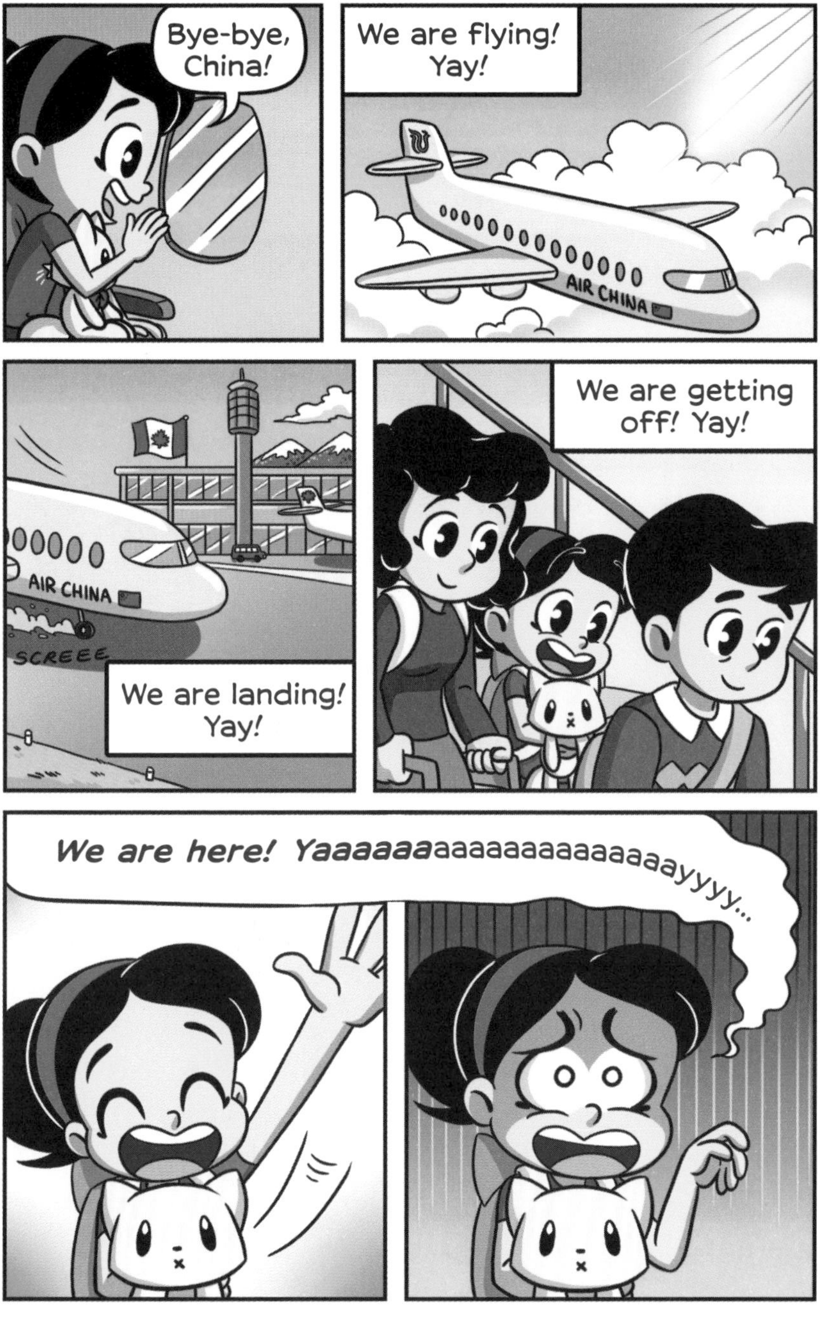
Bye-bye, China!
We are flying! Yay!
AIR CHINA
AIR CHINA
SCREEE
We are landing! Yay!
We are getting off! Yay!
We are here! Yaaaaaaaaaaaaaaaaaaaaayyyy...

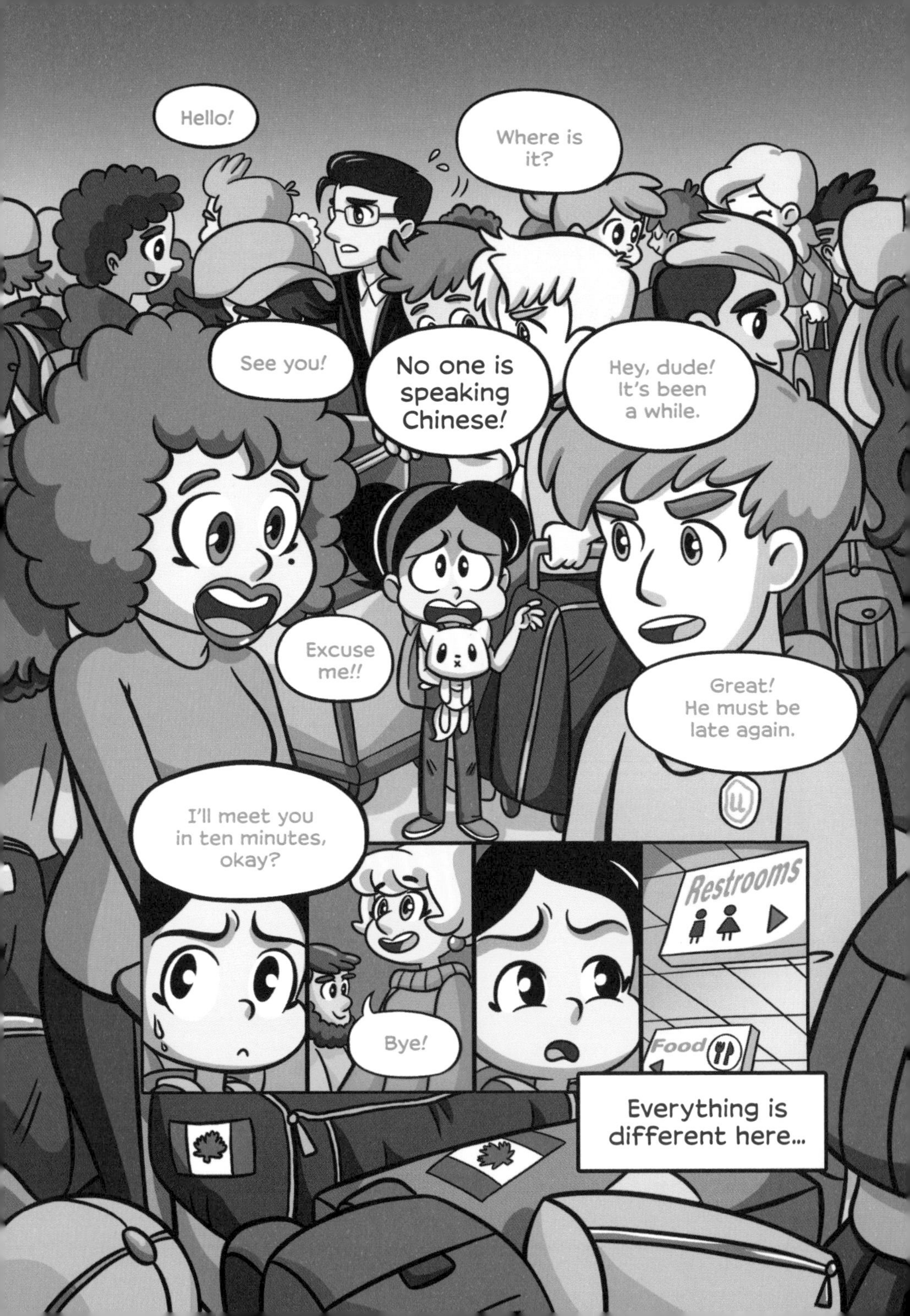

Hello!
Where is it?
See you!
No one is speaking Chinese!
Hey, dude! It's been a while.
Excuse me!!
Great! He must be late again.
I'll meet you in ten minutes, okay?
Bye!
Restrooms
Food
Everything is different here...

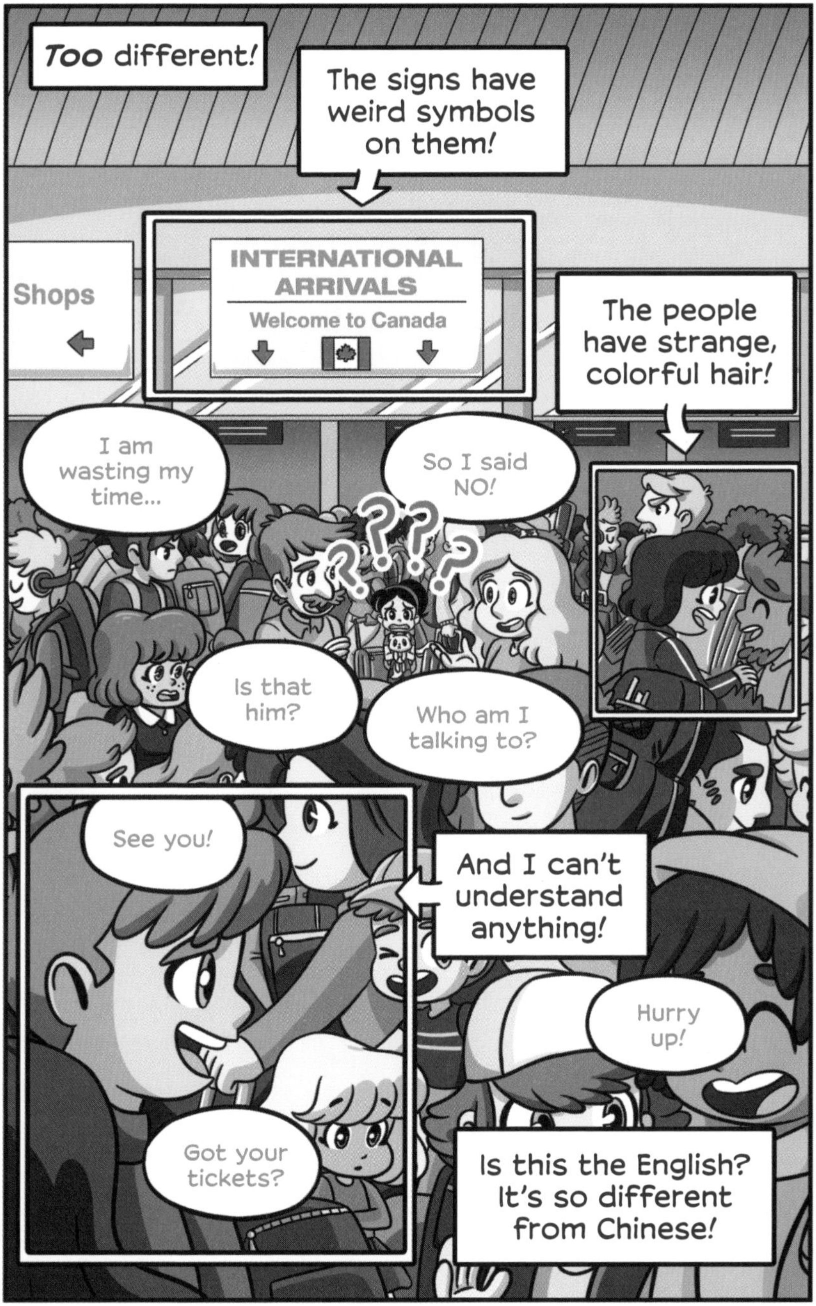

Too different!
The signs have weird symbols on them!
Shops
INTERNATIONAL ARRIVALS
Welcome to Canada
The people have strange, colorful hair!
I am wasting my time...
So I said NO!
Is that him?
Who am I talking to?
See you!
And I can't understand anything!
Hurry up!
Got your tickets?
Is this the English? It's so different from Chinese!

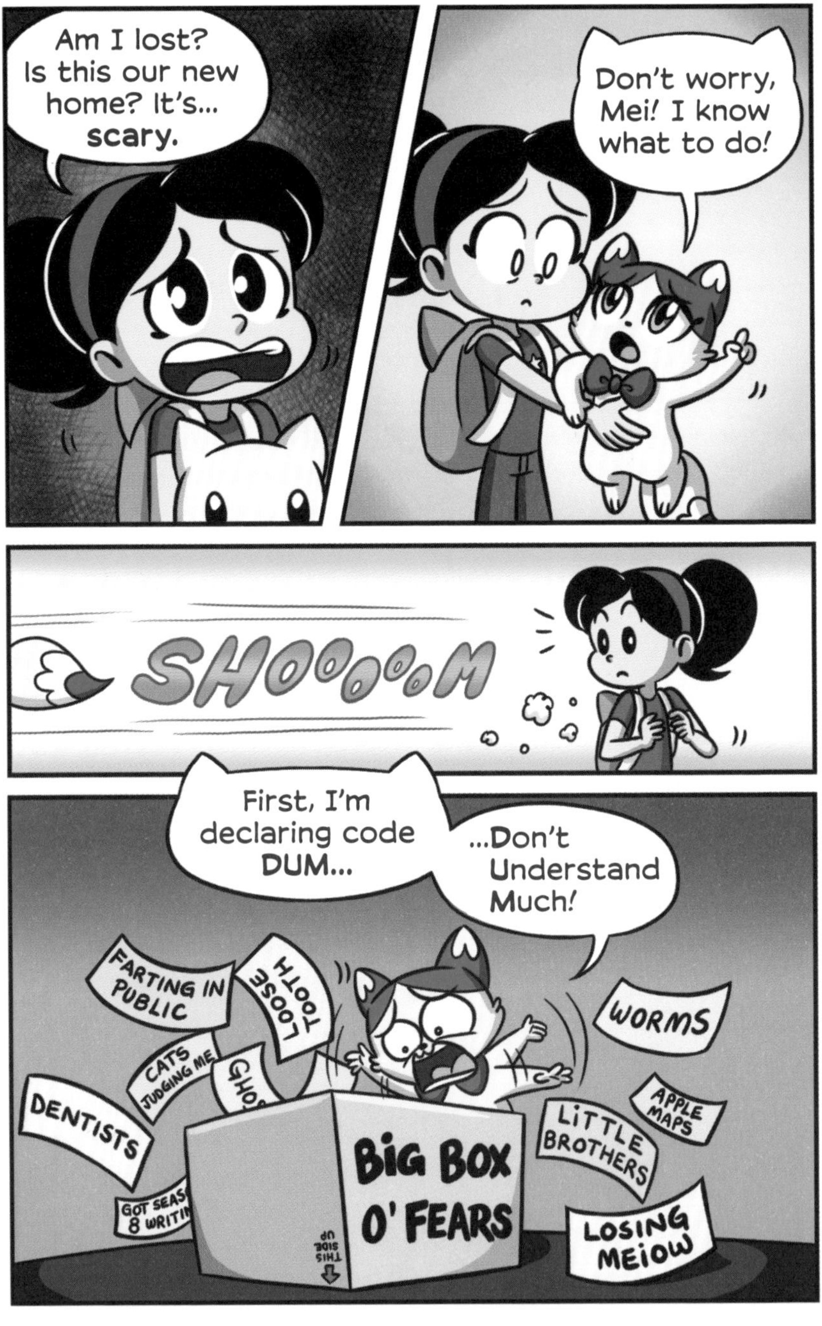

Am I lost? Is this our new home? It's... **scary.**
Don't worry, Mei! I know what to do!
SHOOOOOM
First, I'm declaring code **DUM...**
...Don't Understand Much!
FARTING IN PUBLIC
LOOSE TOOTH
WORMS
CATS JUDGING ME
DENTISTS
APPLE MAPS
LITTLE BROTHERS
BIG BOX O' FEARS
THIS SIDE UP
LOSING MEIOW

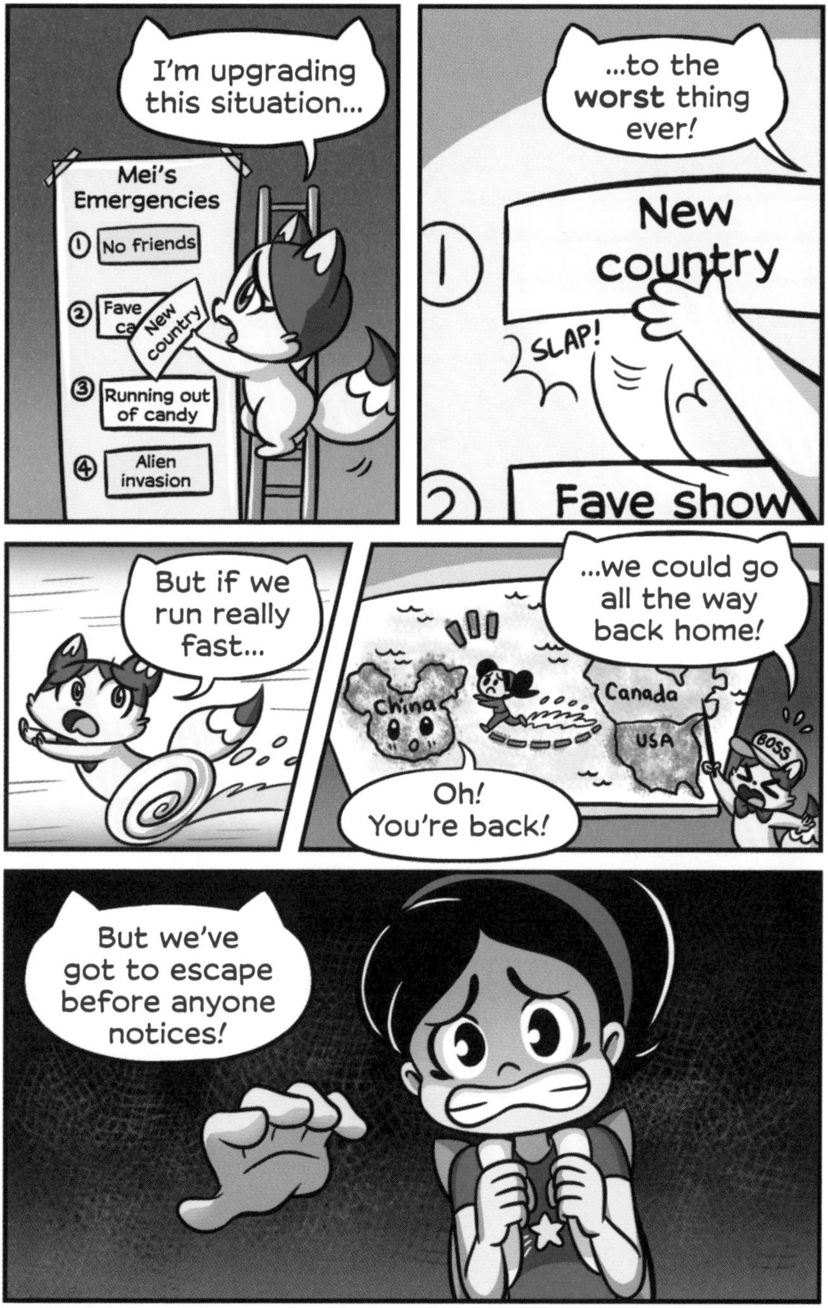
I'm upgrading this situation...
Mei's Emergencies
1 No friends
2 Fave
New country
3 Running out of candy
4 Alien invasion
...to the **worst** thing ever!
1 New country
SLAP!
2 Fave show
But if we run really fast...
...we could go all the way back home!
China
Canada
USA
BOSS
Oh! You're back!
But we've got to escape before anyone notices!

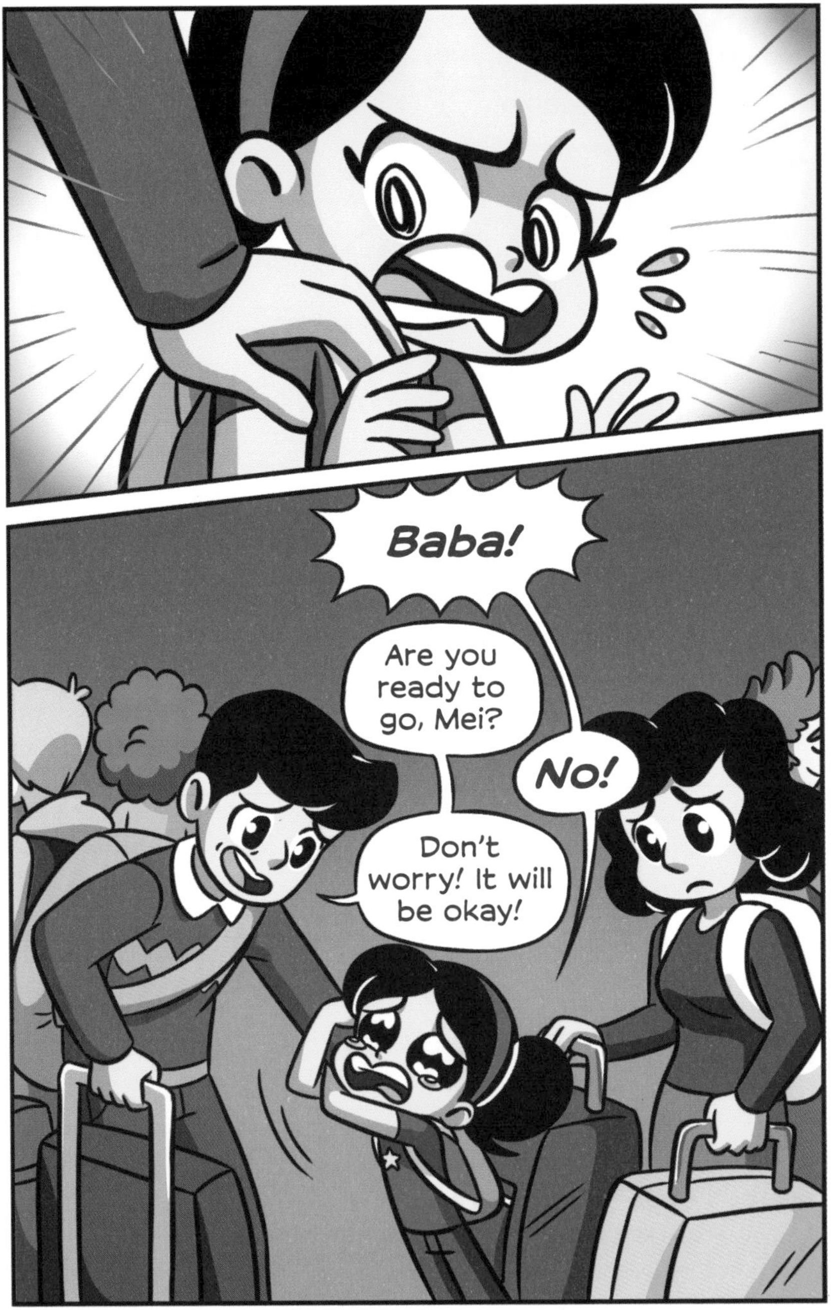
Baba!
Are you ready to go, Mei?
Don't worry! It will be okay!
No!

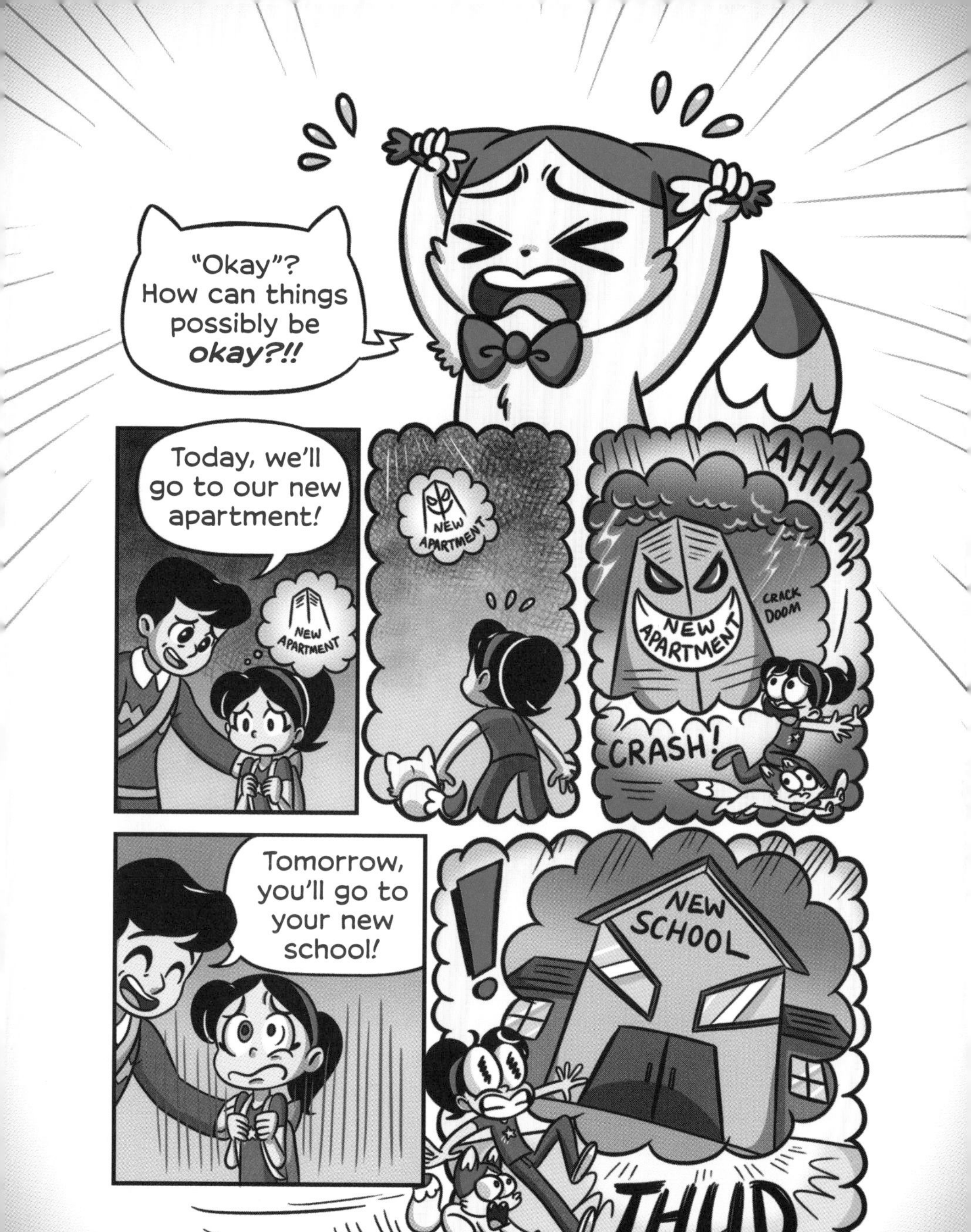
"Okay"? How can things possibly be ***okay?!!***
Today, we'll go to our new apartment!
NEW APARTMENT
NEW APARTMENT
AHHHhhh
NEW APARTMENT
CRACK DOOM
CRASH!
Tomorrow, you'll go to your new school!
NEW SCHOOL
THUD

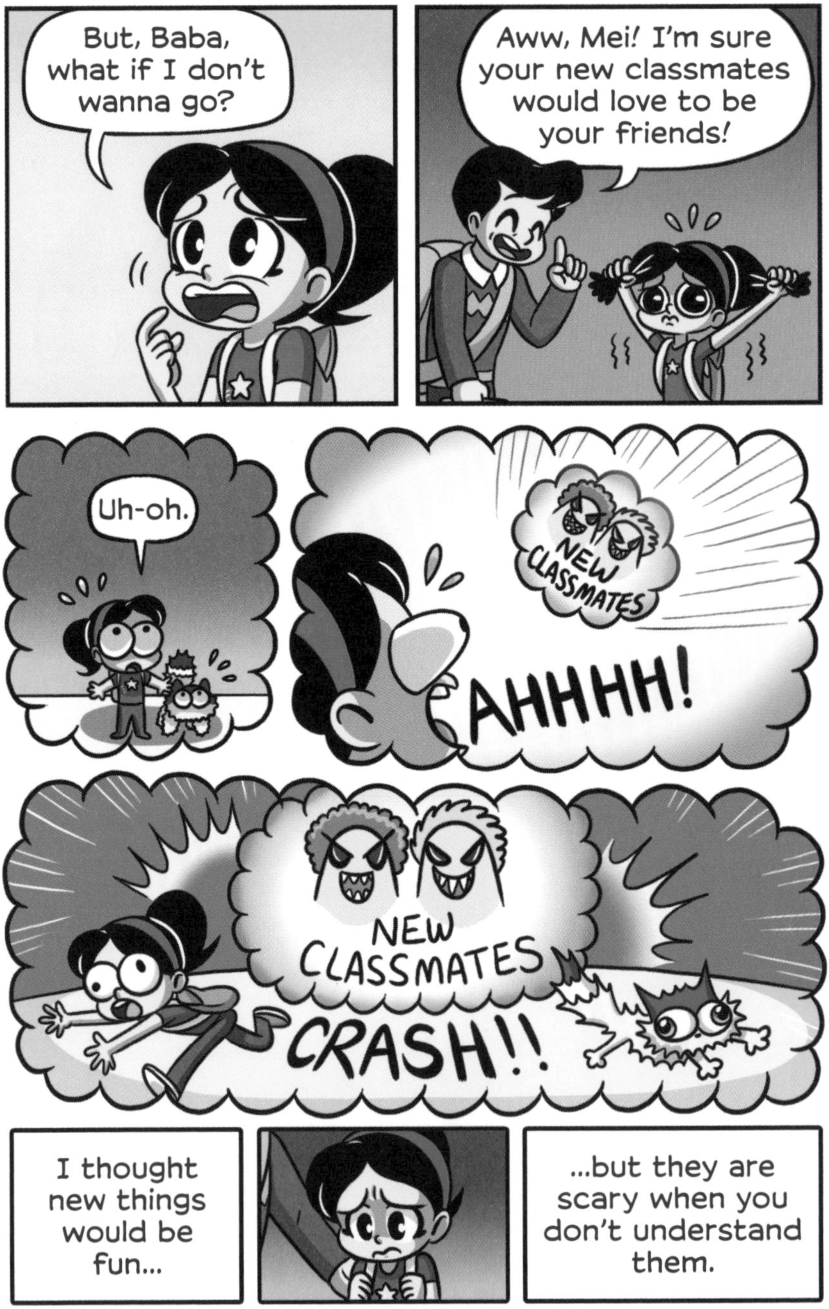
But, Baba, what if I don't wanna go?
Aww, Mei! I'm sure your new classmates would love to be your friends!
Uh-oh.
NEW CLASSMATES
AHHHH!
NEW CLASSMATES
CRASH!!
I thought new things would be fun...
...but they are scary when you don't understand them.

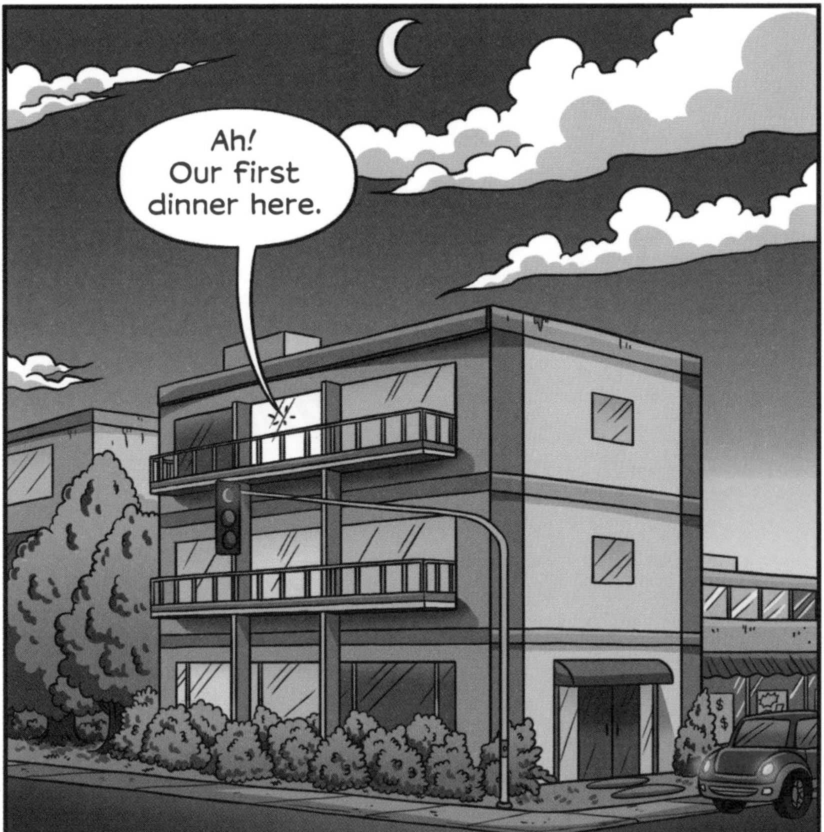
Ah! Our first dinner here.

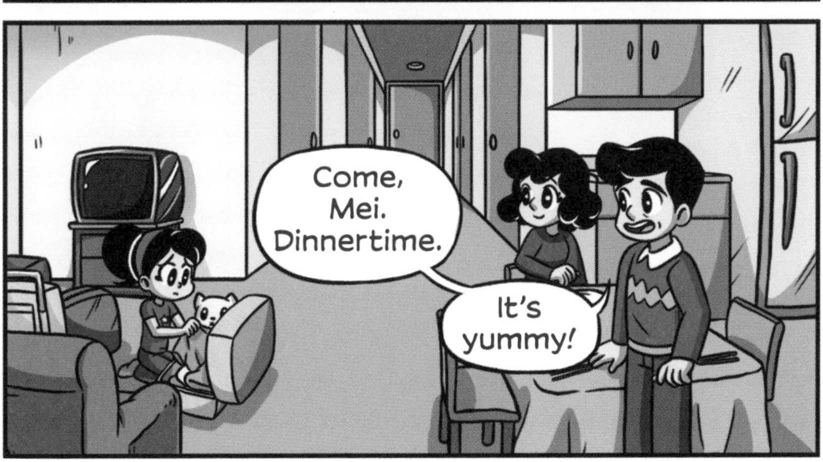
Come, Mei. Dinnertime.
It's yummy!

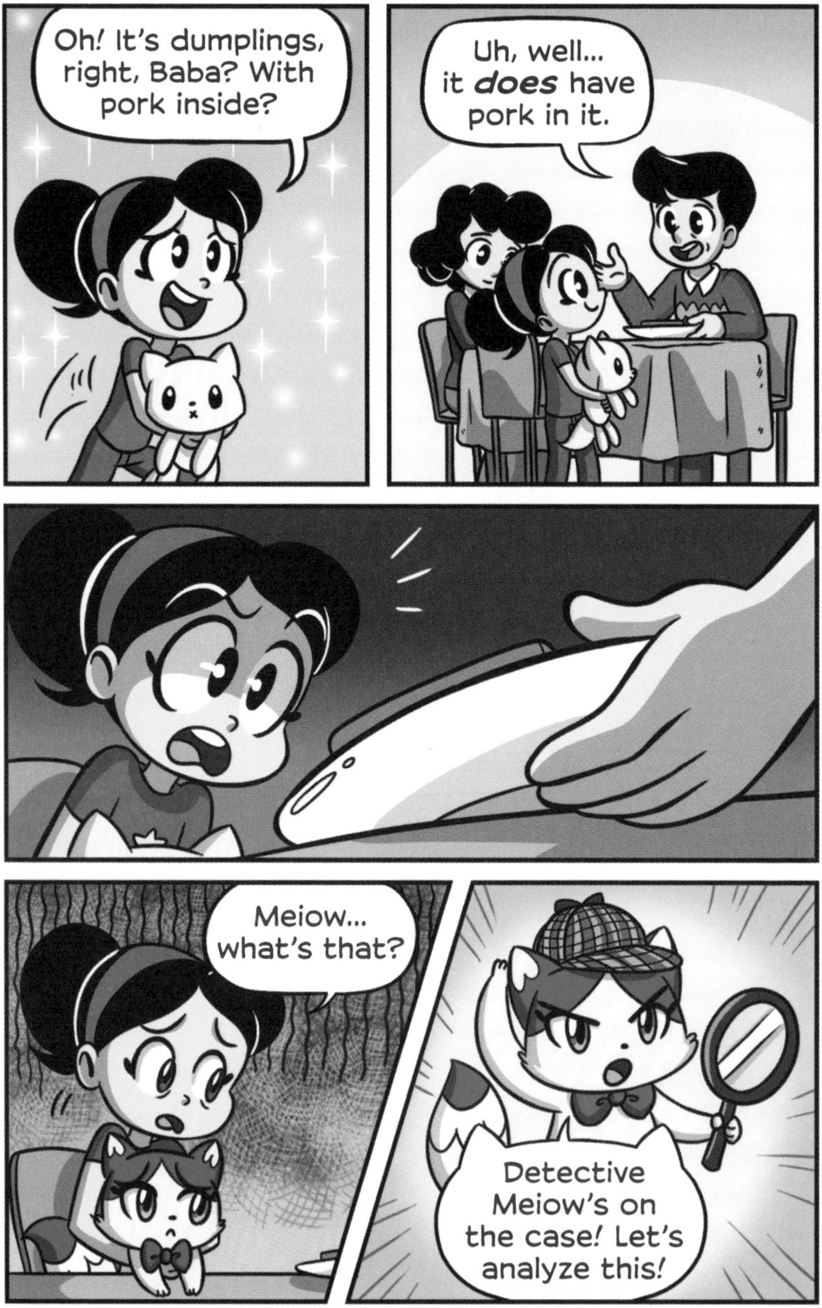
Oh! It's dumplings, right, Baba? With pork inside?
Uh, well... it *does* have pork in it.
Meiow... what's that?
Detective Meiow's on the case! Let's analyze this!

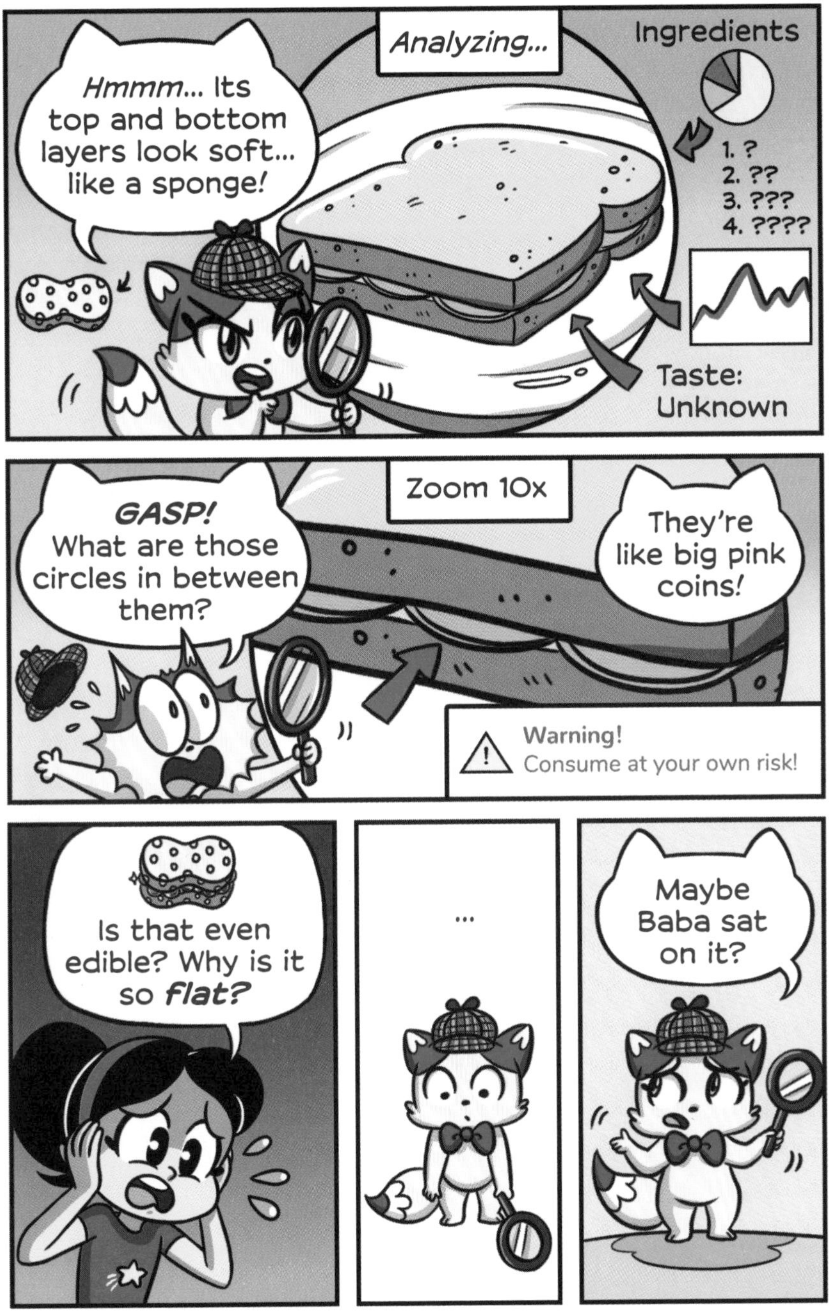
Analyzing...
Ingredients
1. ?
2. ??
3. ???
4. ????
Taste: Unknown
Hmmm... Its top and bottom layers look soft... like a sponge!
Zoom 10x
GASP! What are those circles in between them?
They're like big pink coins!
Warning!
Consume at your own risk!
Is that even edible? Why is it so flat?
...
Maybe Baba sat on it?

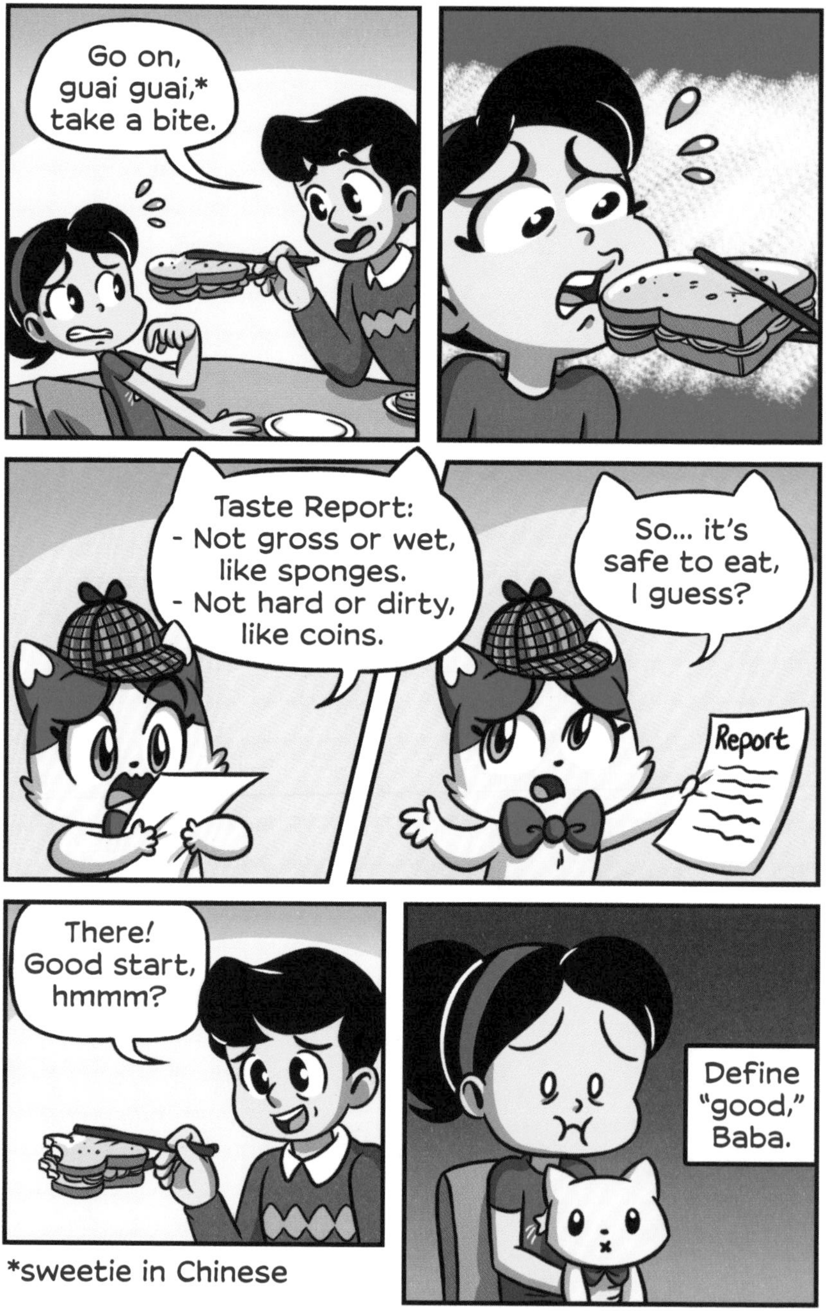
Go on, guai guai,* take a bite.
Taste Report: - Not gross or wet, like sponges. - Not hard or dirty, like coins.
Report
So... it's safe to eat, I guess?
There! Good start, hmmm?
Define "good," Baba.

*sweetie in Chinese

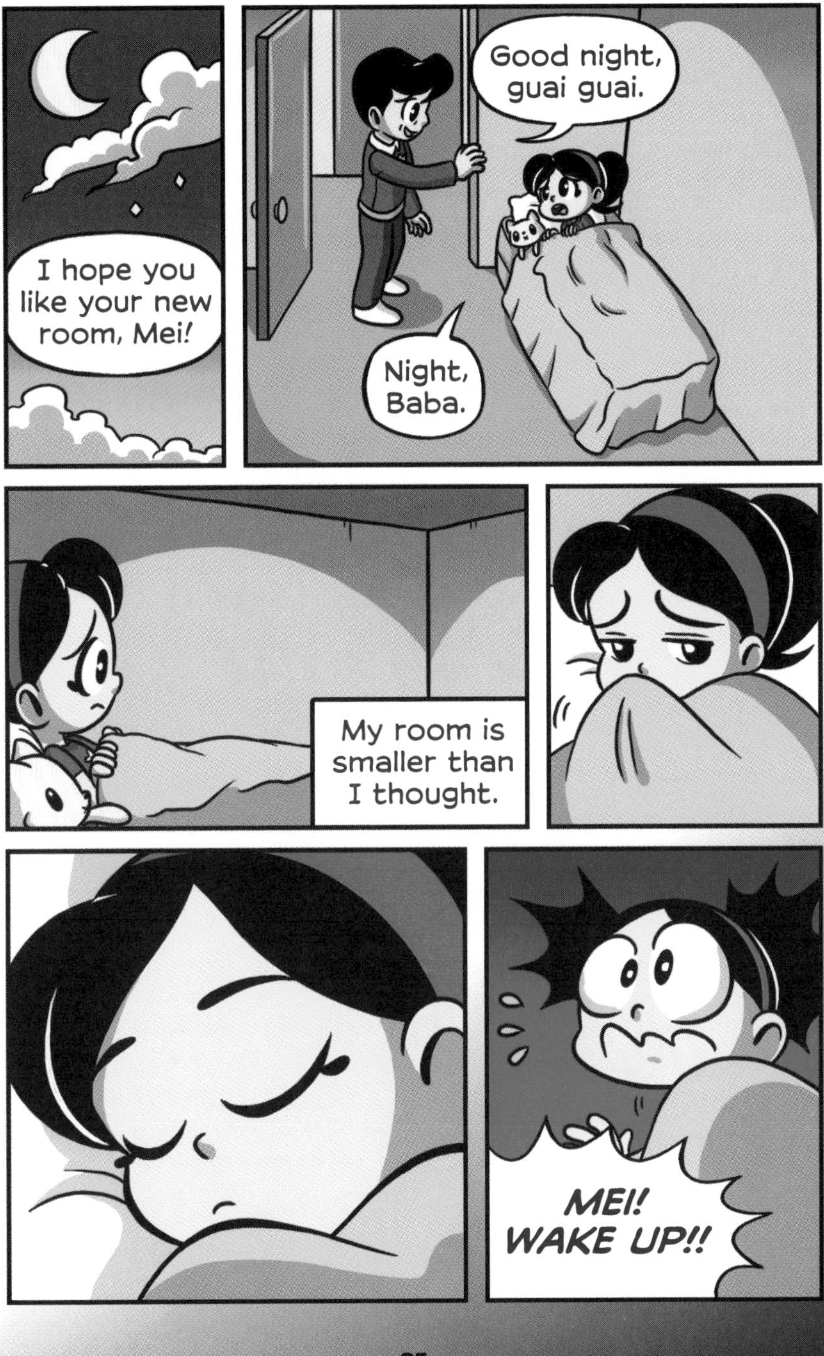
I hope you like your new room, Mei!
Good night, guai guai.
Night, Baba.
My room is smaller than I thought.
MEI! WAKE UP!!

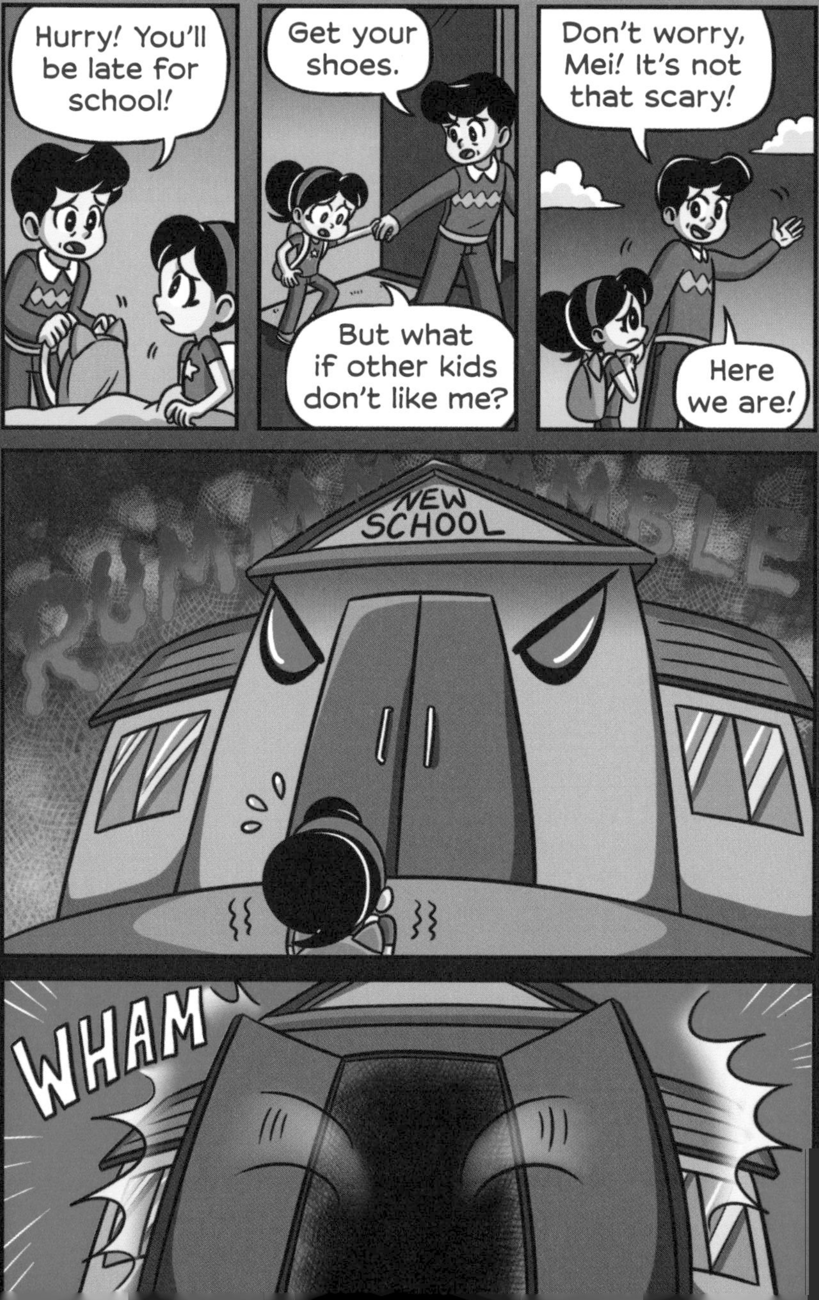
Hurry! You'll be late for school!
Get your shoes.
But what if other kids don't like me?
Don't worry, Mei! It's not that scary!
Here we are!
NEW SCHOOL
WHAM

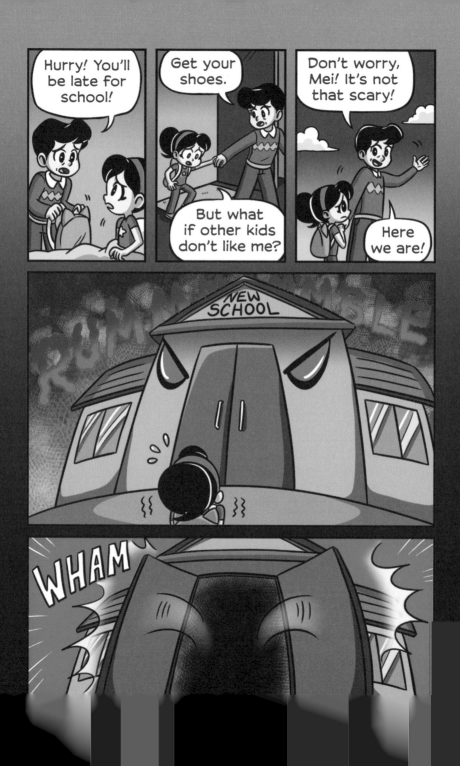

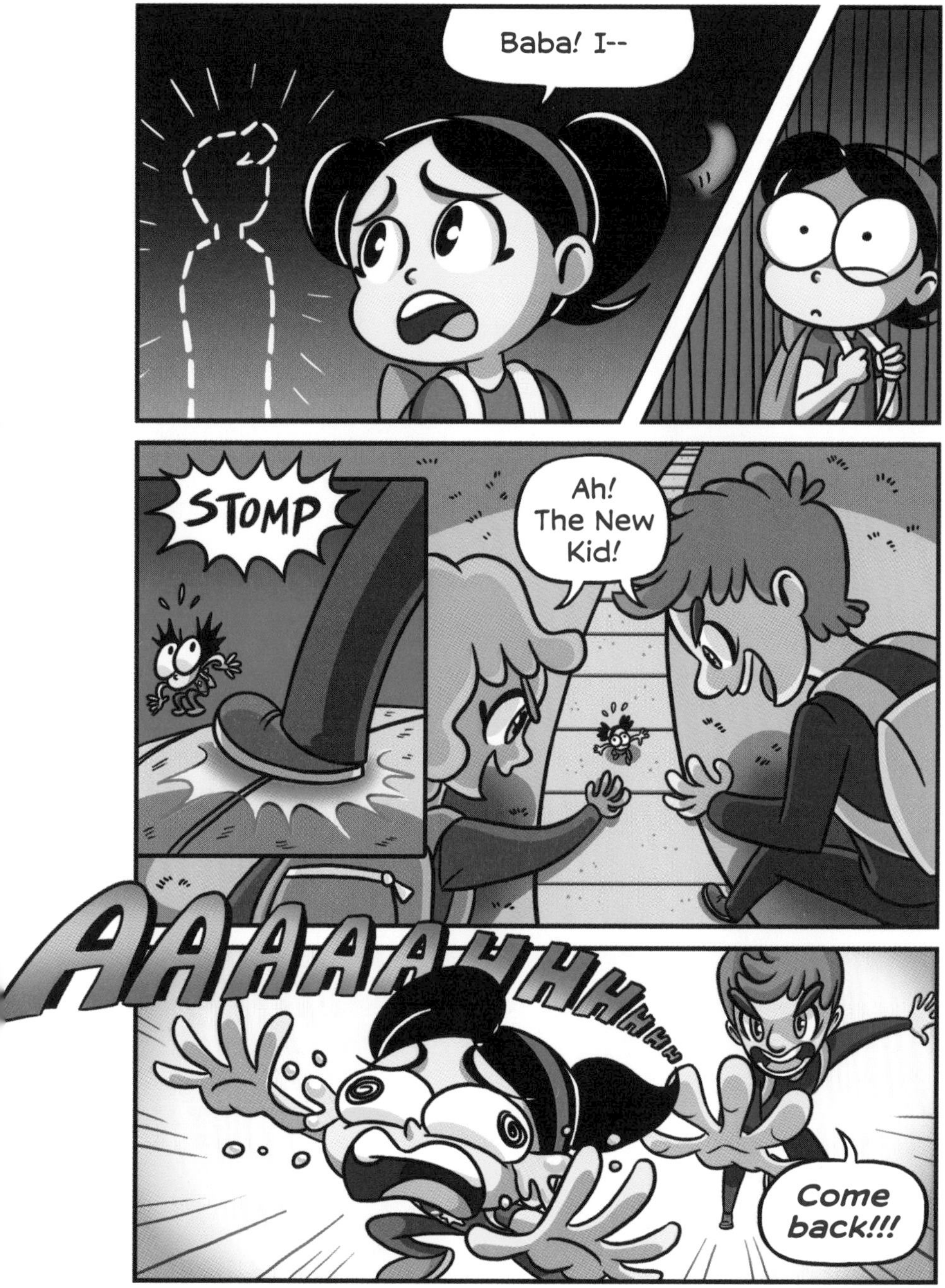
Baba! I--
STOMP
Ah! The New Kid!
AAAAAAHHHHHH
Come back!!!

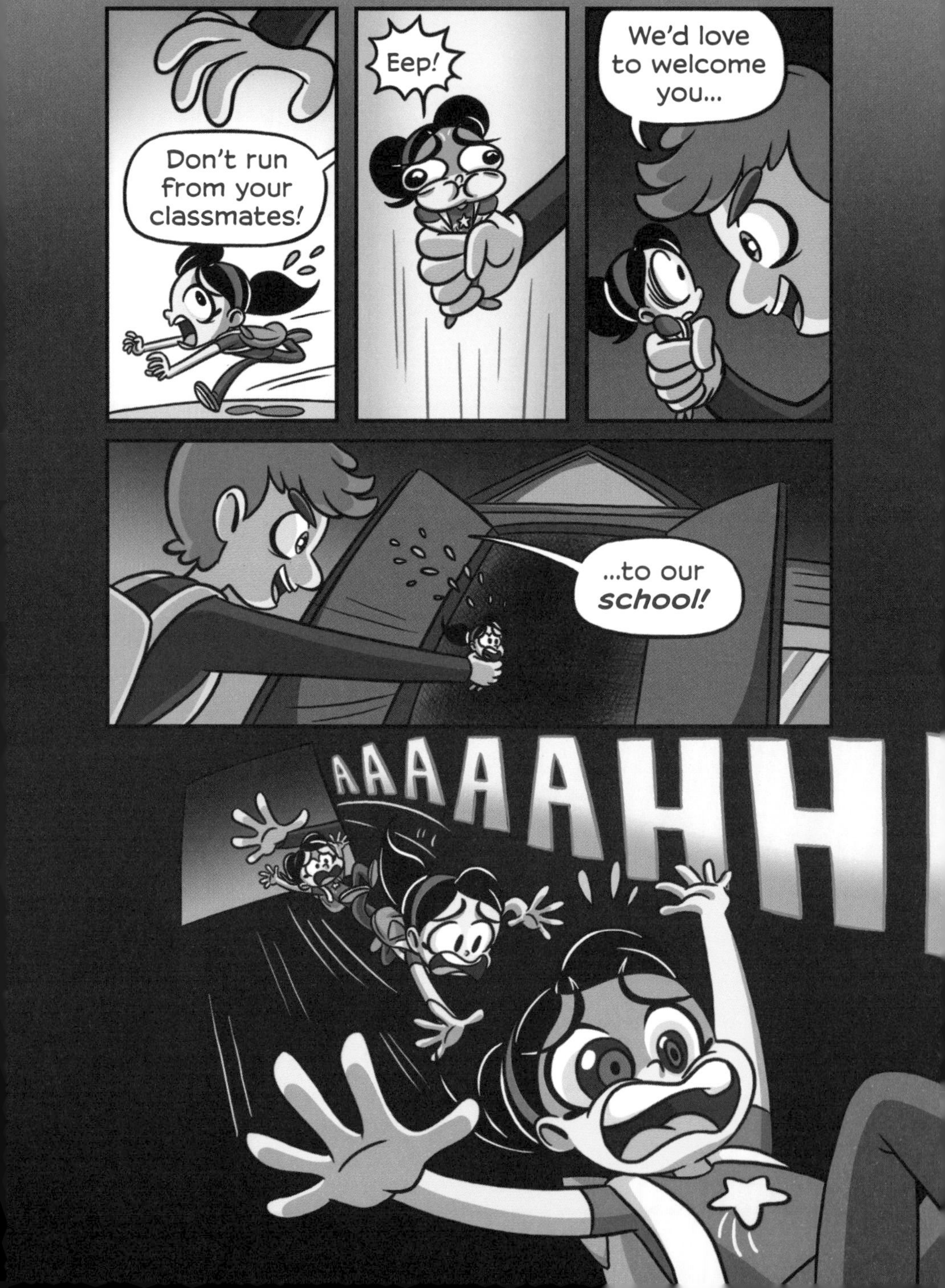
Don't run from your classmates!
Eep!
We'd love to welcome you...
...to our *school!*
AAAAAHHH

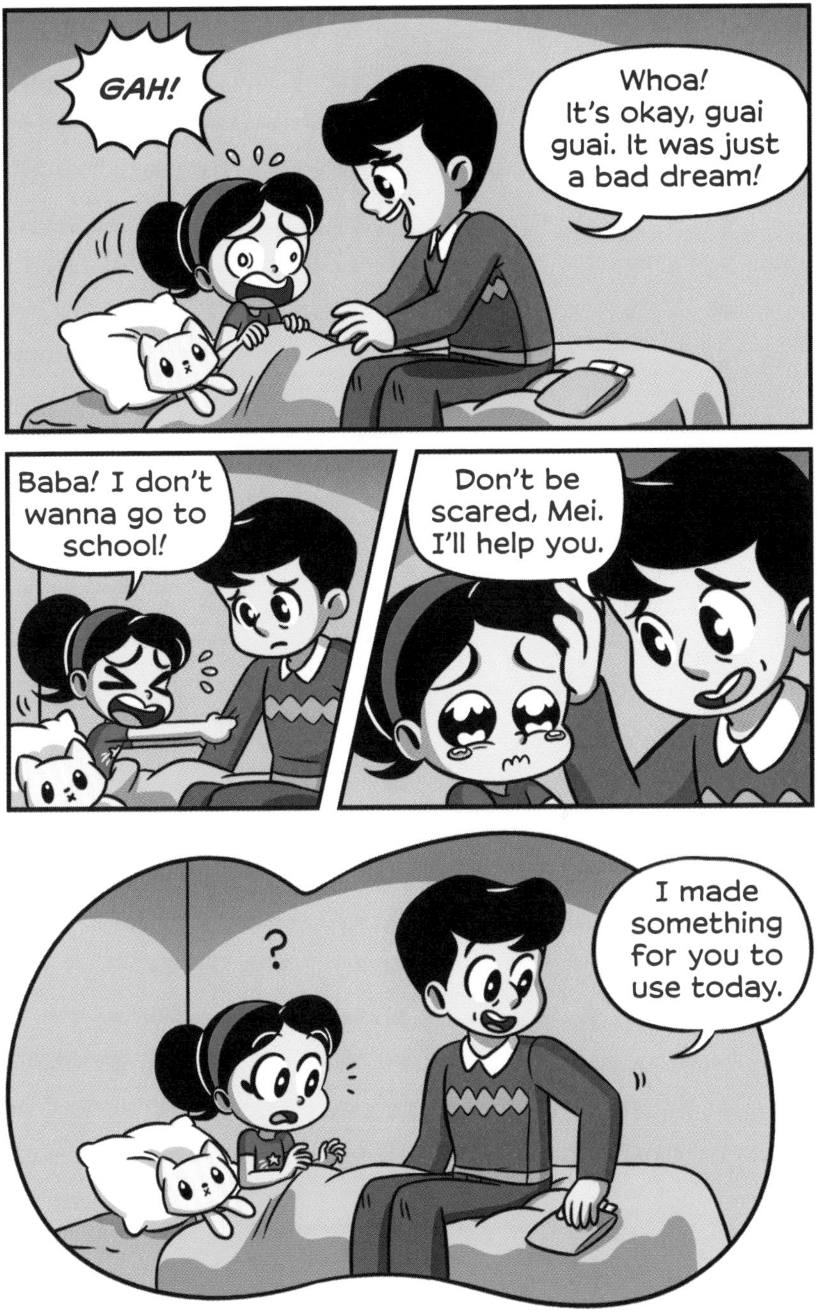
GAH!
Whoa! It's okay, guai guai. It was just a bad dream!
Baba! I don't wanna go to school!
Don't be scared, Mei. I'll help you.
?
I made something for you to use today.

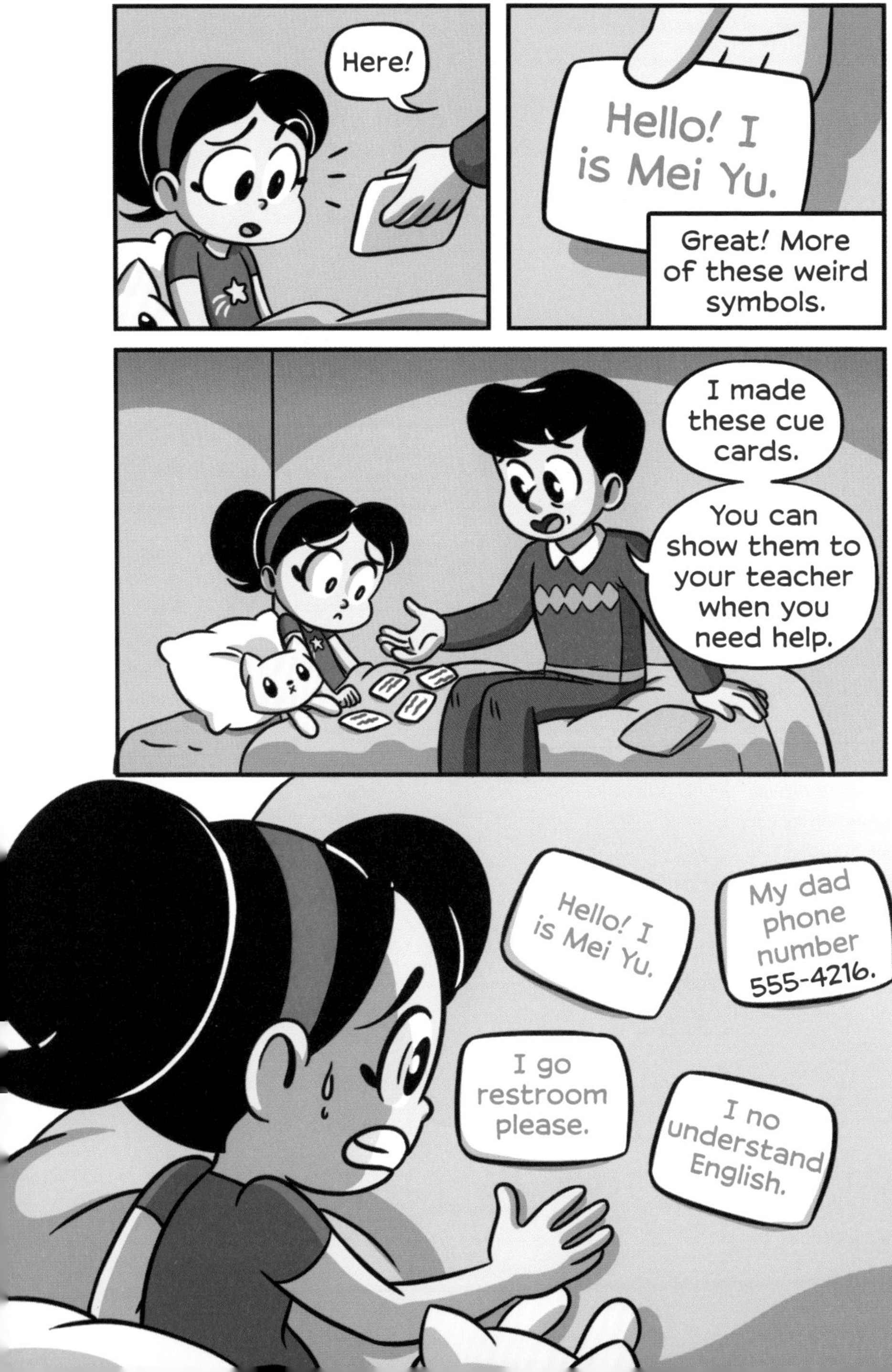
Here!
Hello! I is Mei Yu.
Great! More of these weird symbols.
I made these cue cards.
You can show them to your teacher when you need help.
Hello! I is Mei Yu.
My dad phone number 555-4216.
I go restroom please.
I no understand English.

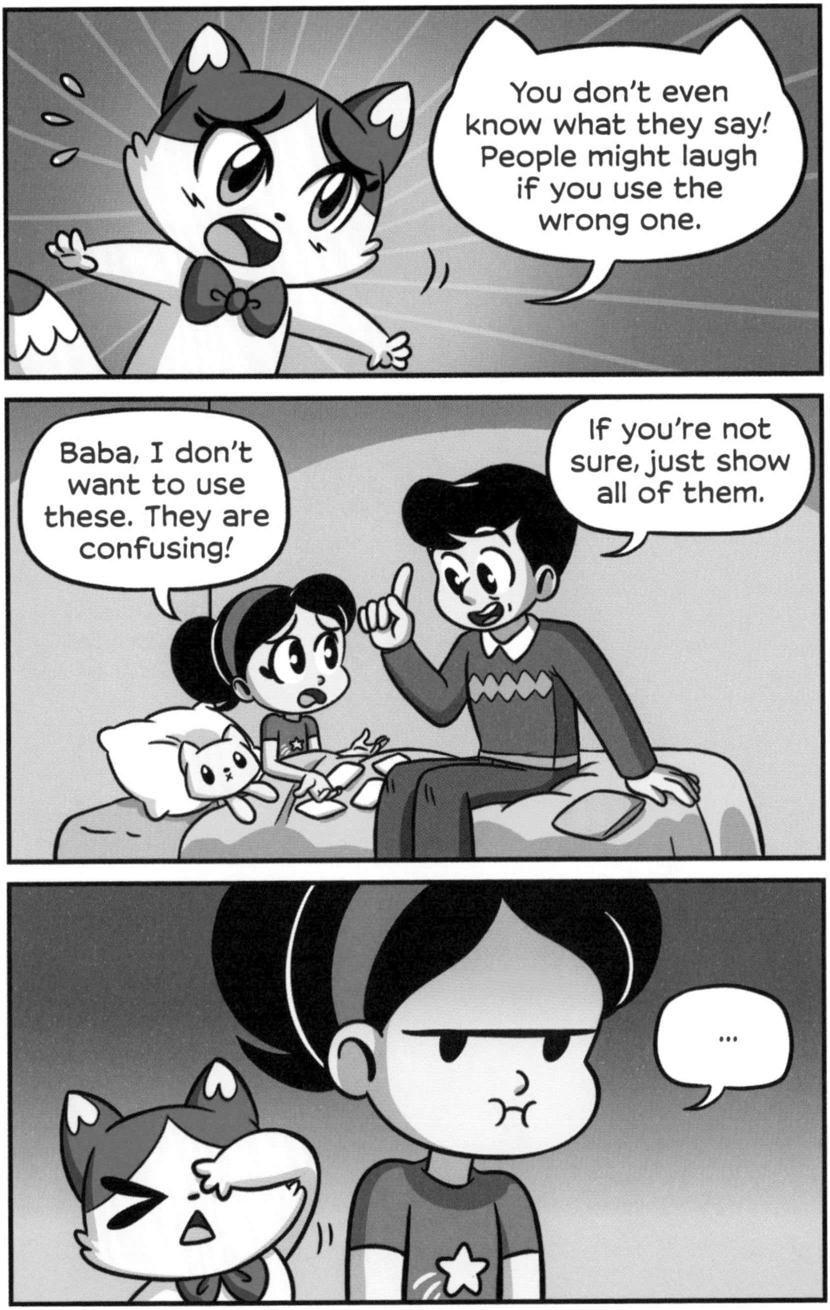
You don't even know what they say! People might laugh if you use the wrong one.
Baba, I don't want to use these. They are confusing!
If you're not sure, just show all of them.
...

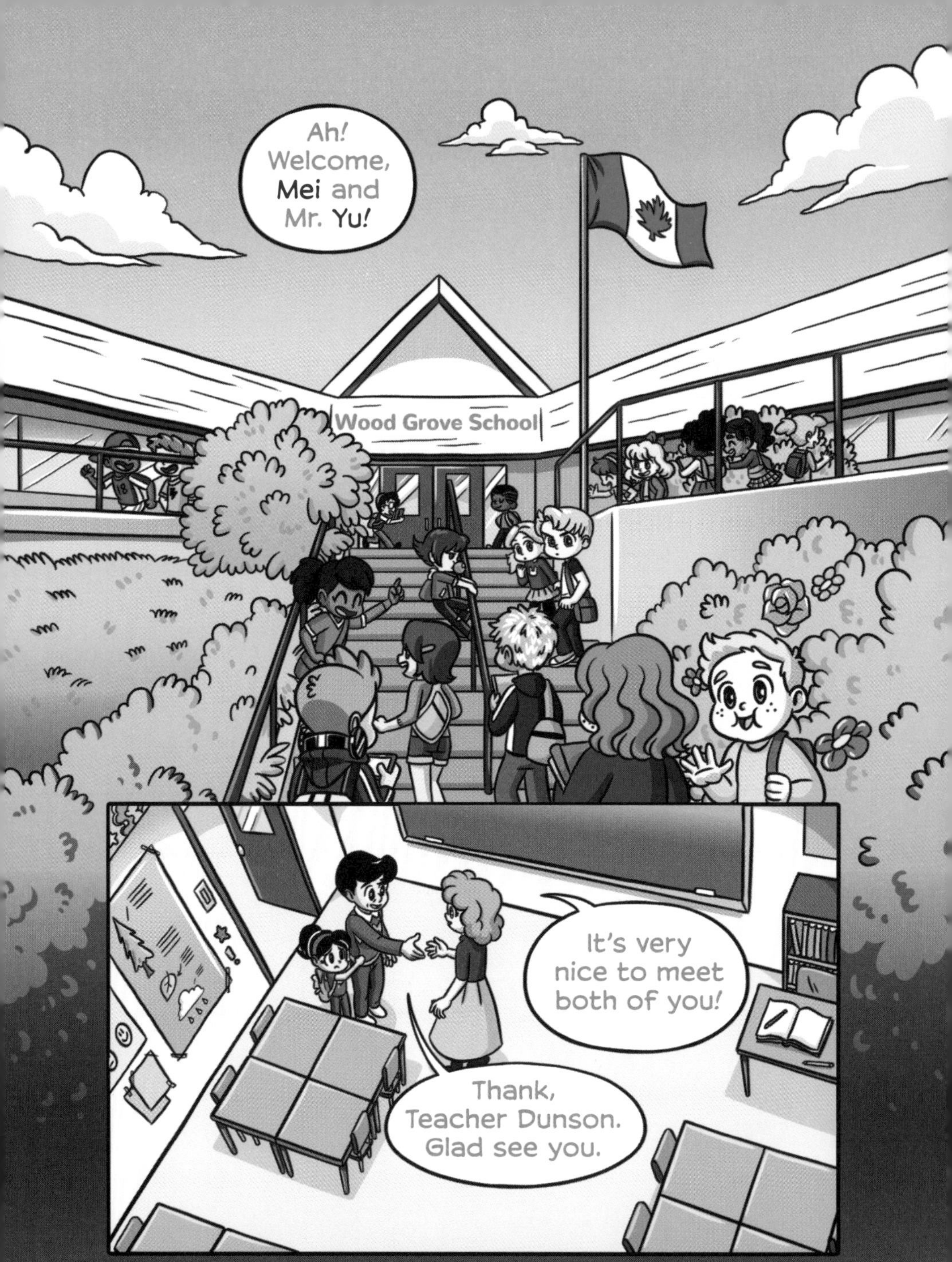
Ah! Welcome, Mei and Mr. Yu!
Wood Grove School
It's very nice to meet both of you!
Thank, Teacher Dunson. Glad see you.

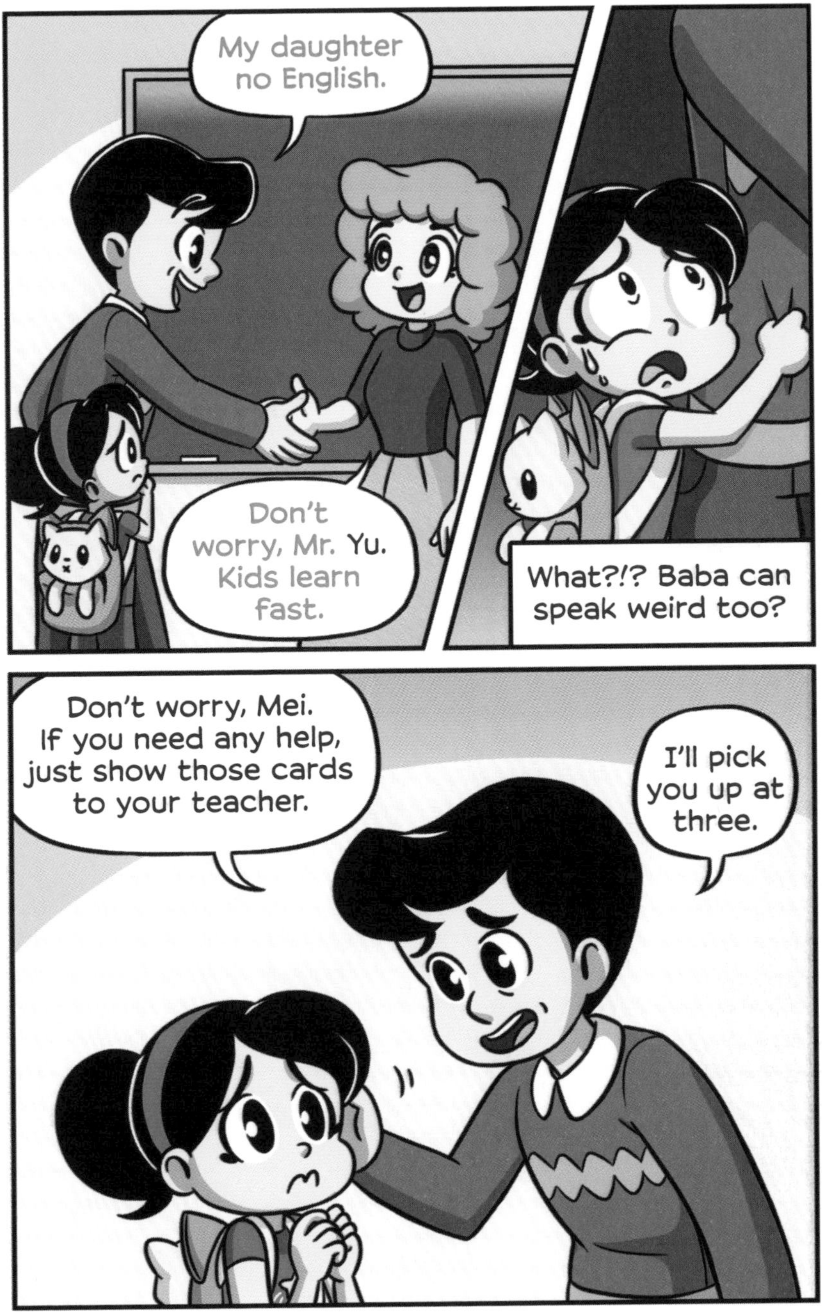
My daughter no English.
Don't worry, Mr. Yu. Kids learn fast.
What?!? Baba can speak weird too?
Don't worry, Mei. If you need any help, just show those cards to your teacher.
I'll pick you up at three.

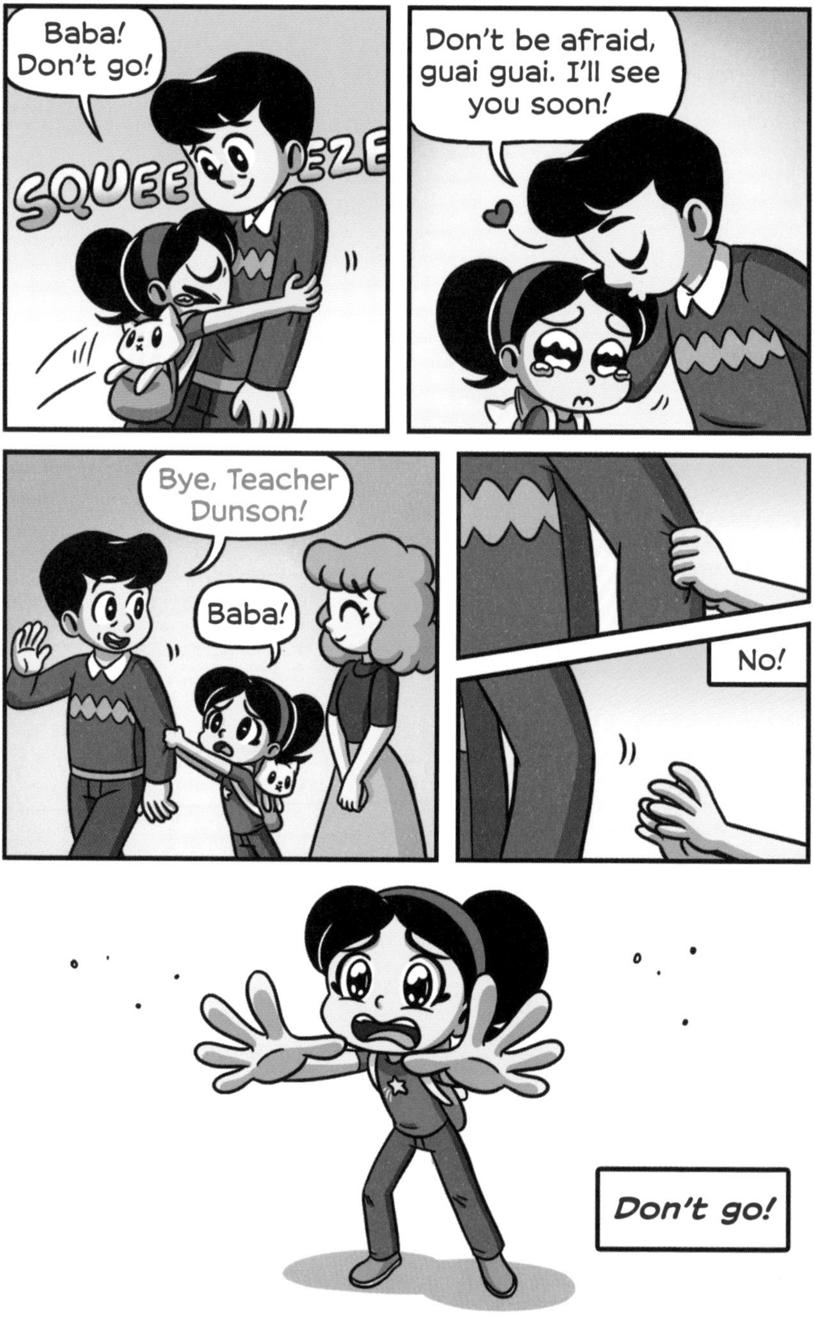
Baba! Don't go!
SQUEEEZE
Don't be afraid, guai guai. I'll see you soon!
Bye, Teacher Dunson!
Baba!
No!
Don't go!

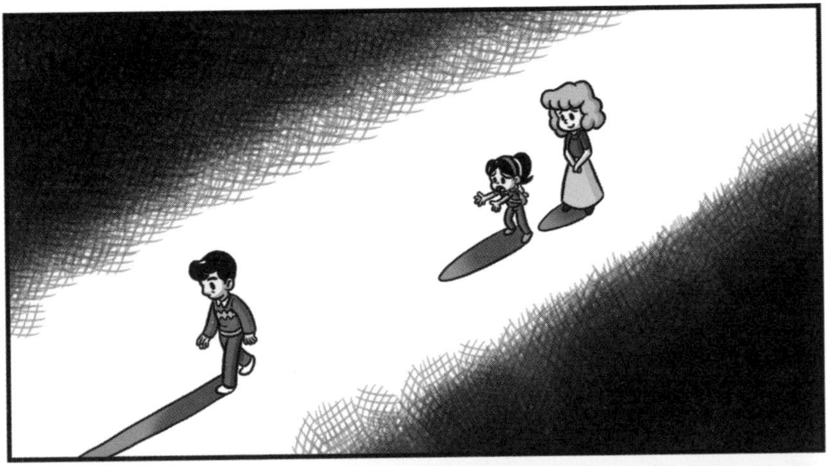

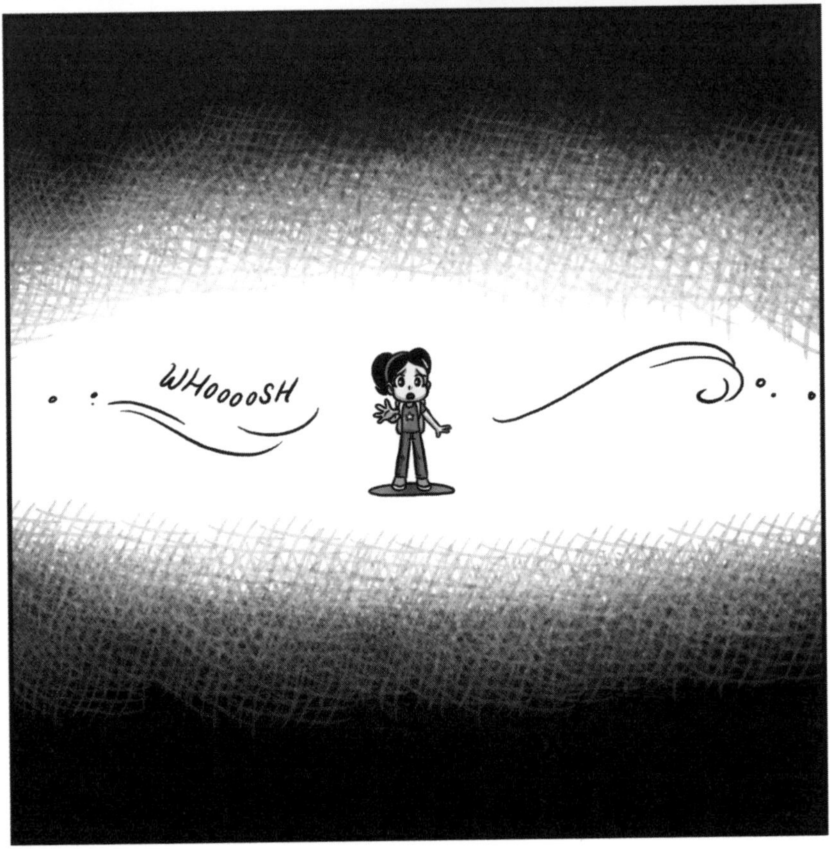
WHooooSH

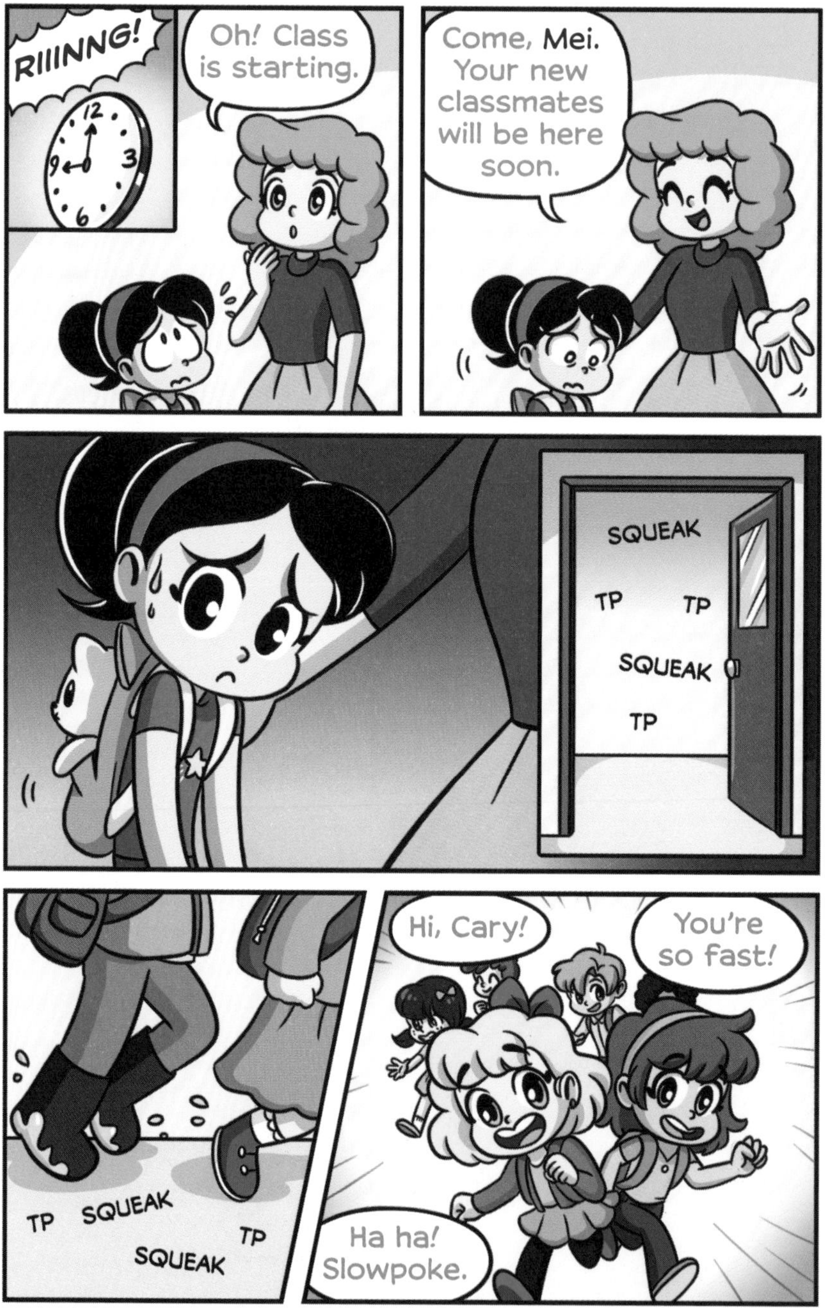
RIIINNG!
Oh! Class is starting.
Come, Mei. Your new classmates will be here soon.
SQUEAK
TP
TP
SQUEAK
TP
TP
SQUEAK
TP
SQUEAK
Hi, Cary!
You're so fast!
Ha ha! Slowpoke.

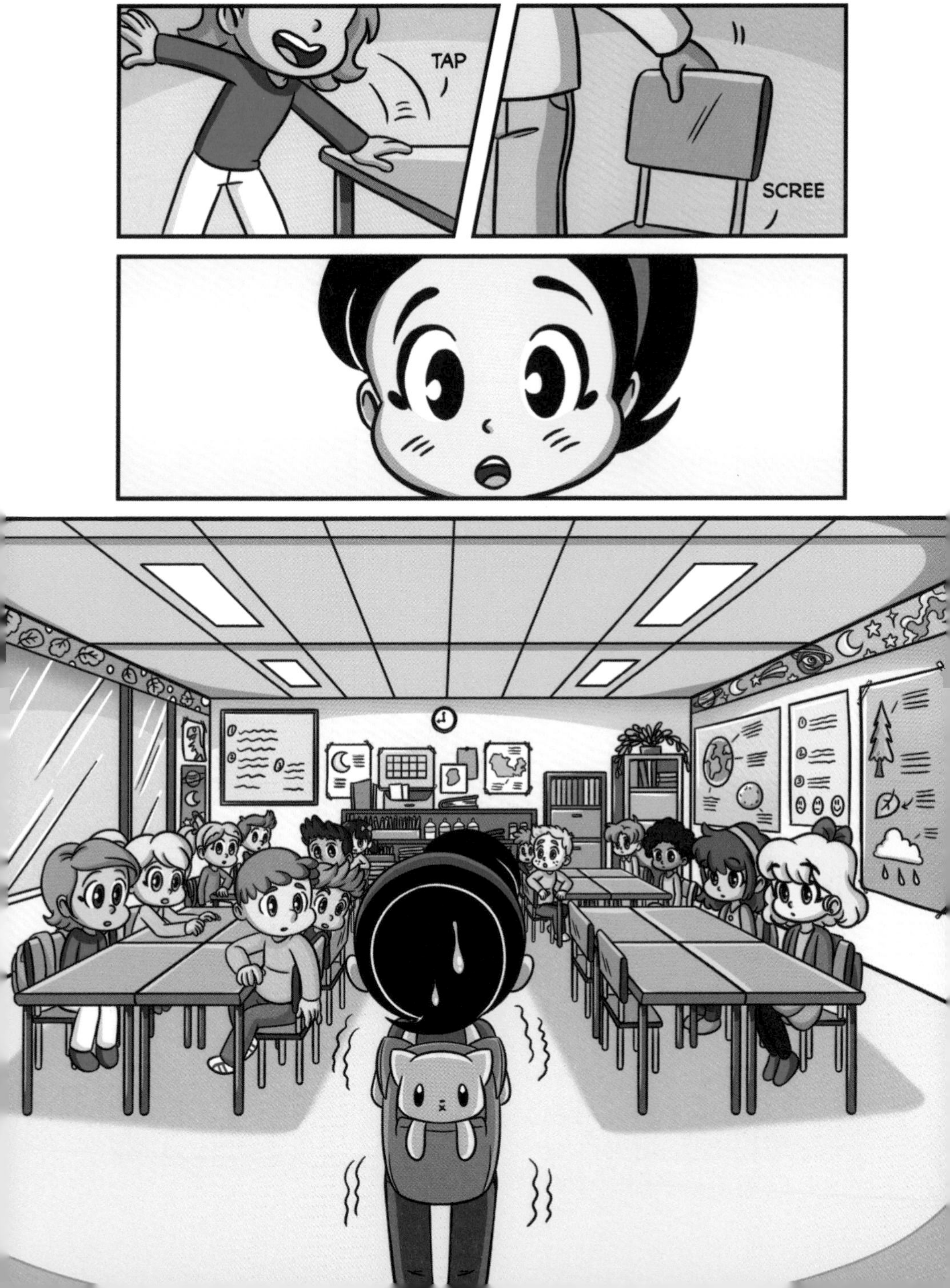
TAP
SCREE

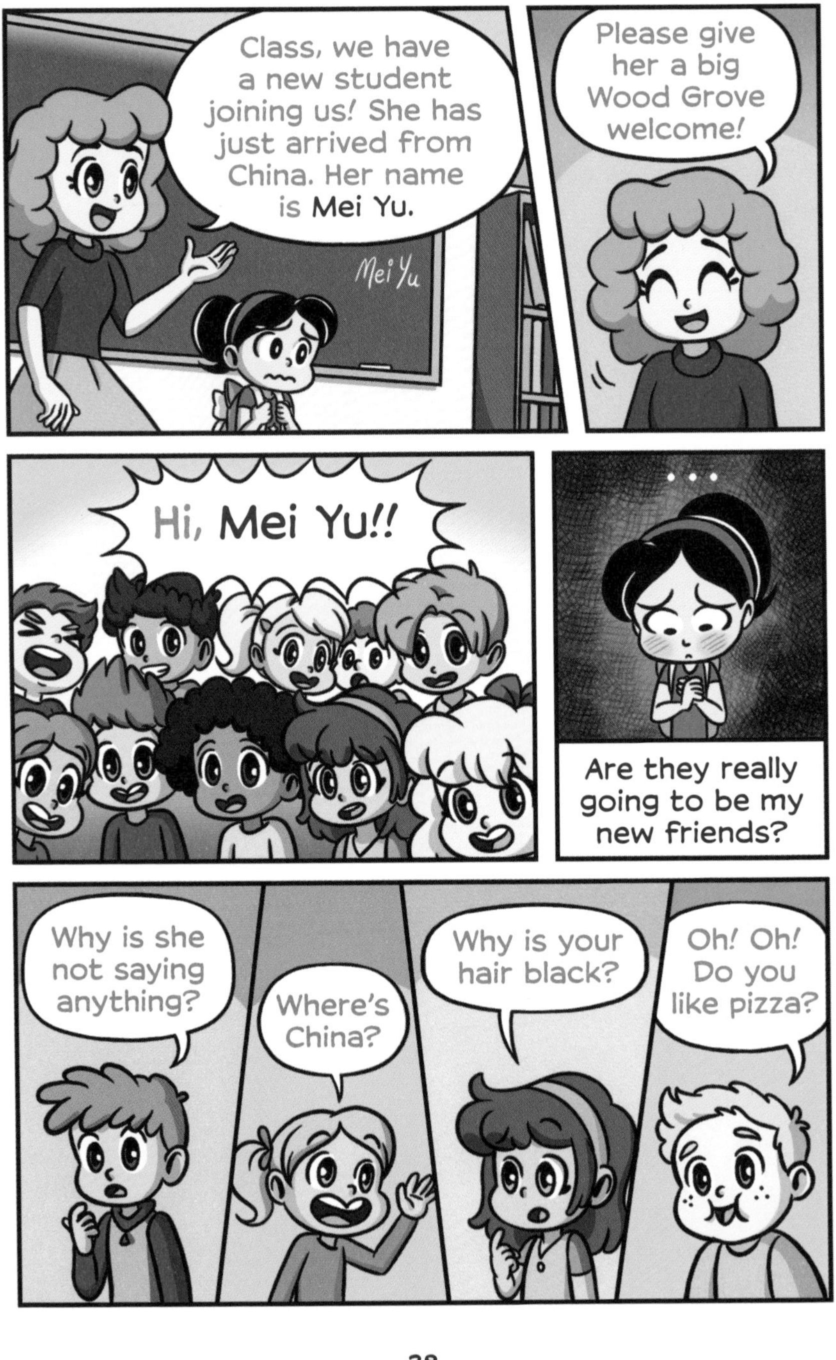
Class, we have a new student joining us! She has just arrived from China. Her name is Mei Yu.
Mei Yu
Please give her a big Wood Grove welcome!
Hi, Mei Yu!!
. . .
Are they really going to be my new friends?
Why is she not saying anything?
Where's China?
Why is your hair black?
Oh! Oh! Do you like pizza?

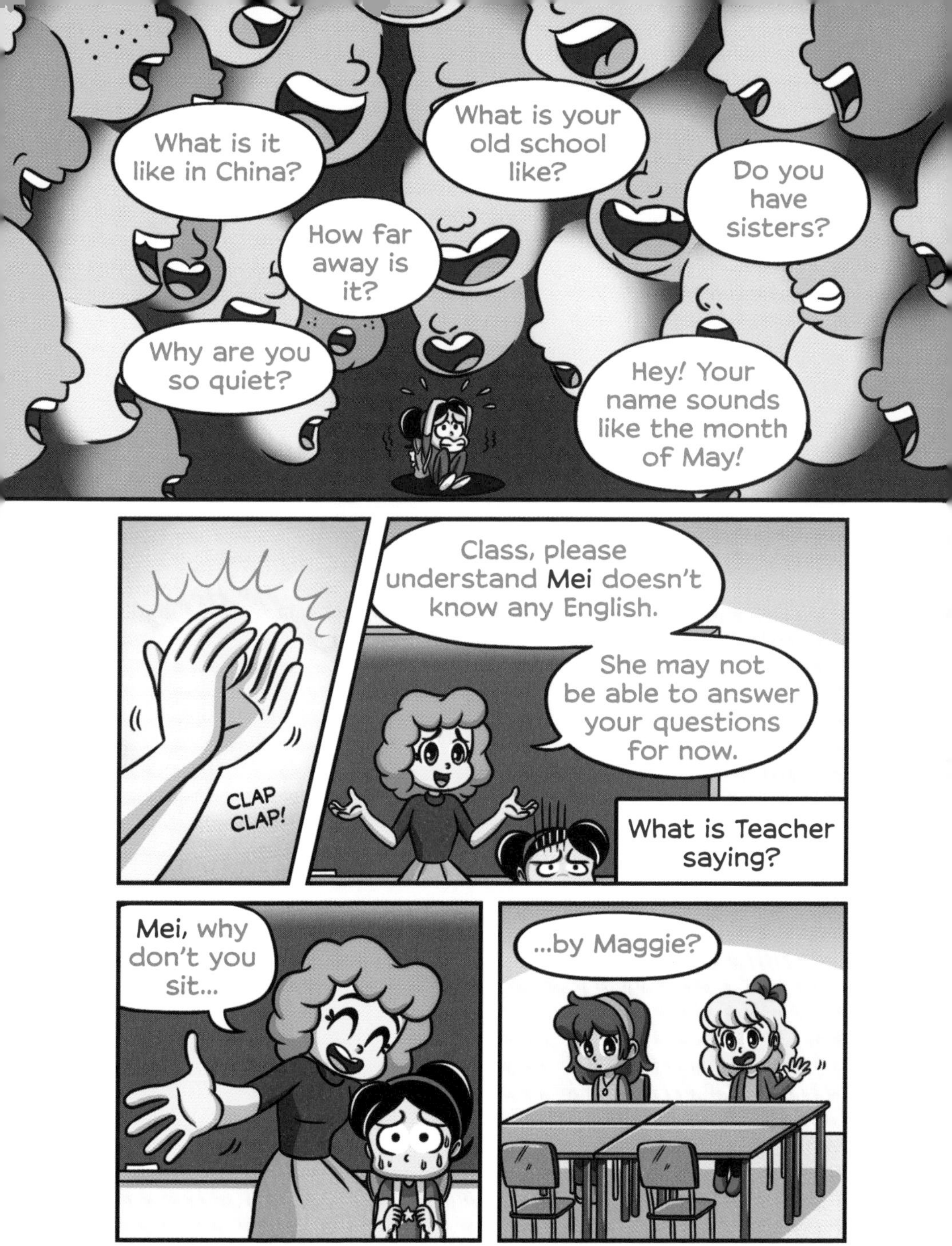
What is it like in China?
What is your old school like?
Do you have sisters?
How far away is it?
Why are you so quiet?
Hey! Your name sounds like the month of May!
CLAP CLAP!
Class, please understand Mei doesn't know any English.
She may not be able to answer your questions for now.
What is Teacher saying?
Mei, why don't you sit...
...by Maggie?

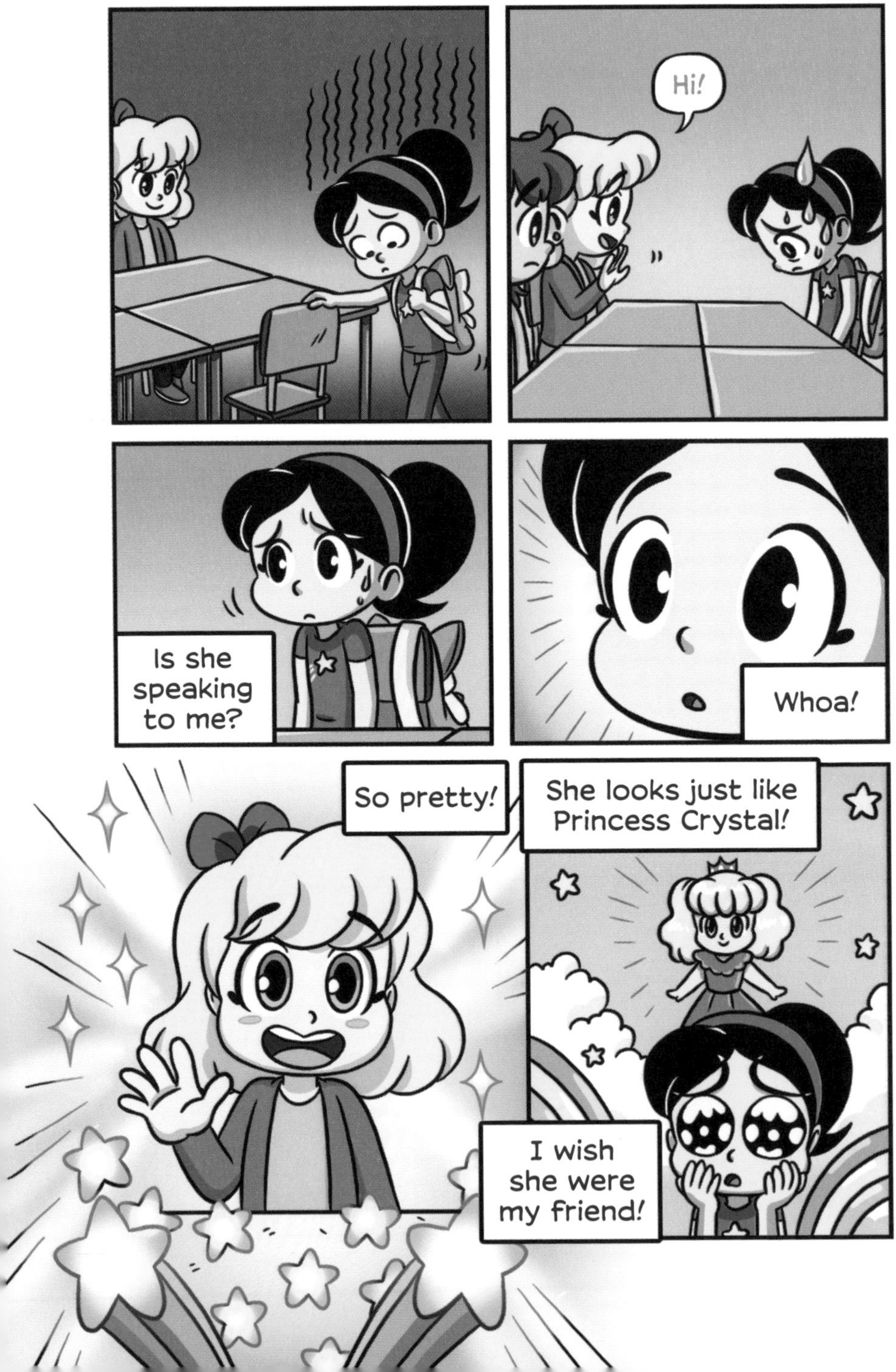
Hi!
Is she speaking to me?
Whoa!
So pretty!
She looks just like Princess Crystal!
I wish she were my friend!

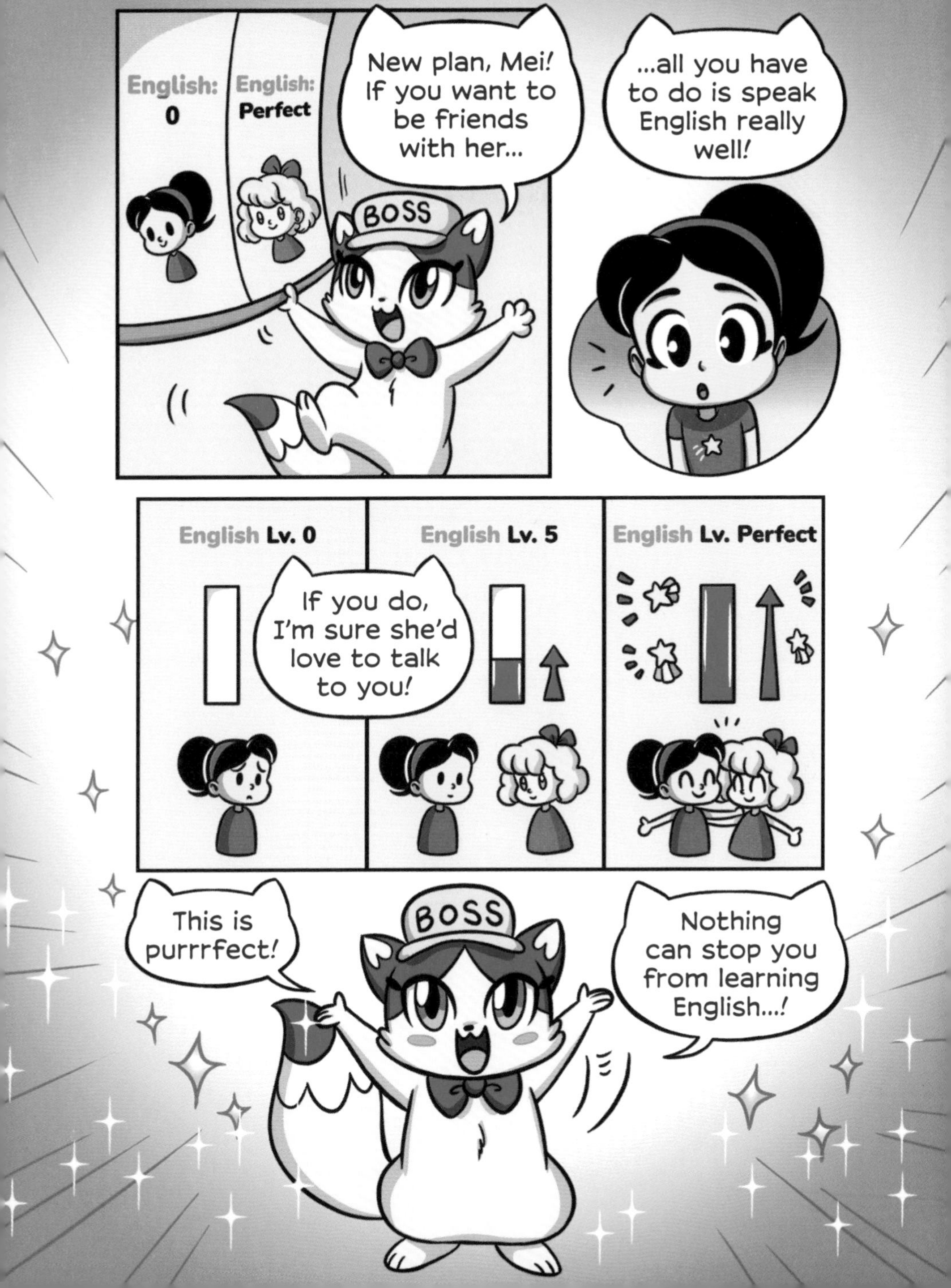
English: 0
English: Perfect
New plan, Mei! If you want to be friends with her...
...all you have to do is speak English really well!
English Lv. 0
English Lv. 5
English Lv. Perfect
If you do, I'm sure she'd love to talk to you!
This is purrrfect!
Nothing can stop you from learning English...!

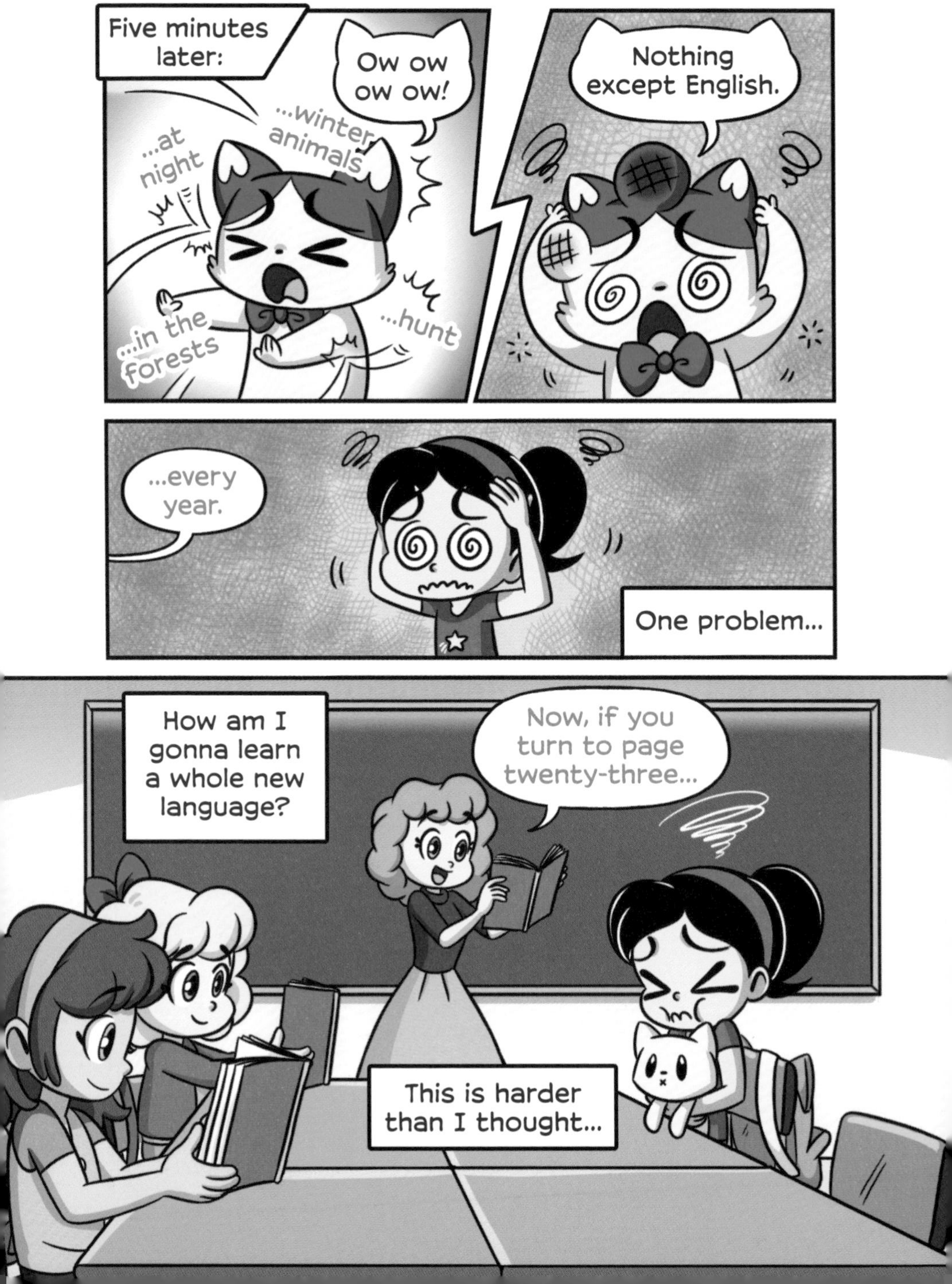
Five minutes later:
Ow ow ow ow!
...winter animals
...at night
...in the forests
...hunt
Nothing except English.
...every year.
One problem...
How am I gonna learn a whole new language?
Now, if you turn to page twenty-three...
This is harder than I thought...

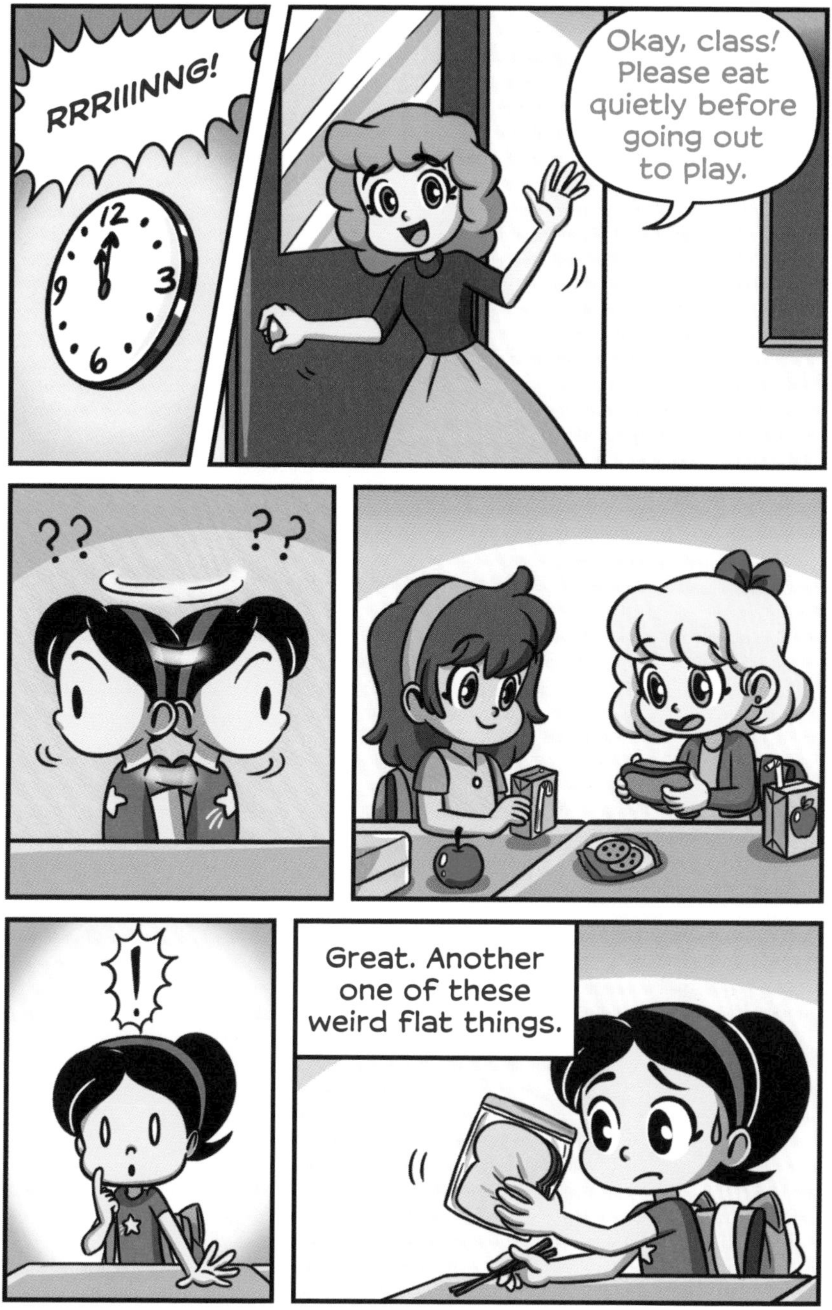
RRRIIINNG!
12
3
6
9
Okay, class! Please eat quietly before going out to play.
??
??
!
Great. Another one of these weird flat things.

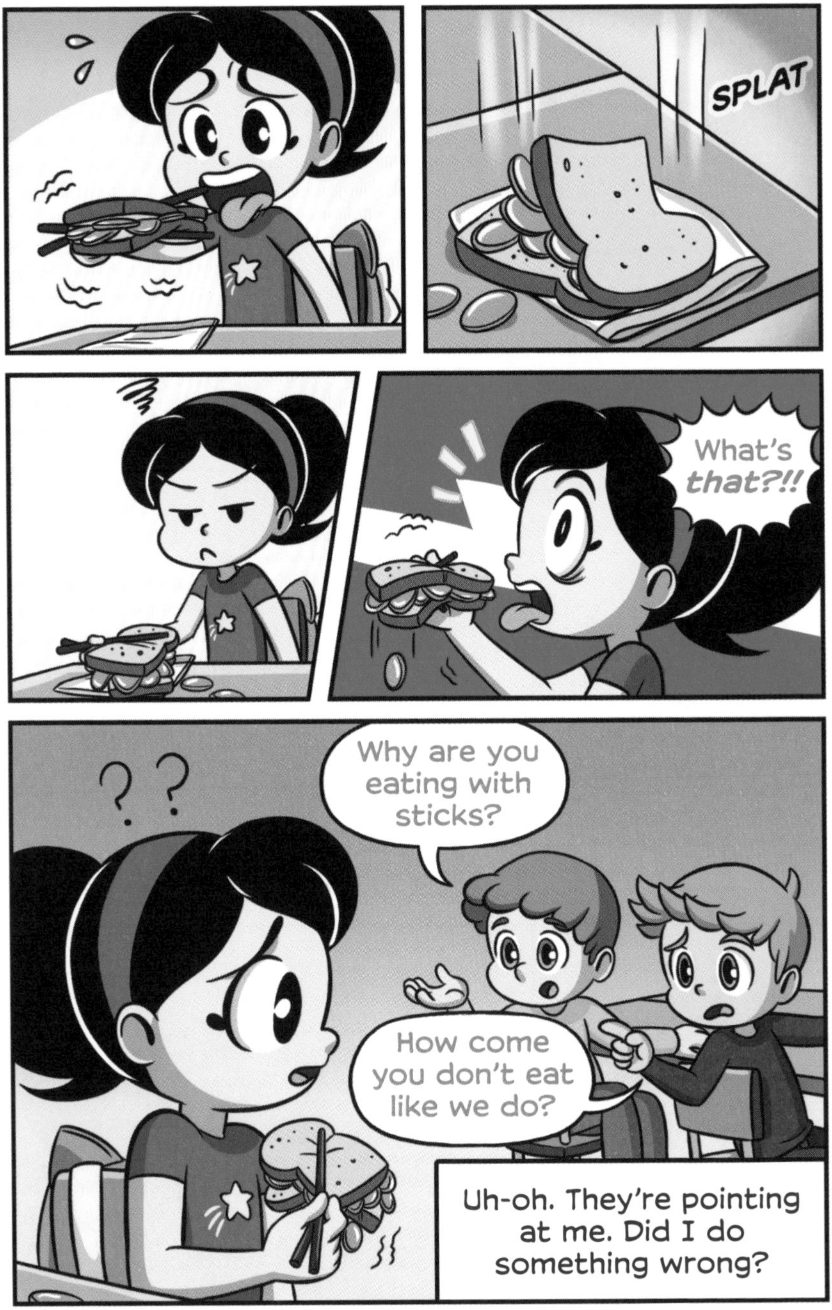
SPLAT
What's *that?!!*
Why are you eating with sticks?
How come you don't eat like we do?
Uh-oh. They're pointing at me. Did I do something wrong?

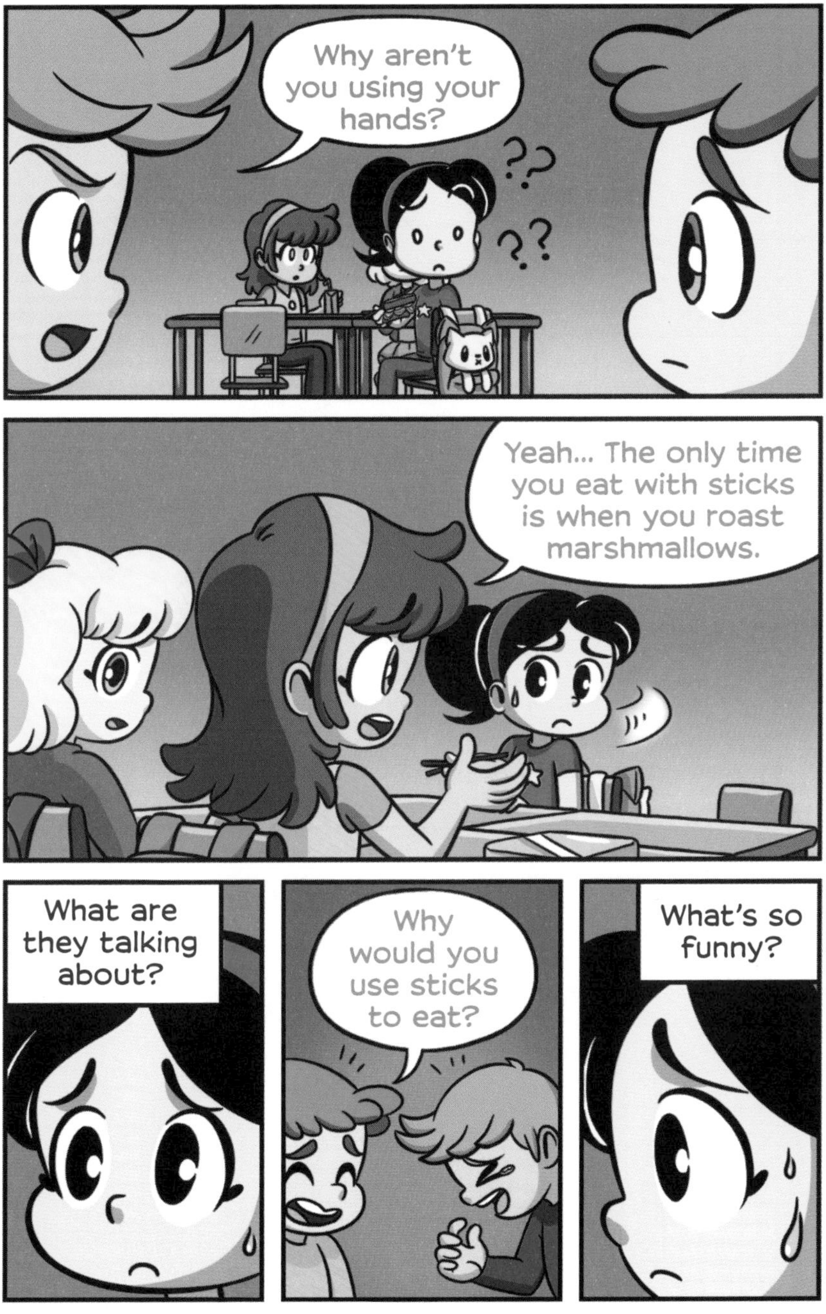

Why aren't you using your hands?
??
??
Yeah... The only time you eat with sticks is when you roast marshmallows.
What are they talking about?
Why would you use sticks to eat?
What's so funny?

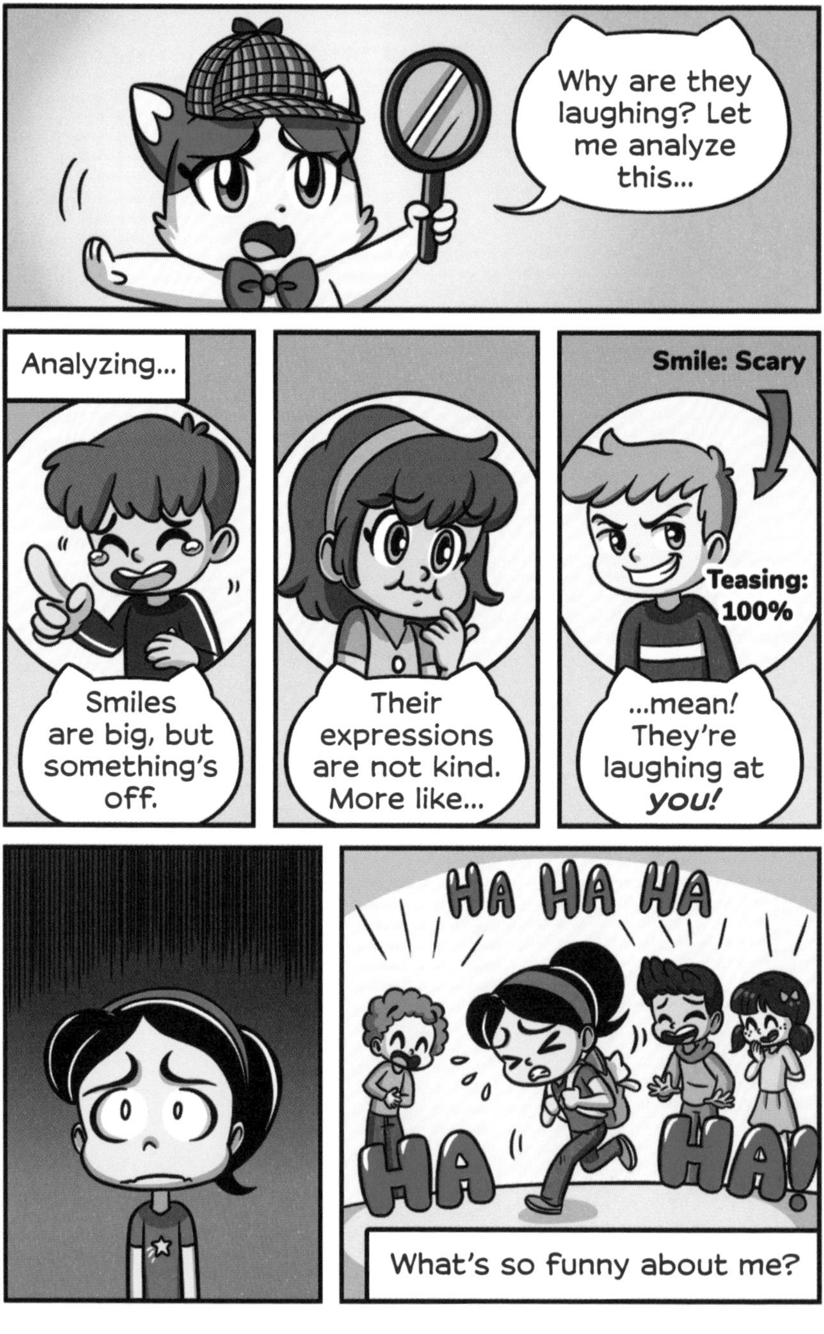

Why are they laughing? Let me analyze this...
Analyzing...
Smiles are big, but something's off.
Their expressions are not kind. More like...
Smile: Scary
Teasing: 100%
...mean! They're laughing at *you!*
HA HA HA
HA HA!
What's so funny about me?

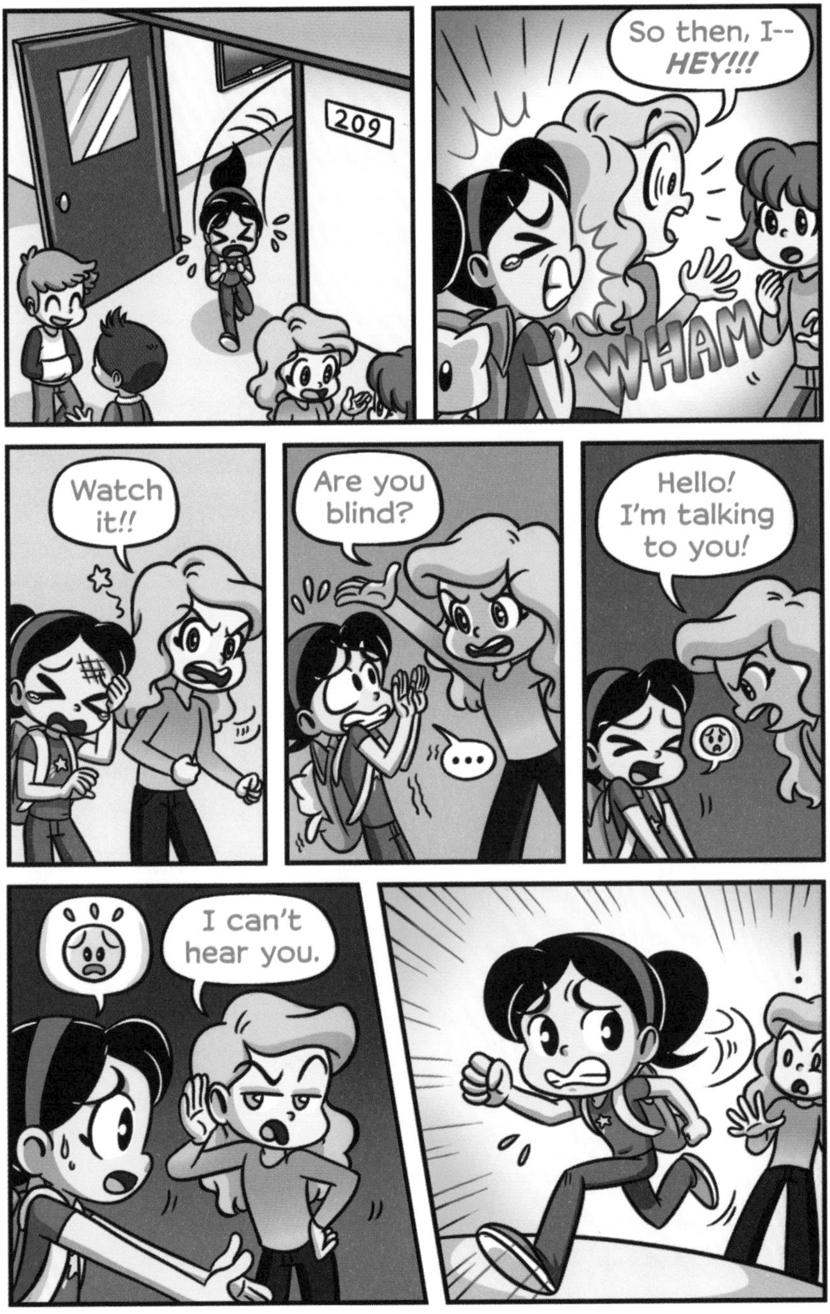
209
So then, I-- *HEY!!!*
WHAM
Watch it!!
Are you blind?
...
Hello! I'm talking to you!
I can't hear you.
!

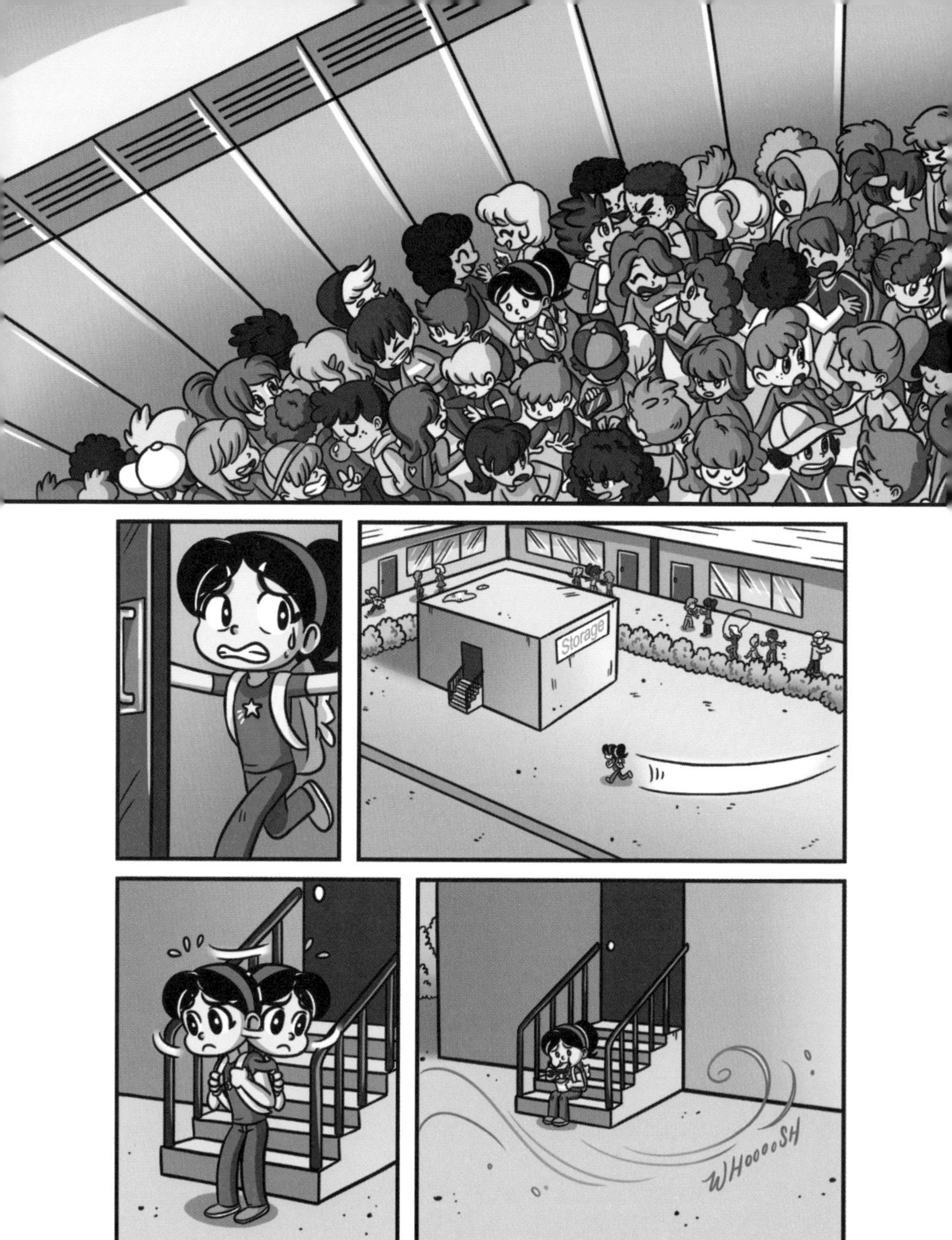
Storage
WHOooooSH

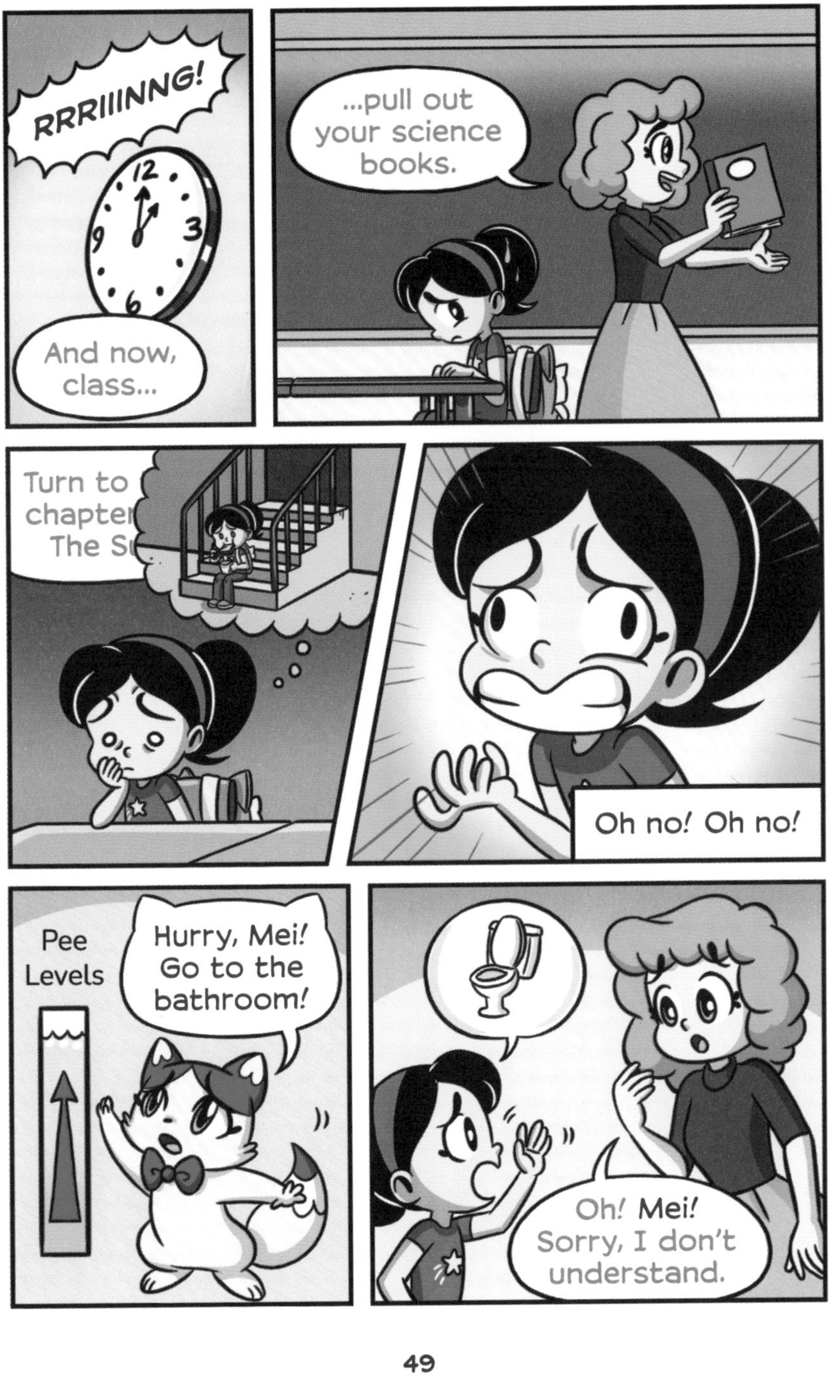
RRRIIINNG!
And now, class...
...pull out your science books.
Turn to chapter The S
Oh no! Oh no!
Pee Levels
Hurry, Mei! Go to the bathroom!
Oh! Mei! Sorry, I don't understand.

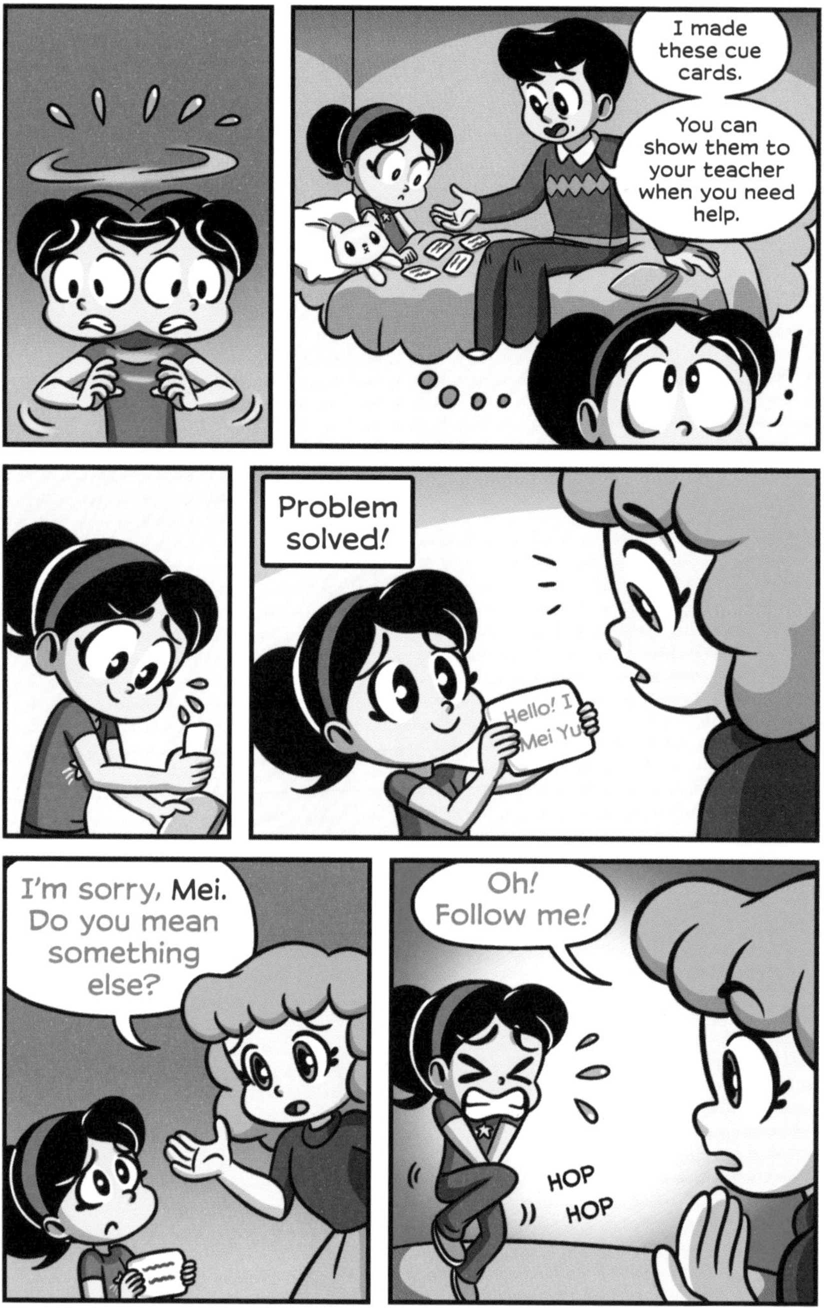
I made these cue cards.
You can show them to your teacher when you need help.
!
Problem solved!
Hello! I Mei Yu
I'm sorry, Mei. Do you mean something else?
Oh! Follow me!
HOP
HOP

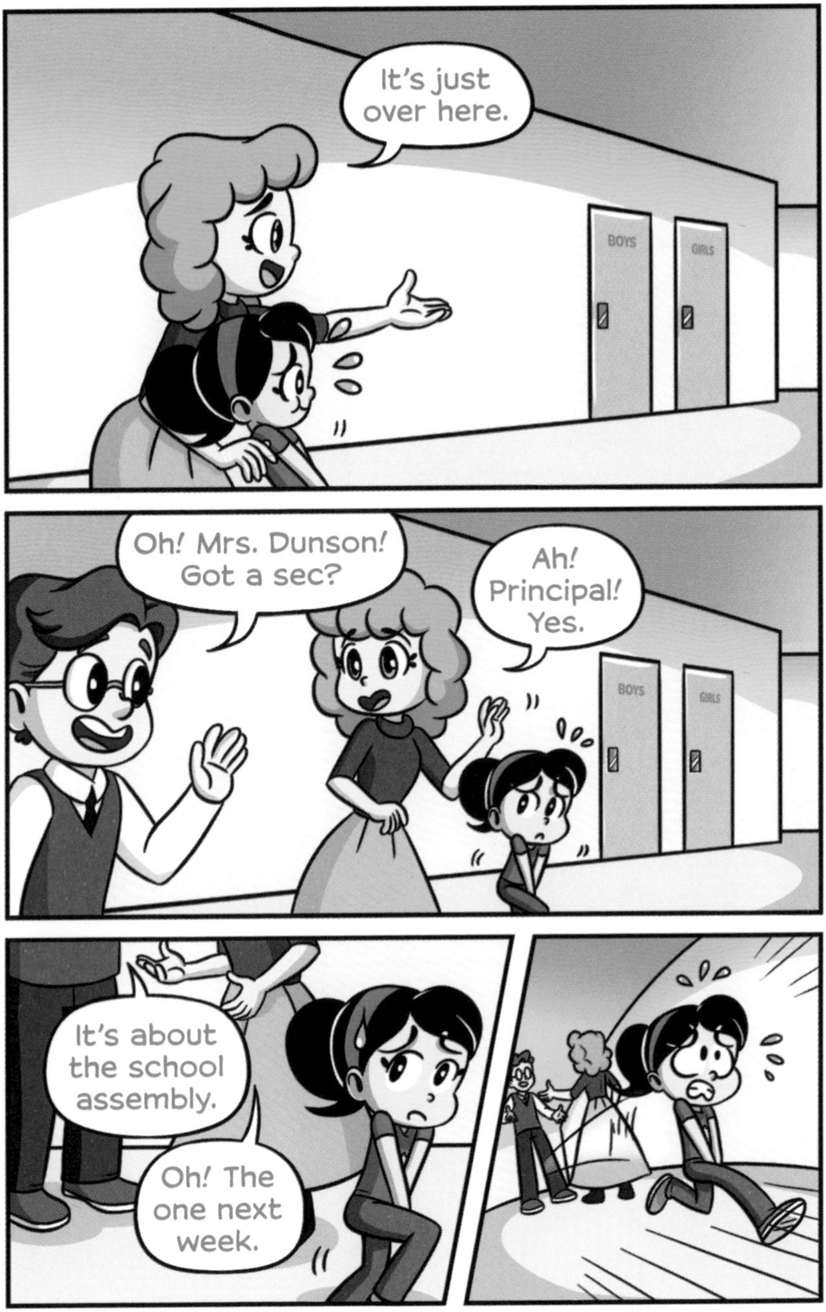
It's just over here.
BOYS
GIRLS
Oh! Mrs. Dunson! Got a sec?
Ah! Principal! Yes.
BOYS
GIRLS
It's about the school assembly.
Oh! The one next week.

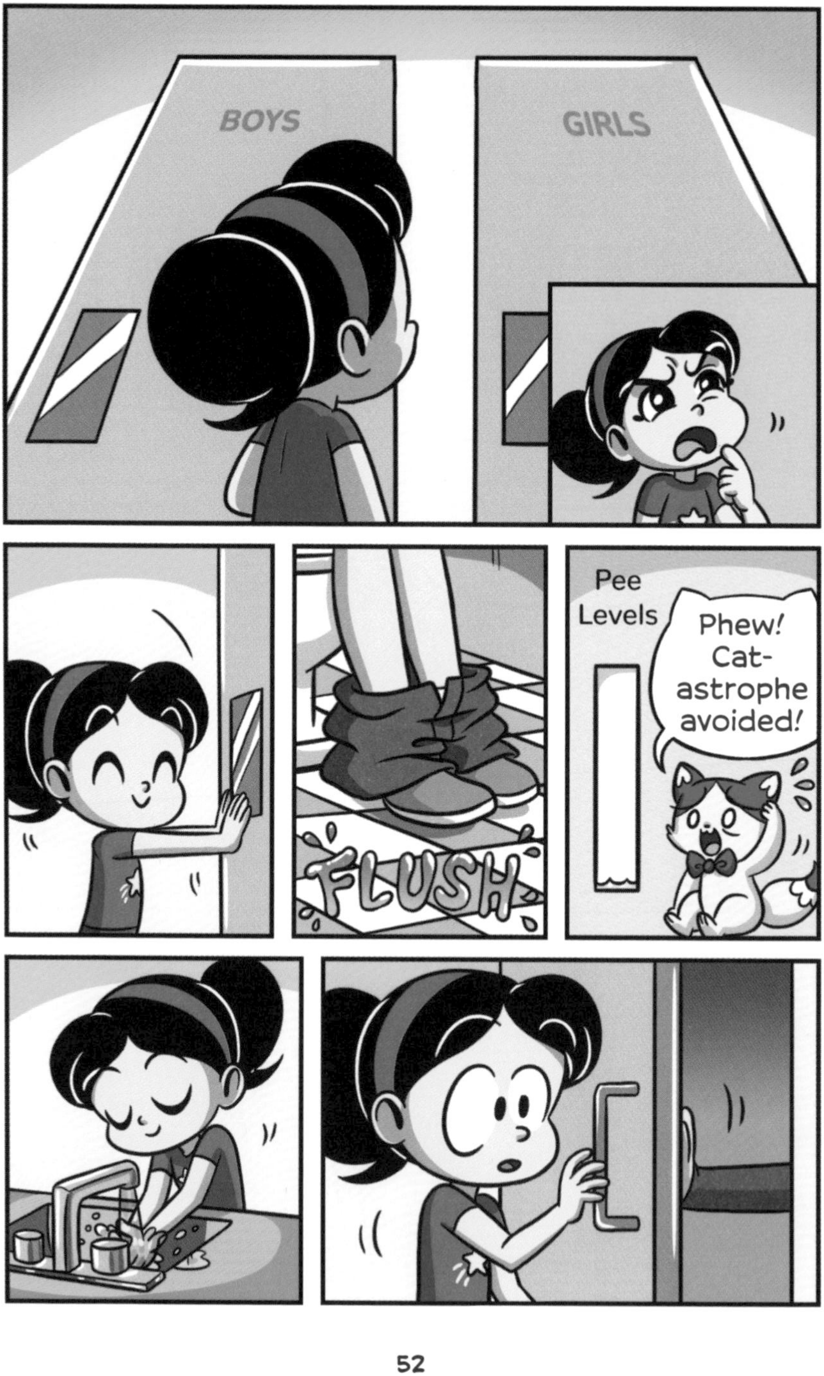
BOYS
GIRLS
FLUSH
Pee Levels
Phew! Cat-astrophe avoided!

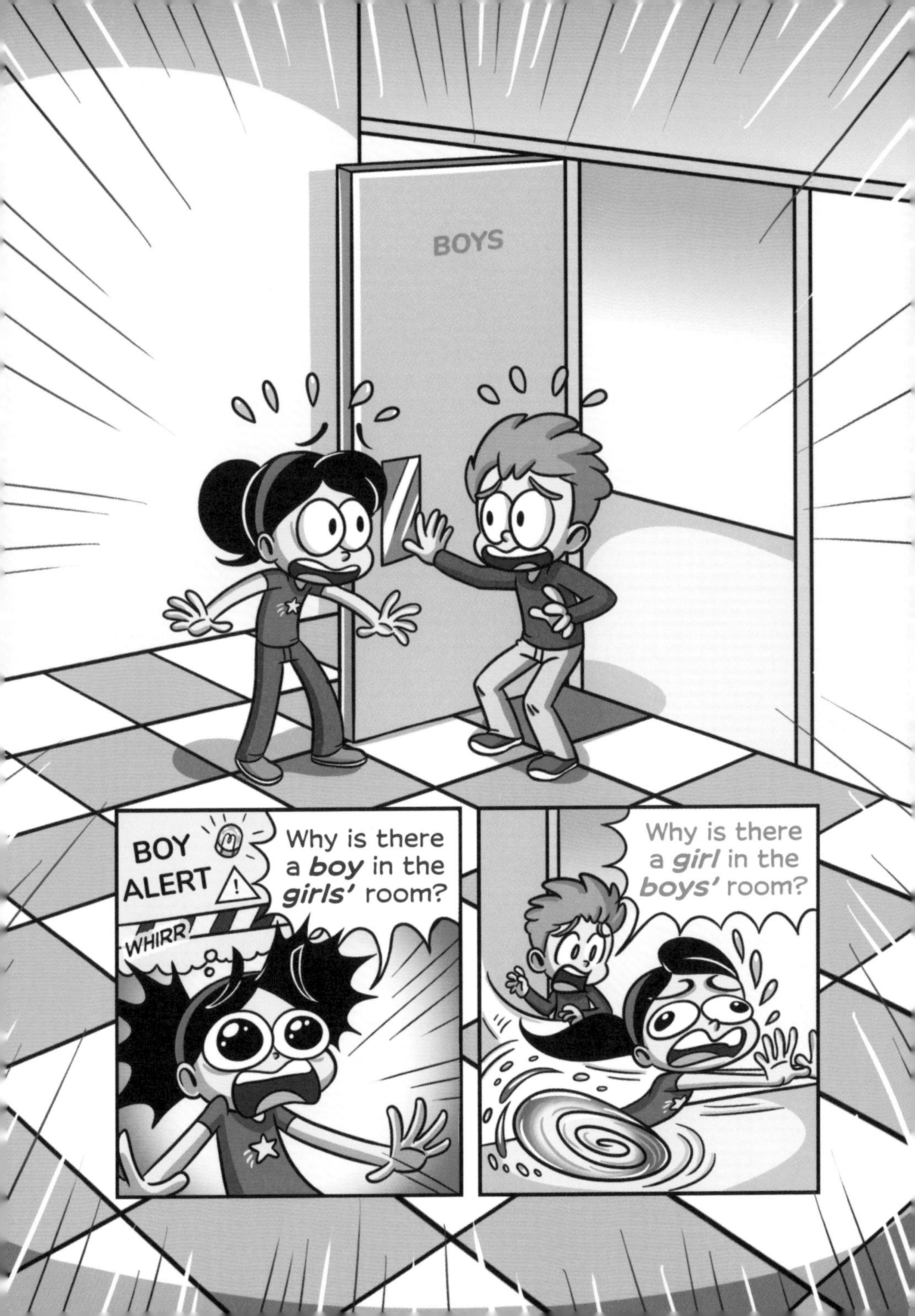
BOYS
BOY ALERT
WHIRR
Why is there a ***boy*** in the ***girls'*** room?
Why is there a ***girl*** in the ***boys'*** room?

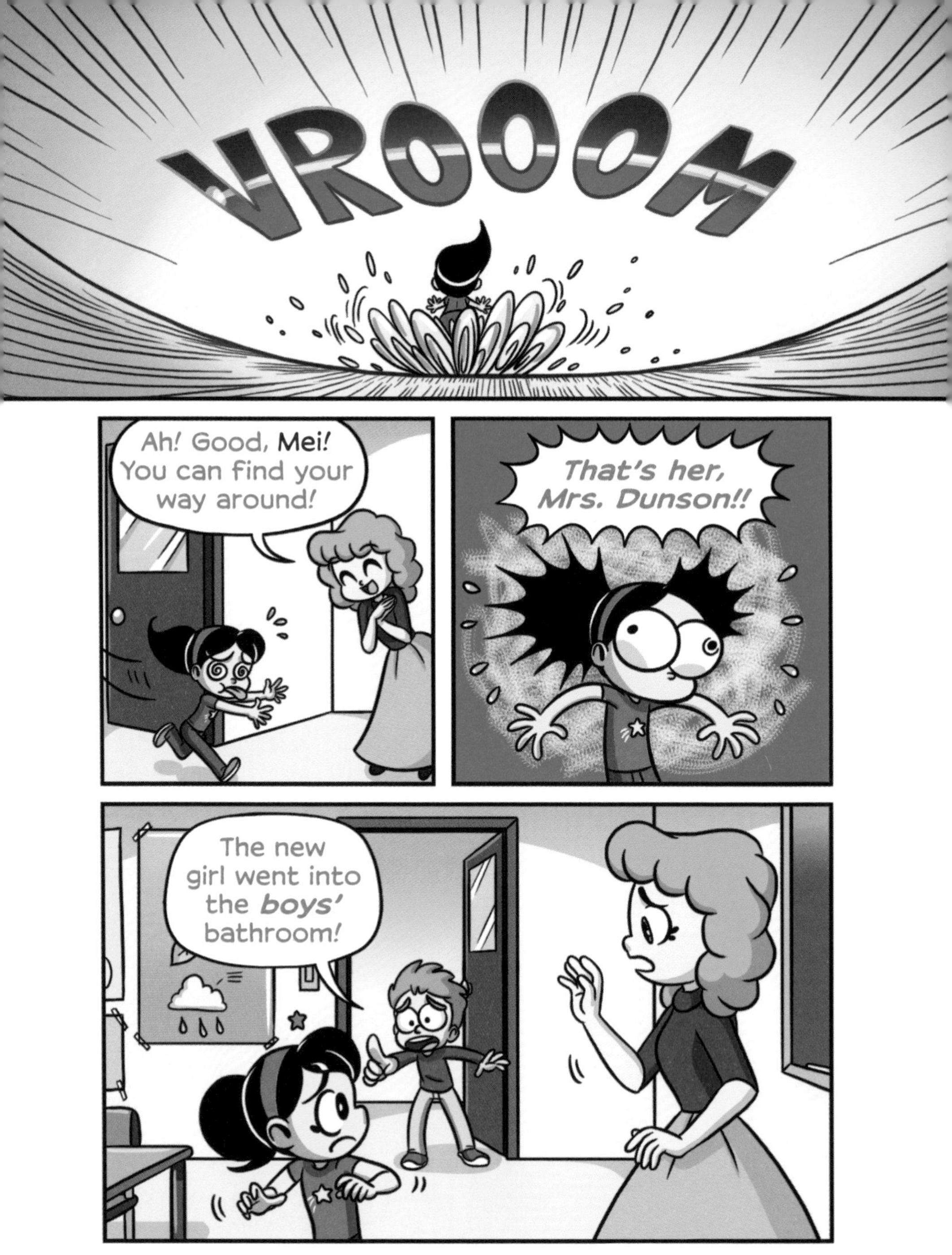
VROOOM
Ah! Good, Mei! You can find your way around!
That's her, Mrs. Dunson!!
The new girl went into the *boys'* bathroom!

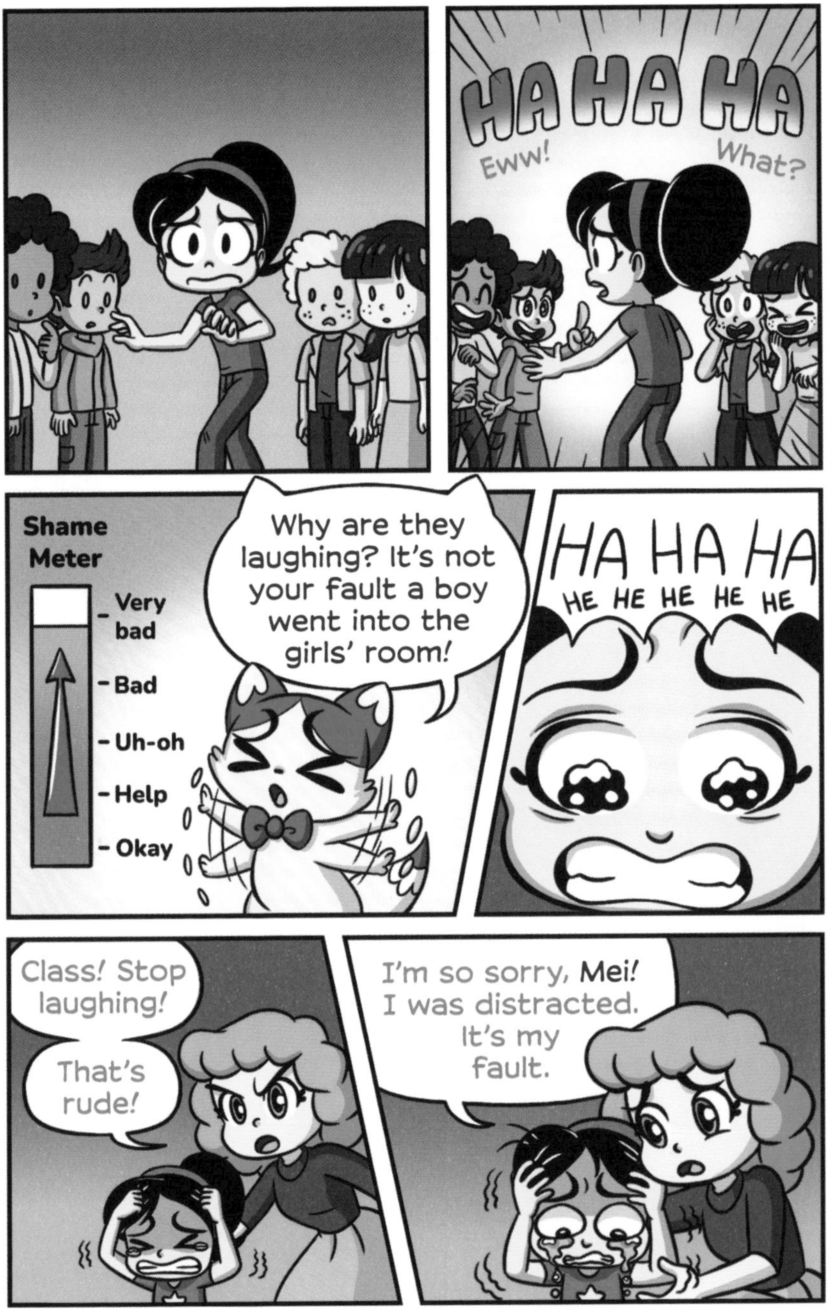
HA HA HA HA
Eww!
What?
Shame Meter
Very bad
Bad
Uh-oh
Help
Okay
Why are they laughing? It's not your fault a boy went into the girls' room!
HA HA HA
HE HE HE HE HE
Class! Stop laughing!
That's rude!
I'm so sorry, Mei! I was distracted. It's my fault.

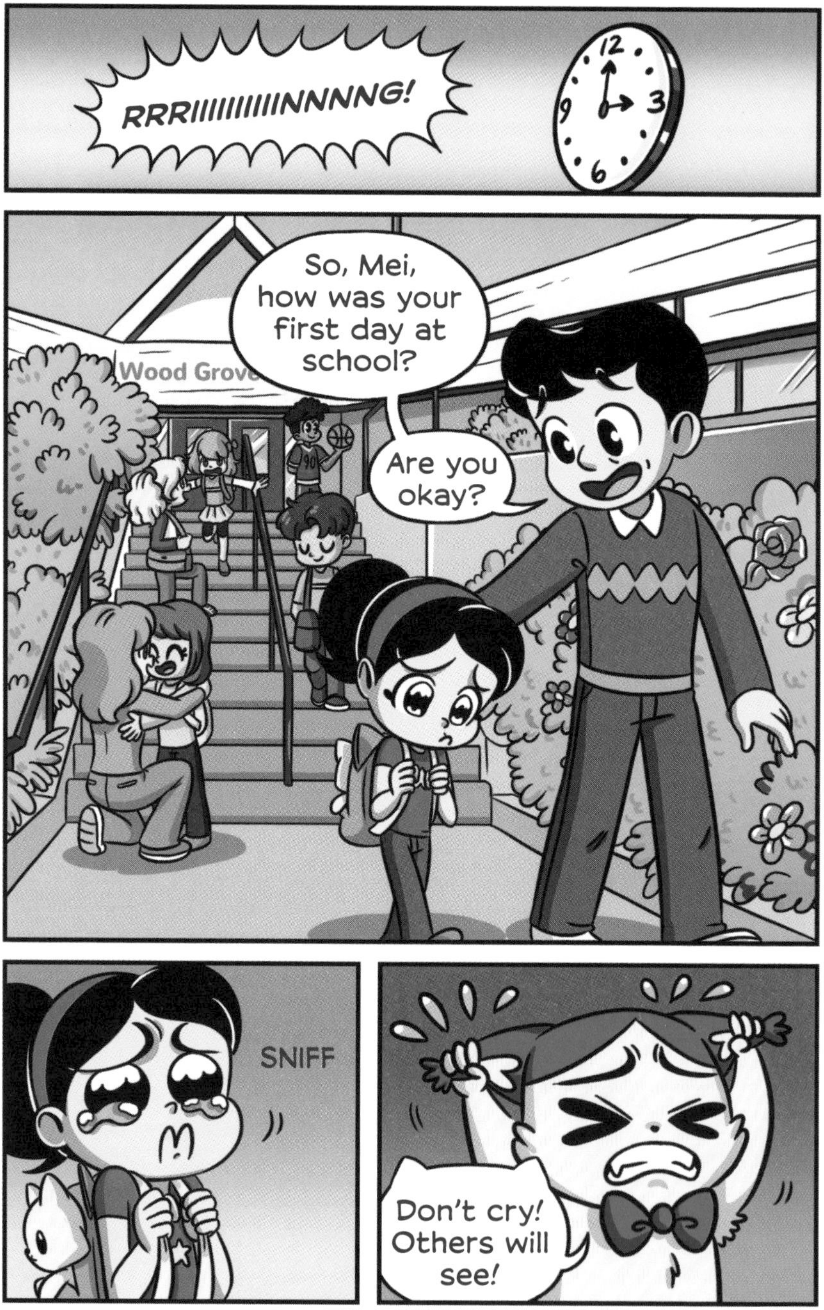
RRRIIIIIIIIIIINNNNG!
12
3
6
9
Wood Grove
So, Mei, how was your first day at school?
Are you okay?
SNIFF
Don't cry! Others will see!

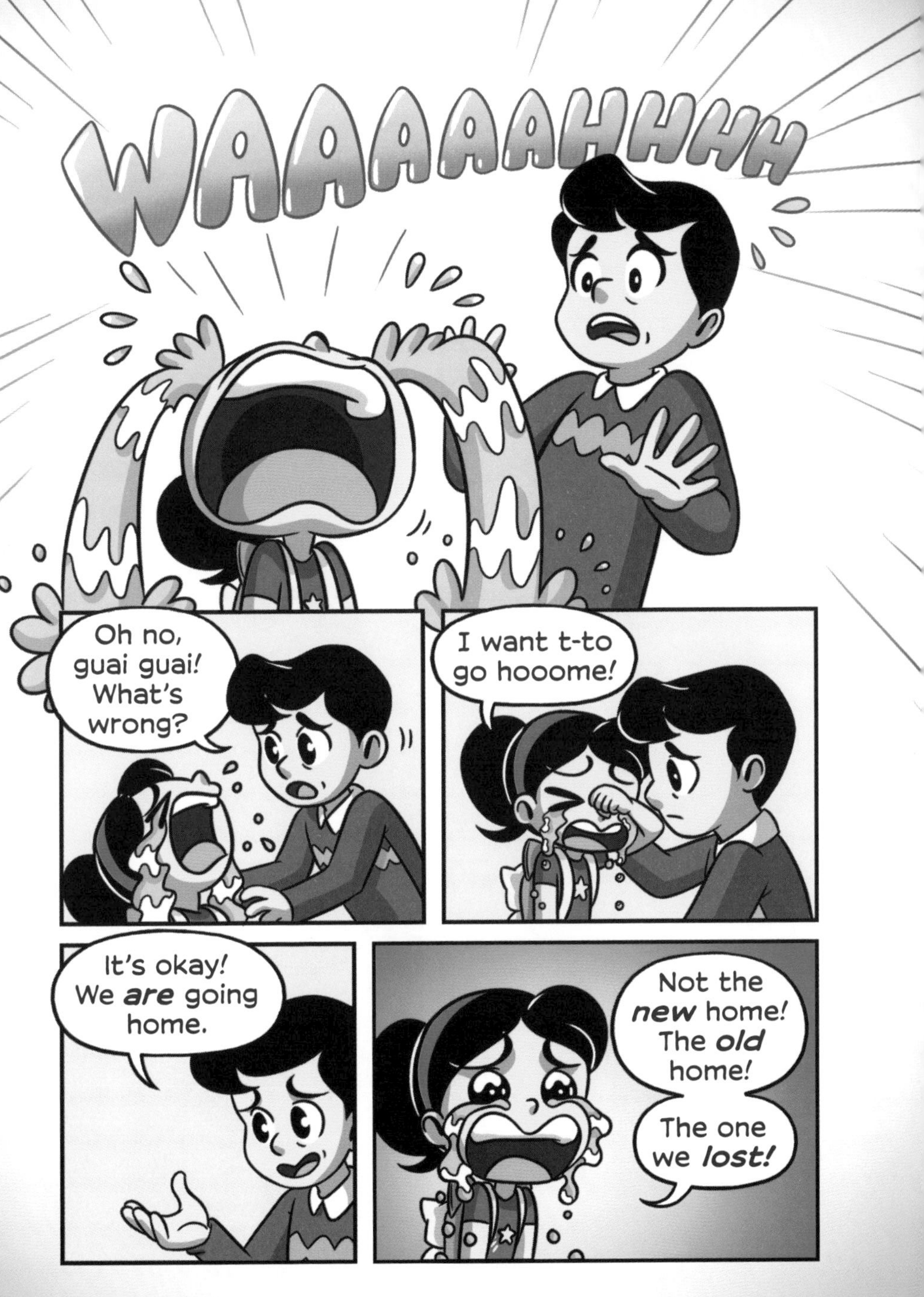
WAAAAAAHHHH
Oh no, guai guai! What's wrong?
I want t-to go hooome!
It's okay! We *are* going home.
Not the ***new*** home! The ***old*** home!
The one we ***lost!***

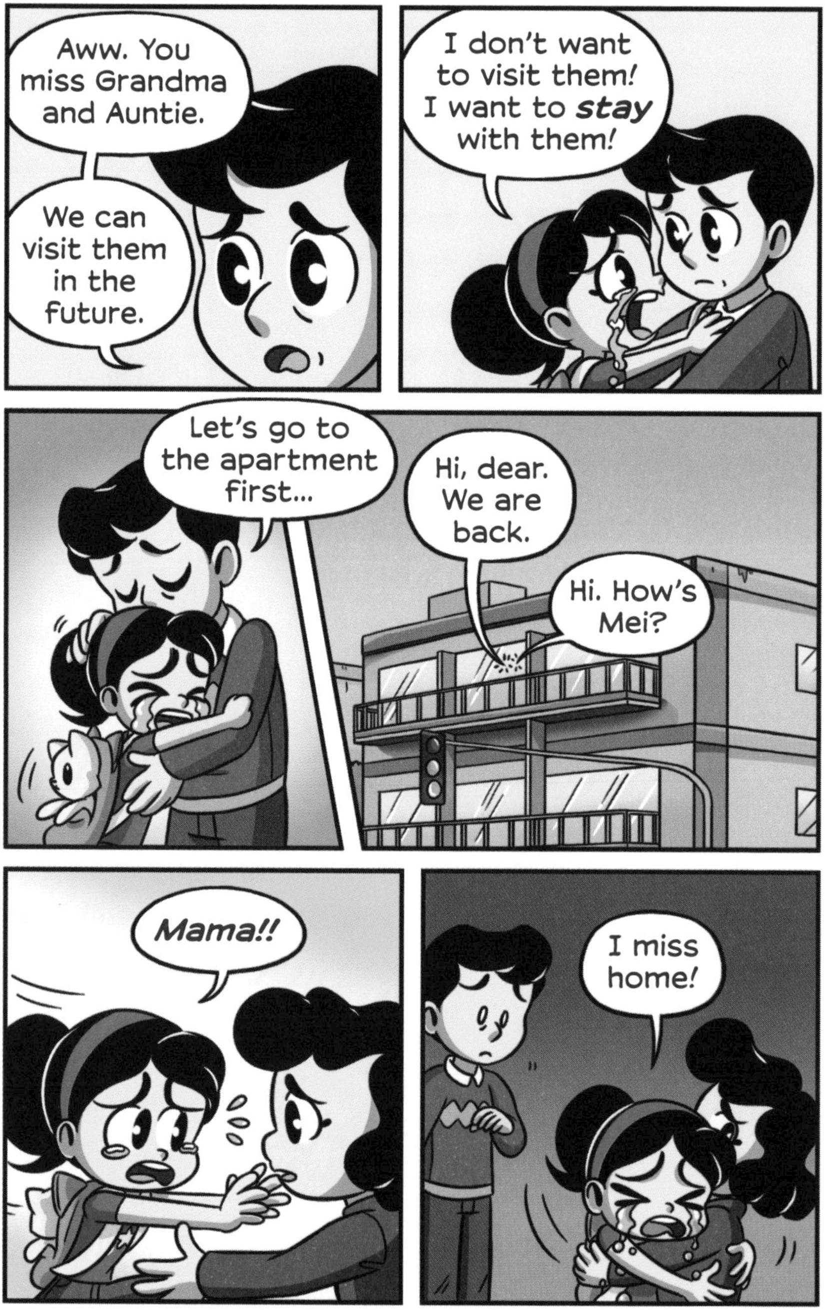
Aww. You miss Grandma and Auntie.
We can visit them in the future.
I don't want to visit them! I want to *stay* with them!
Let's go to the apartment first...
Hi, dear. We are back.
Hi. How's Mei?
Mama!!
I miss home!

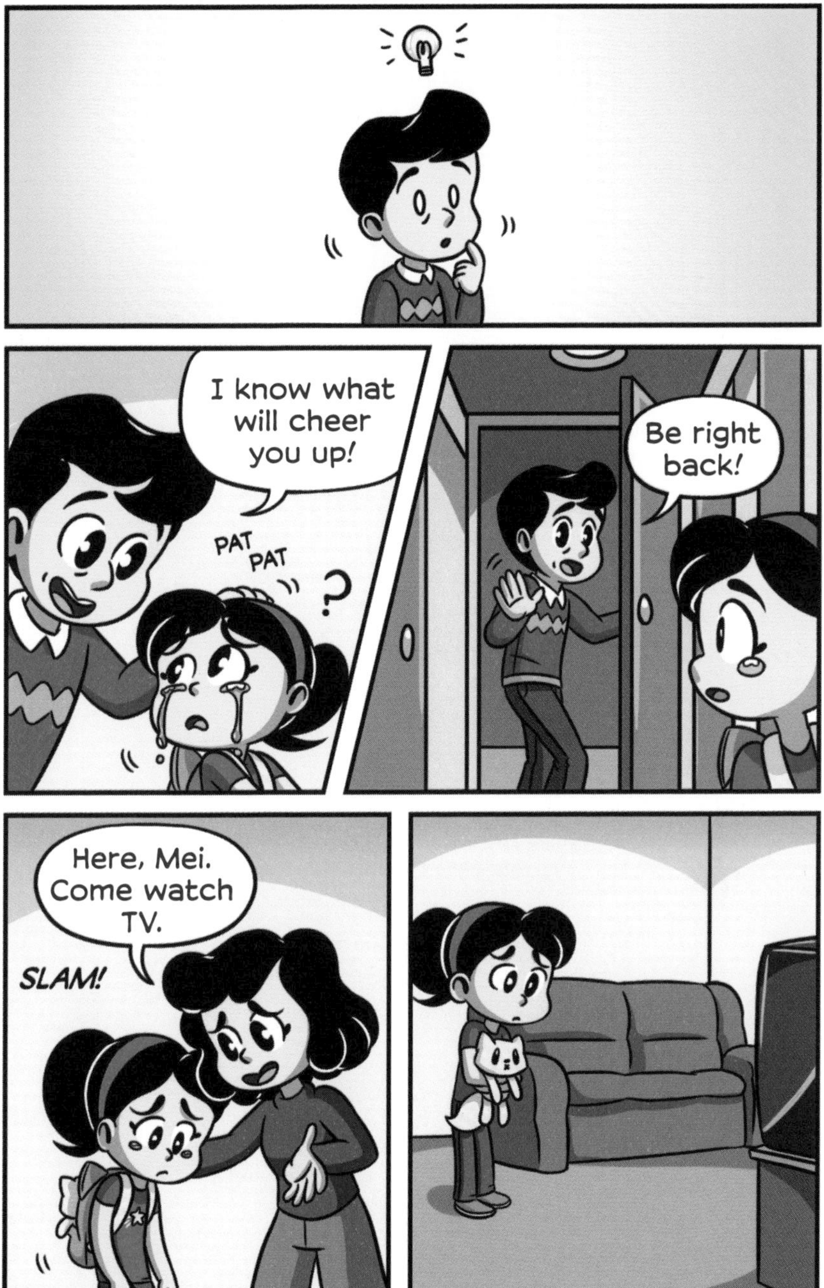
I know what will cheer you up!
PAT PAT
?
Be right back!
Here, Mei. Come watch TV.
SLAM!

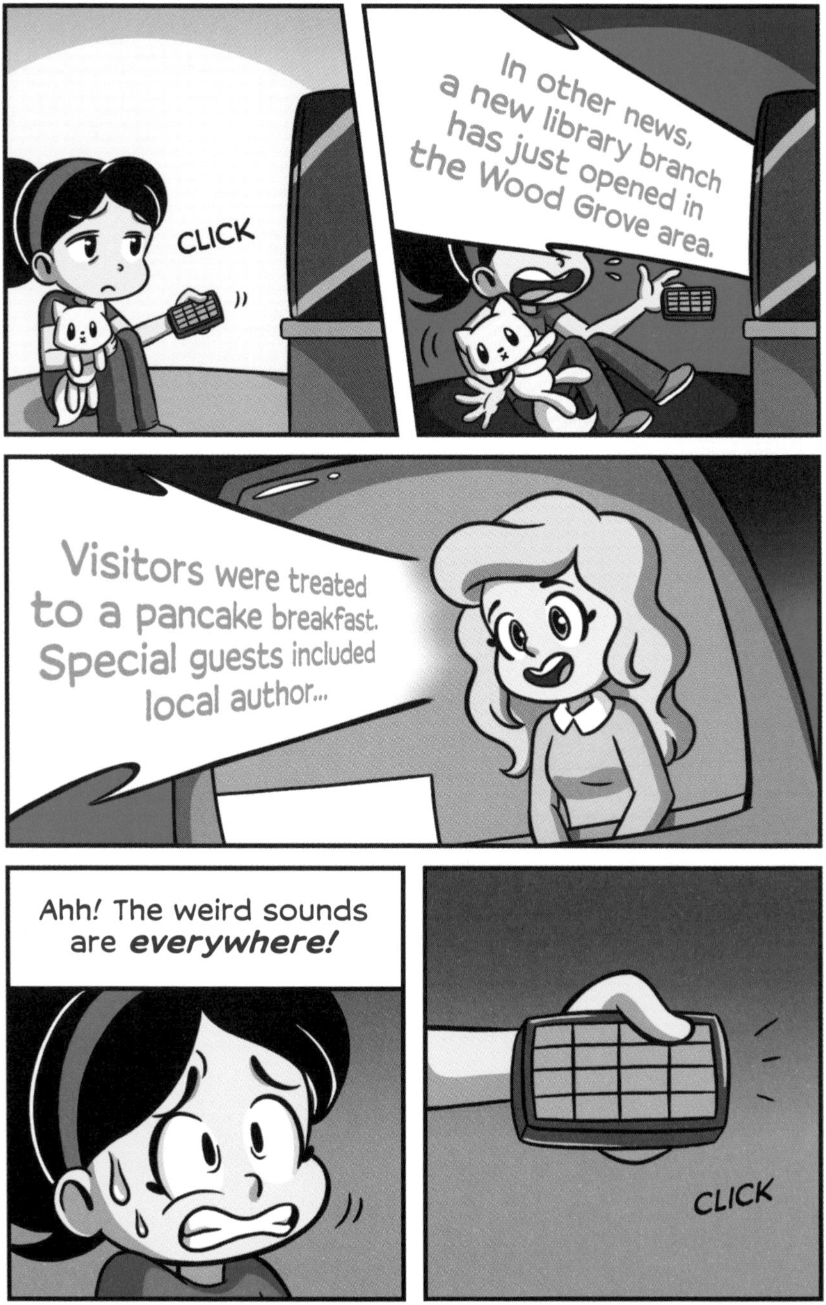
CLICK
In other news, a new library branch has just opened in the Wood Grove area.
Visitors were treated to a pancake breakfast. Special guests included local author...
Ahh! The weird sounds are ***everywhere!***
CLICK

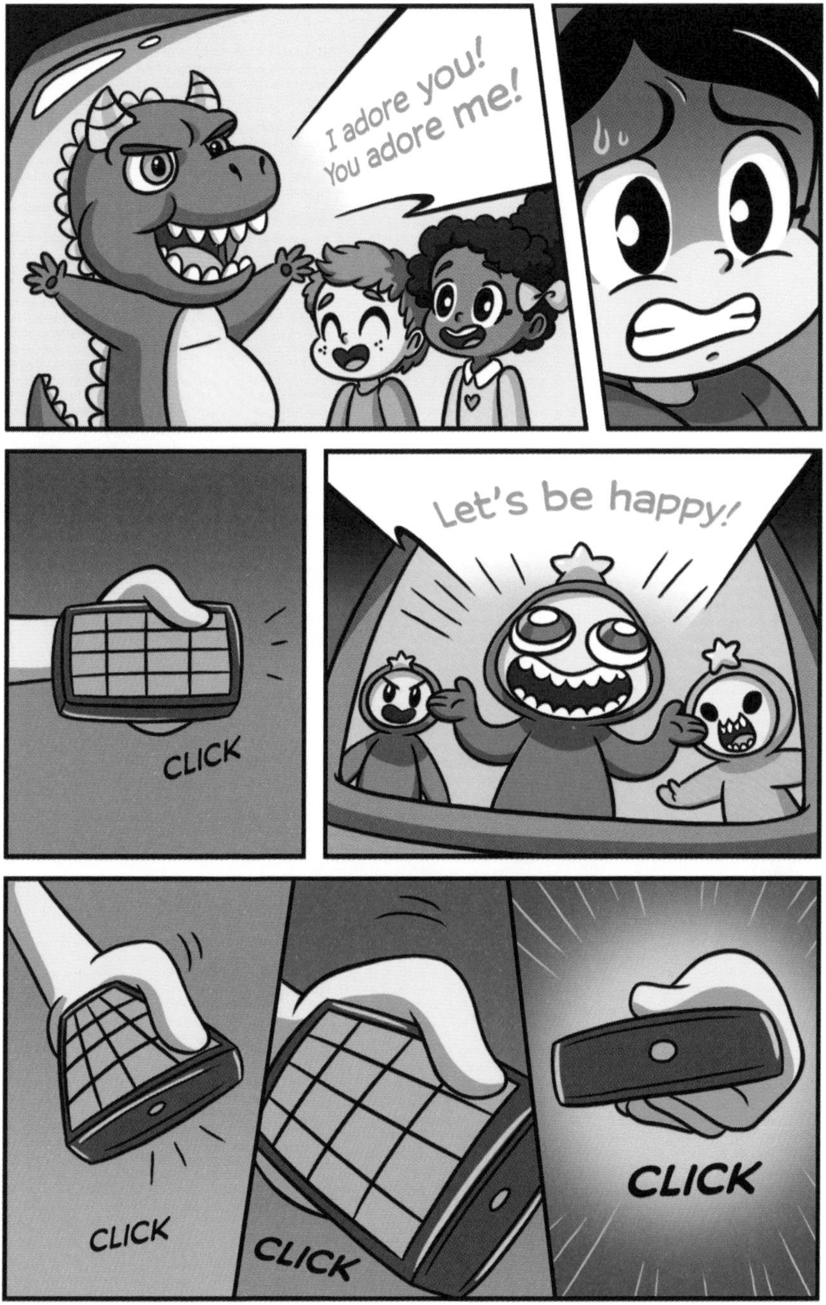
I adore you! You adore me!
CLICK
Let's be happy!
CLICK
CLICK
CLICK

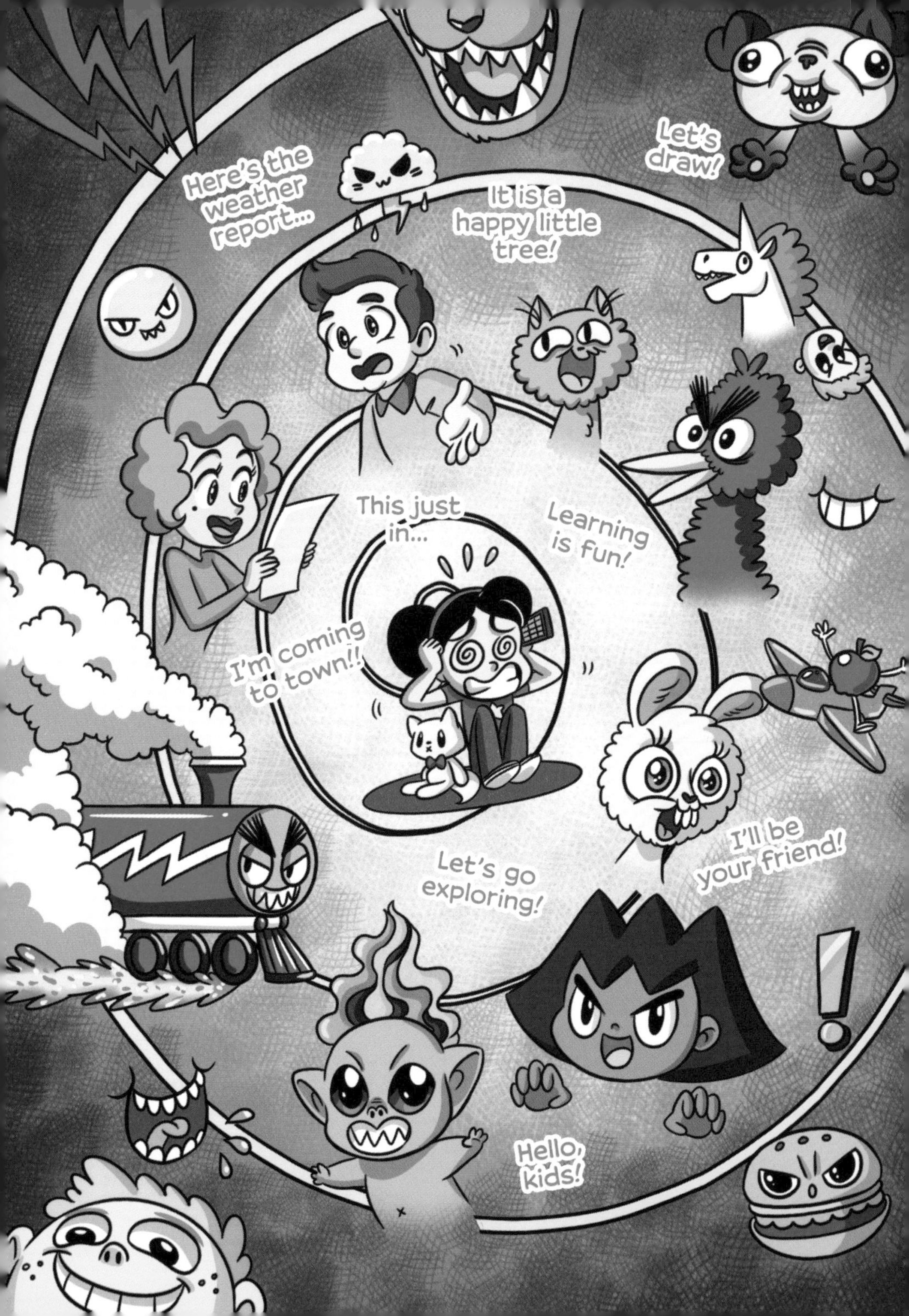
Here's the weather report...
It is a happy little tree!
Let's draw!
This just in...
Learning is fun!
I'm coming to town!!
I'll be your friend!
Let's go exploring!
Hello, kids!

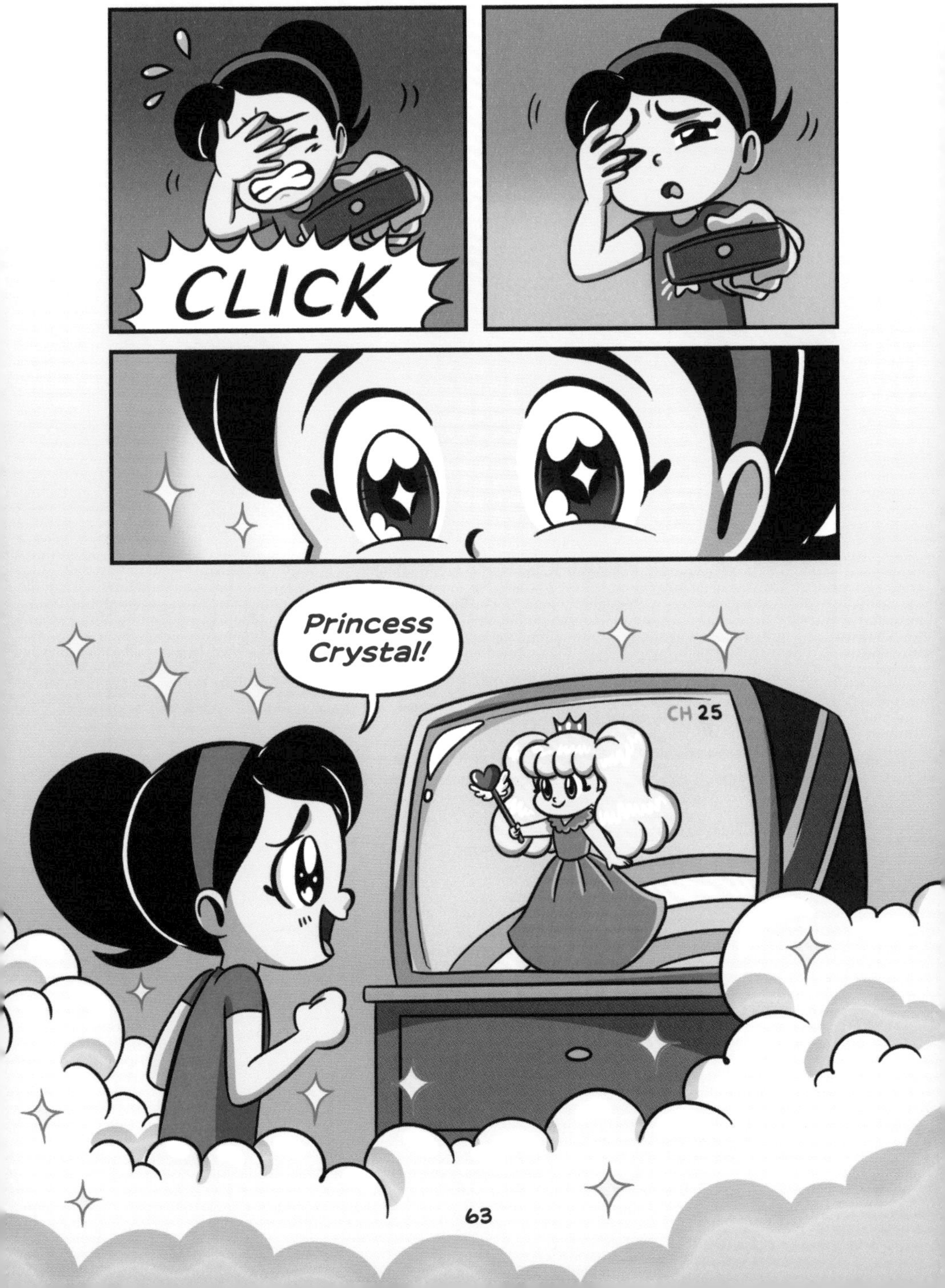
CLICK
Princess Crystal!
CH 25

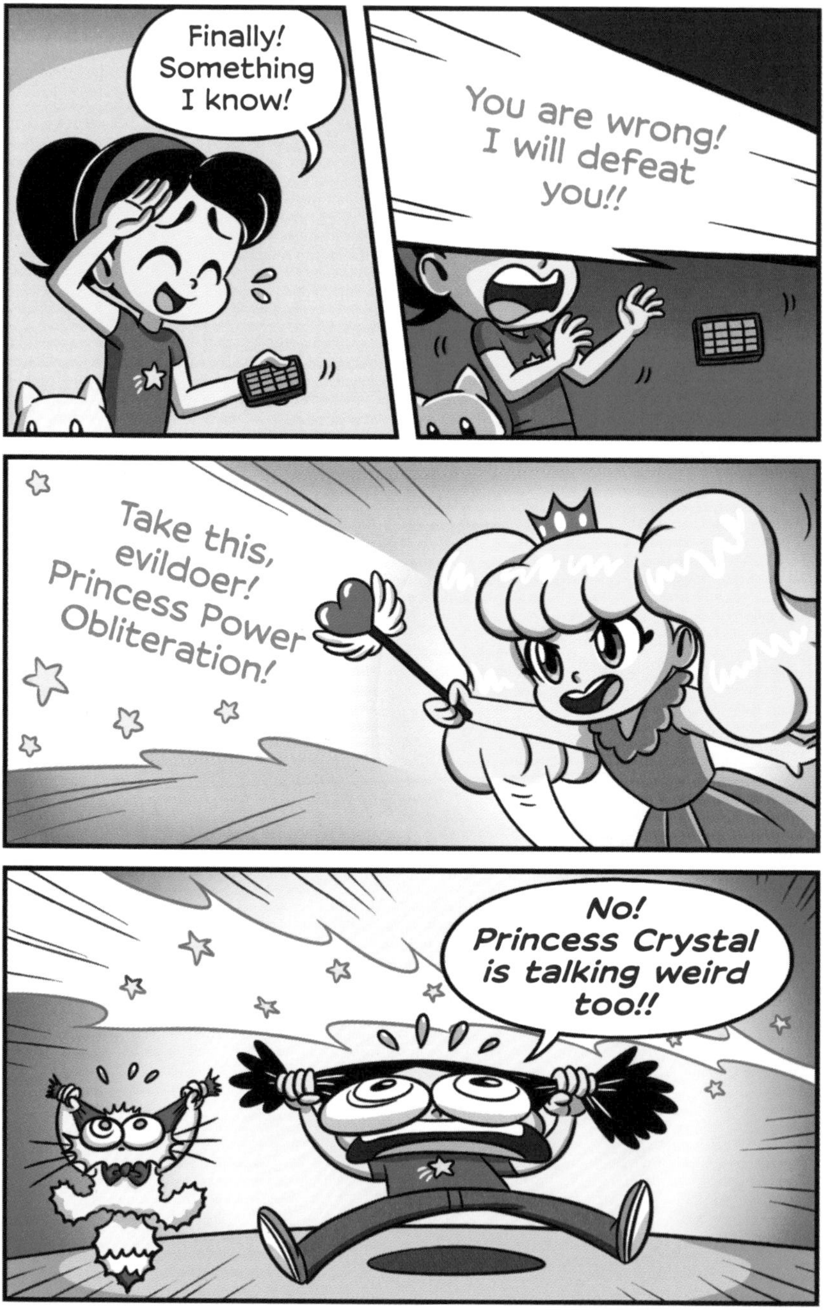
Finally! Something I know!
You are wrong! I will defeat you!!
Take this, evildoer! Princess Power Obliteration!
No! Princess Crystal is talking weird too!!

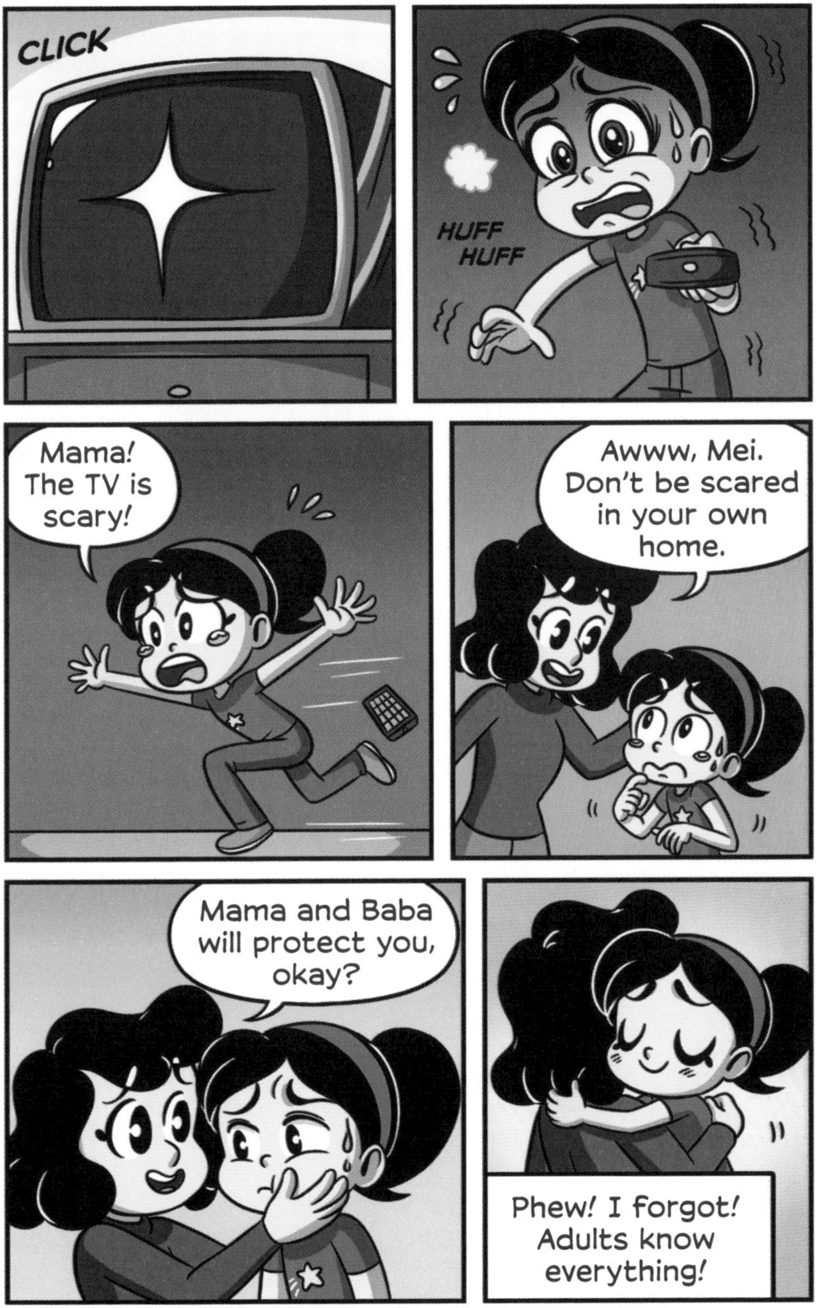
CLICK
HUFF HUFF
Mama! The TV is scary!
Awww, Mei. Don't be scared in your own home.
Mama and Baba will protect you, okay?
Phew! I forgot! Adults know everything!

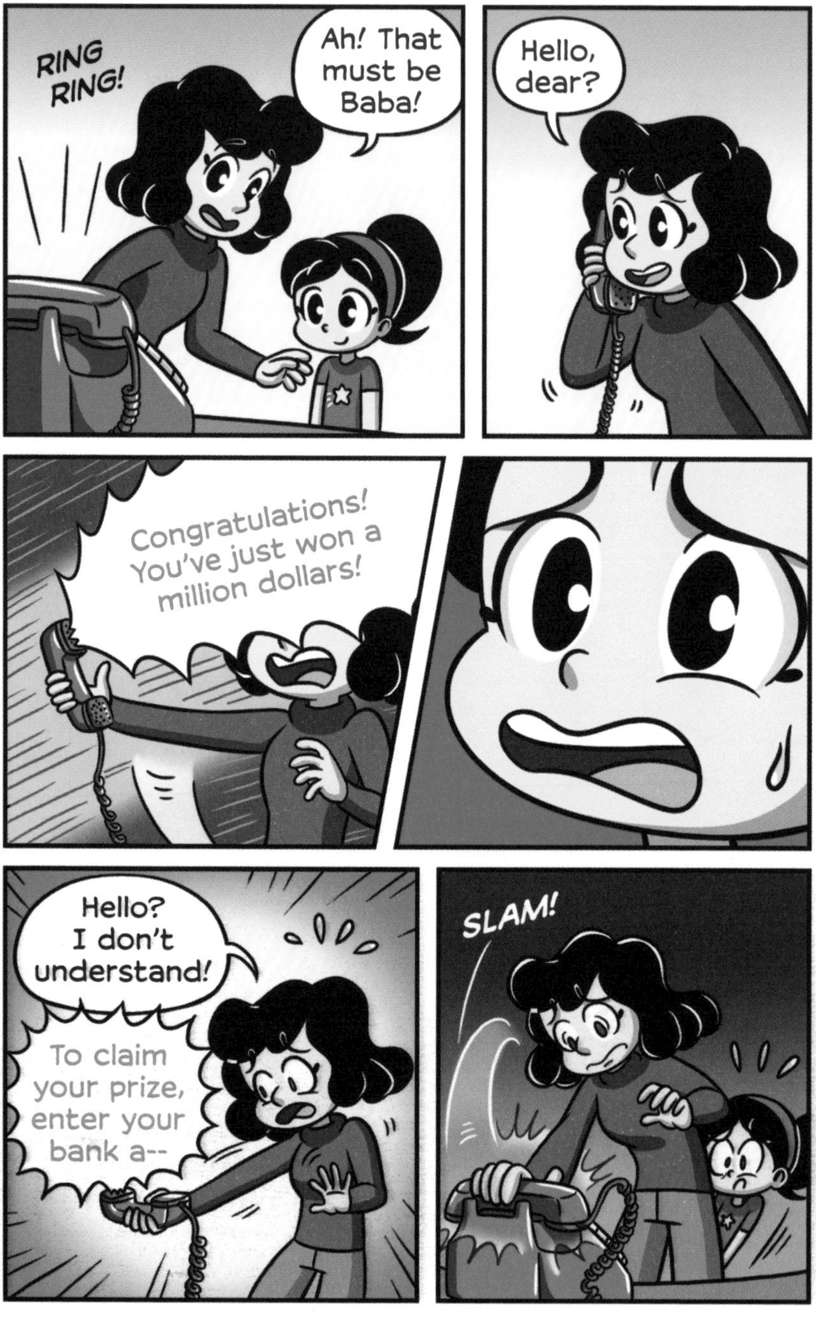
RING RING!
Ah! That must be Baba!
Hello, dear?
Congratulations! You've just won a million dollars!
Hello? I don't understand!
To claim your prize, enter your bank a--
SLAM!

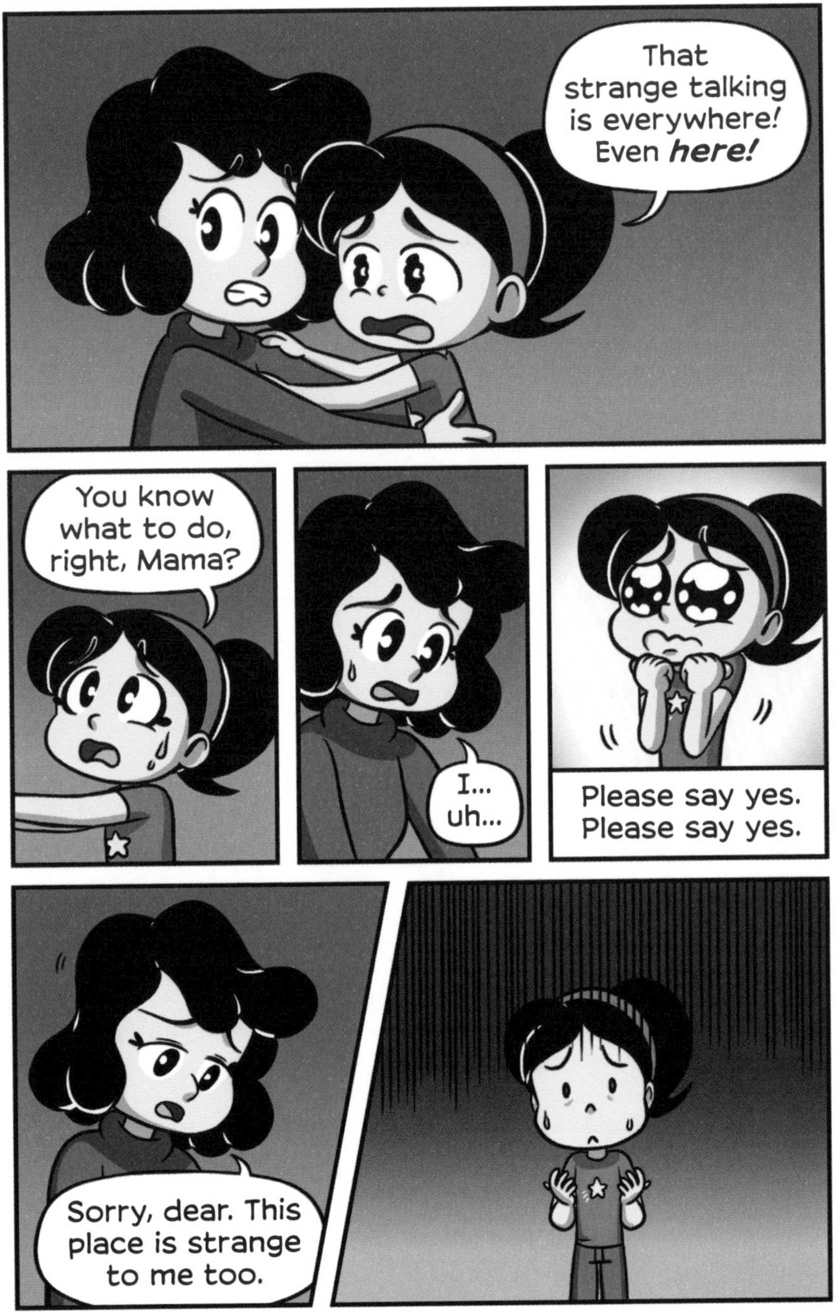
That strange talking is everywhere! Even ***here!***
You know what to do, right, Mama?
I... uh...
Please say yes. Please say yes.
Sorry, dear. This place is strange to me too.

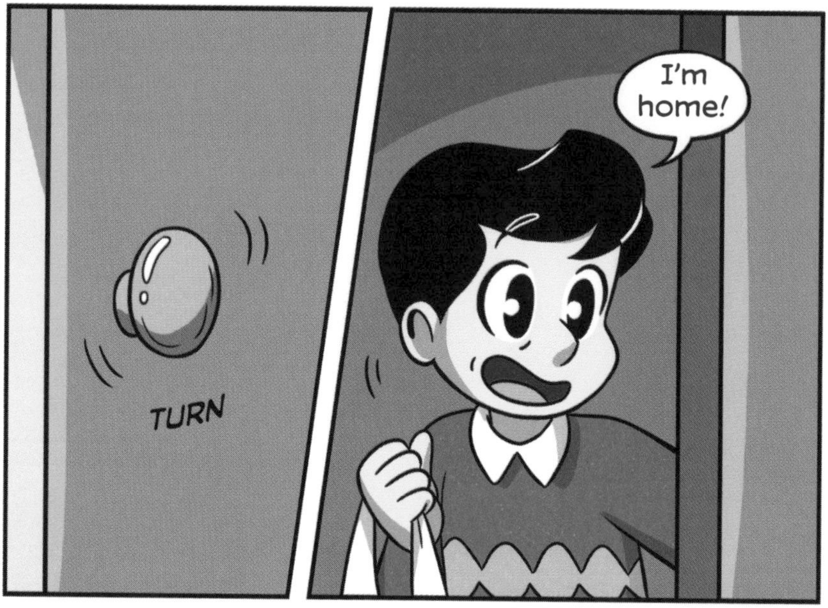
TURN
I'm home!

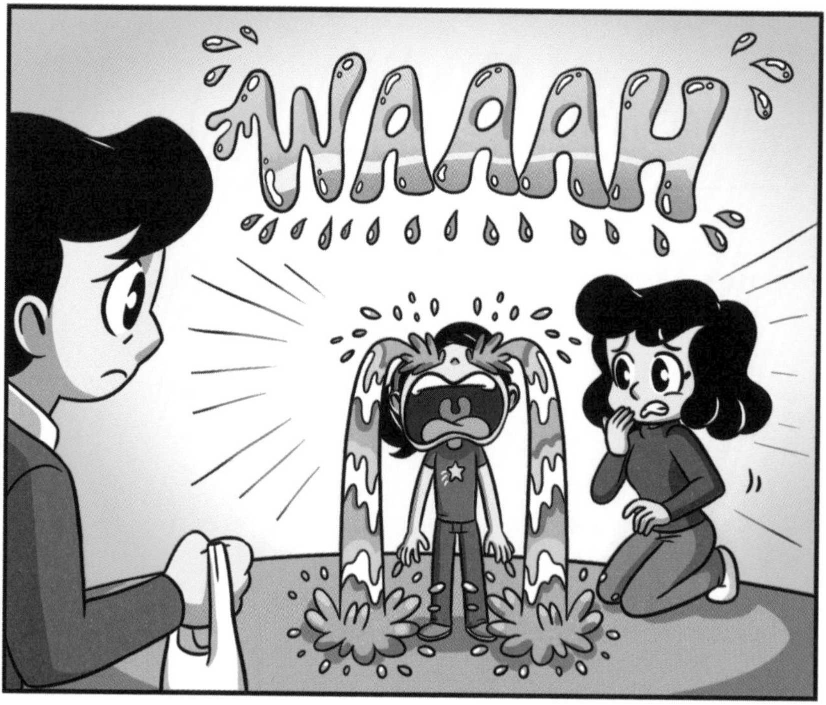
WAAAH

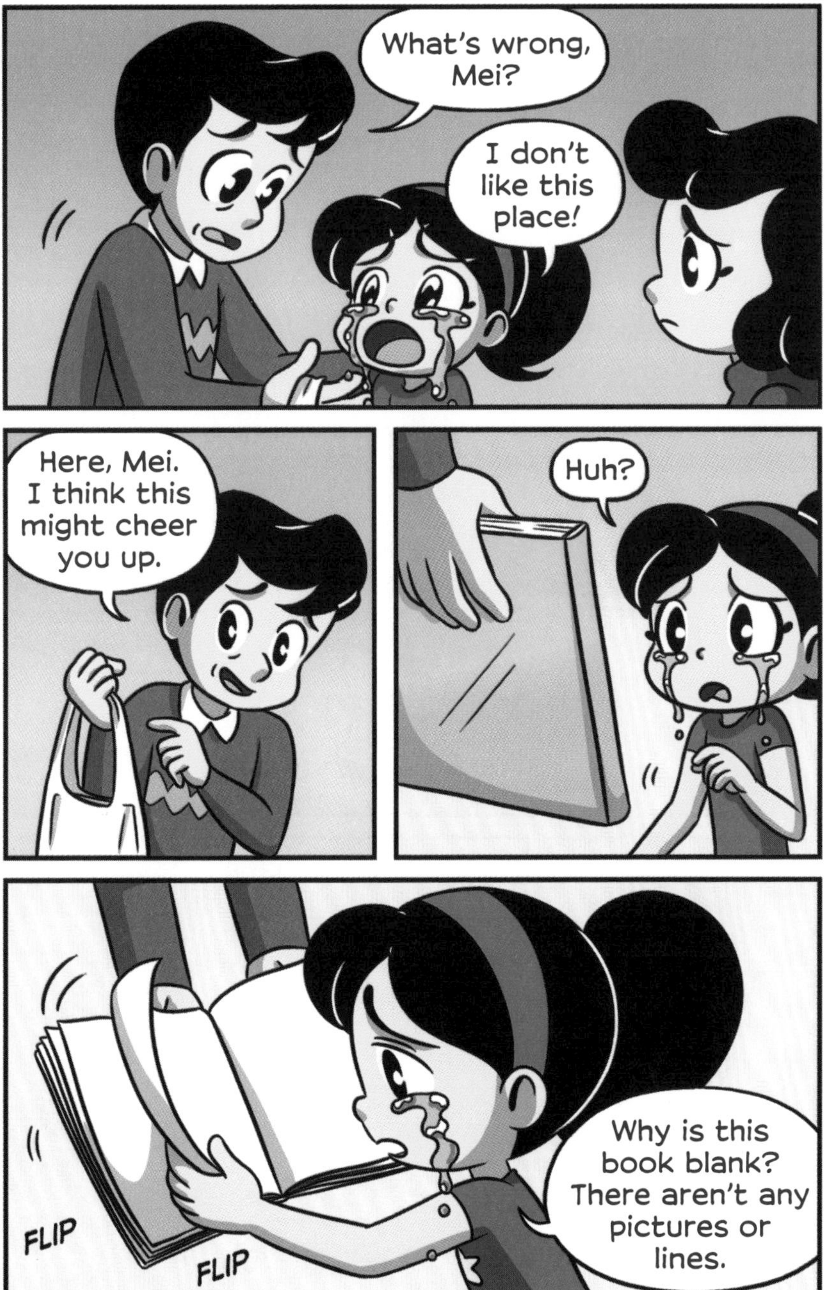
What's wrong, Mei?
I don't like this place!
Here, Mei. I think this might cheer you up.
Huh?
Why is this book blank? There aren't any pictures or lines.
FLIP
FLIP

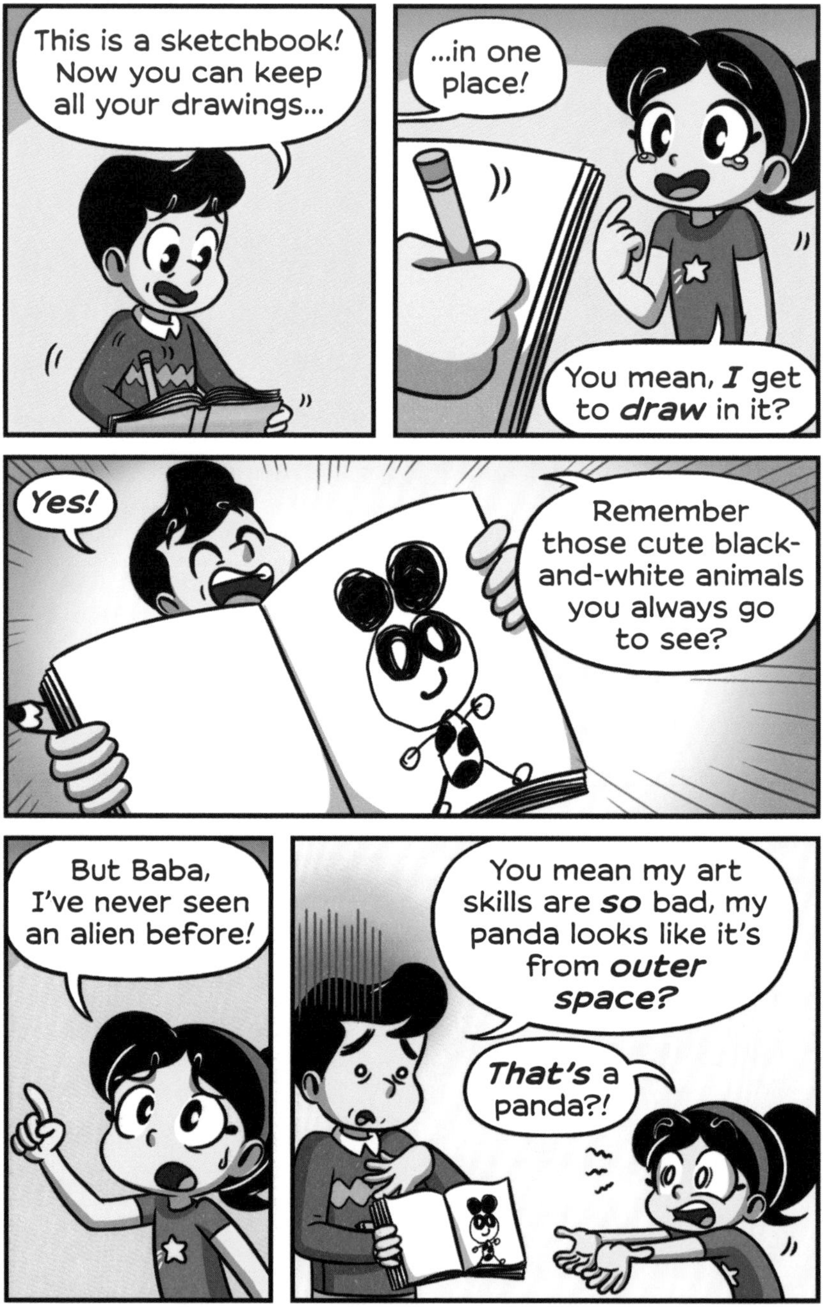

This is a sketchbook! Now you can keep all your drawings...
...in one place!
You mean, *I* get to *draw* in it?
Yes!
Remember those cute black-and-white animals you always go to see?
But Baba, I've never seen an alien before!
You mean my art skills are *so* bad, my panda looks like it's from *outer space?*
That's a panda?!

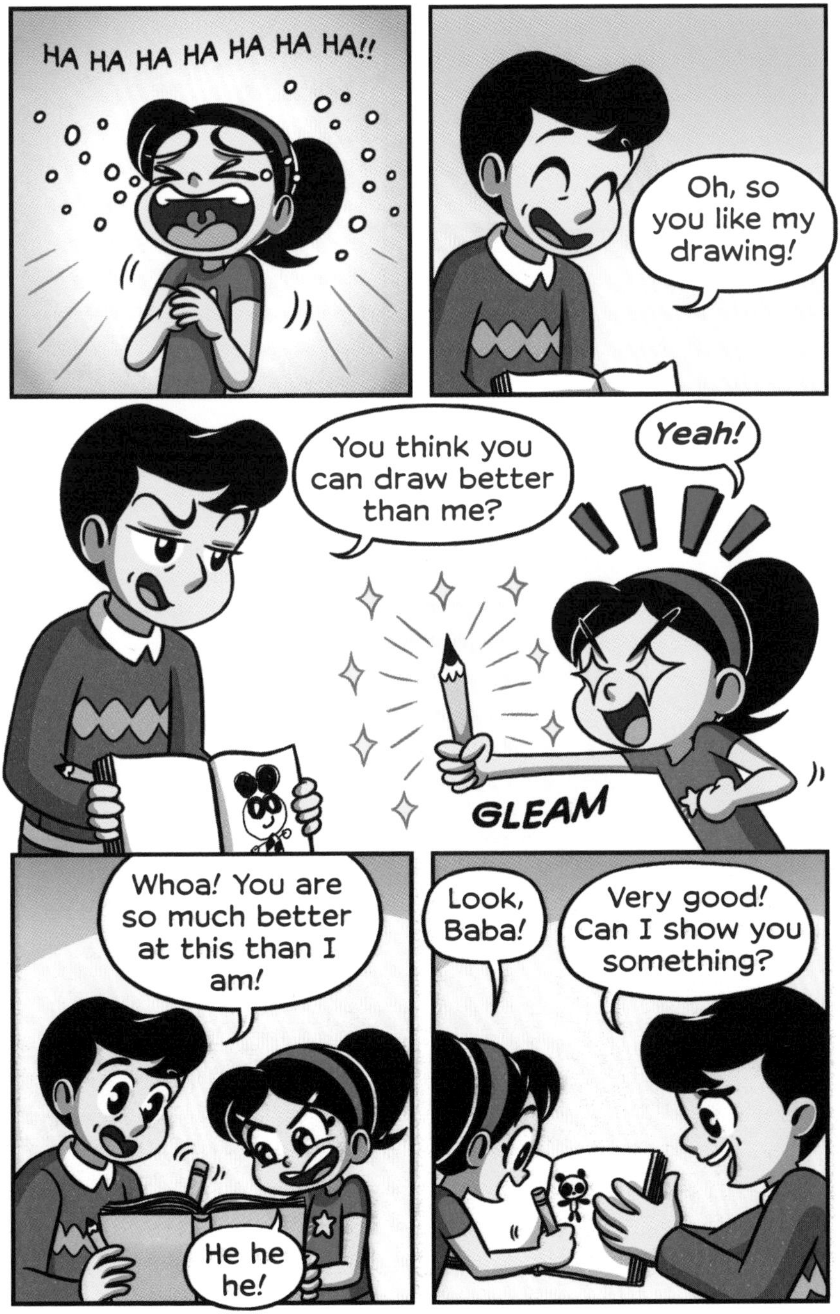
HA HA HA HA HA HA HA!!
Oh, so you like my drawing!
You think you can draw better than me?
Yeah!
GLEAM
Whoa! You are so much better at this than I am!
He he he!
Look, Baba!
Very good! Can I show you something?

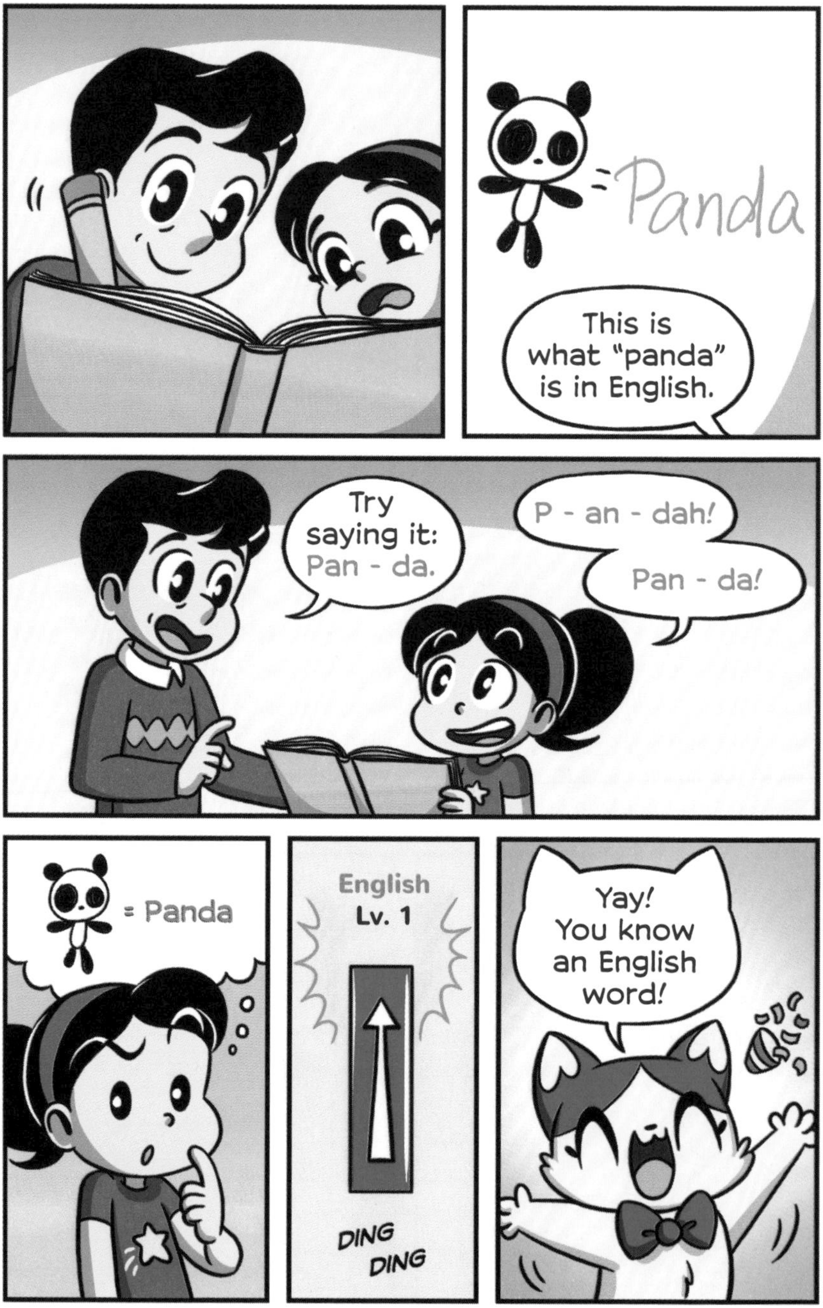
Panda
This is what "panda" is in English.
Try saying it: Pan - da.
P - an - dah!
Pan - da!
= Panda
English
Lv. 1
DING
DING
Yay! You know an English word!

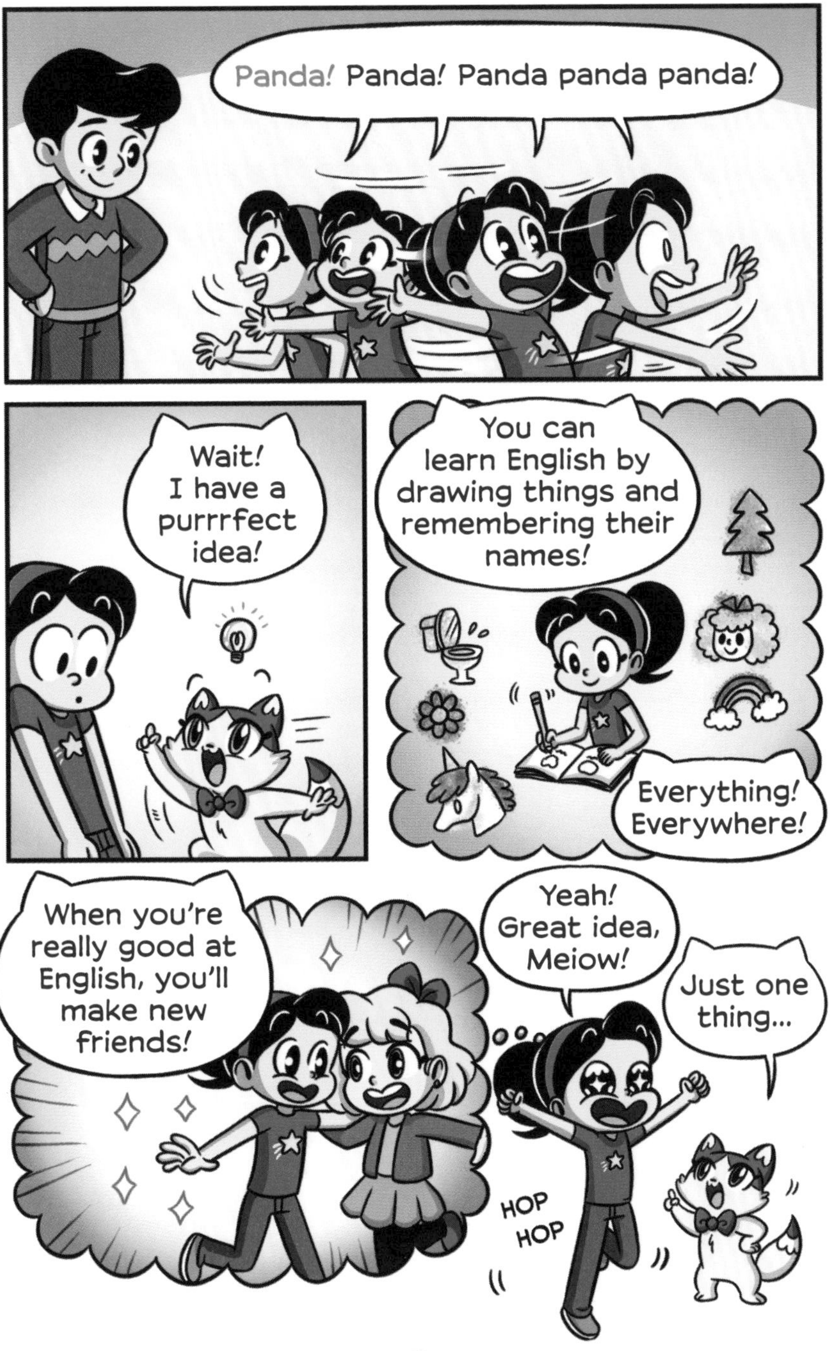

Panda! Panda! Panda panda panda!
Wait! I have a purrrfect idea!
You can learn English by drawing things and remembering their names!
Everything! Everywhere!
When you're really good at English, you'll make new friends!
Yeah! Great idea, Meiow!
Just one thing...
HOP HOP

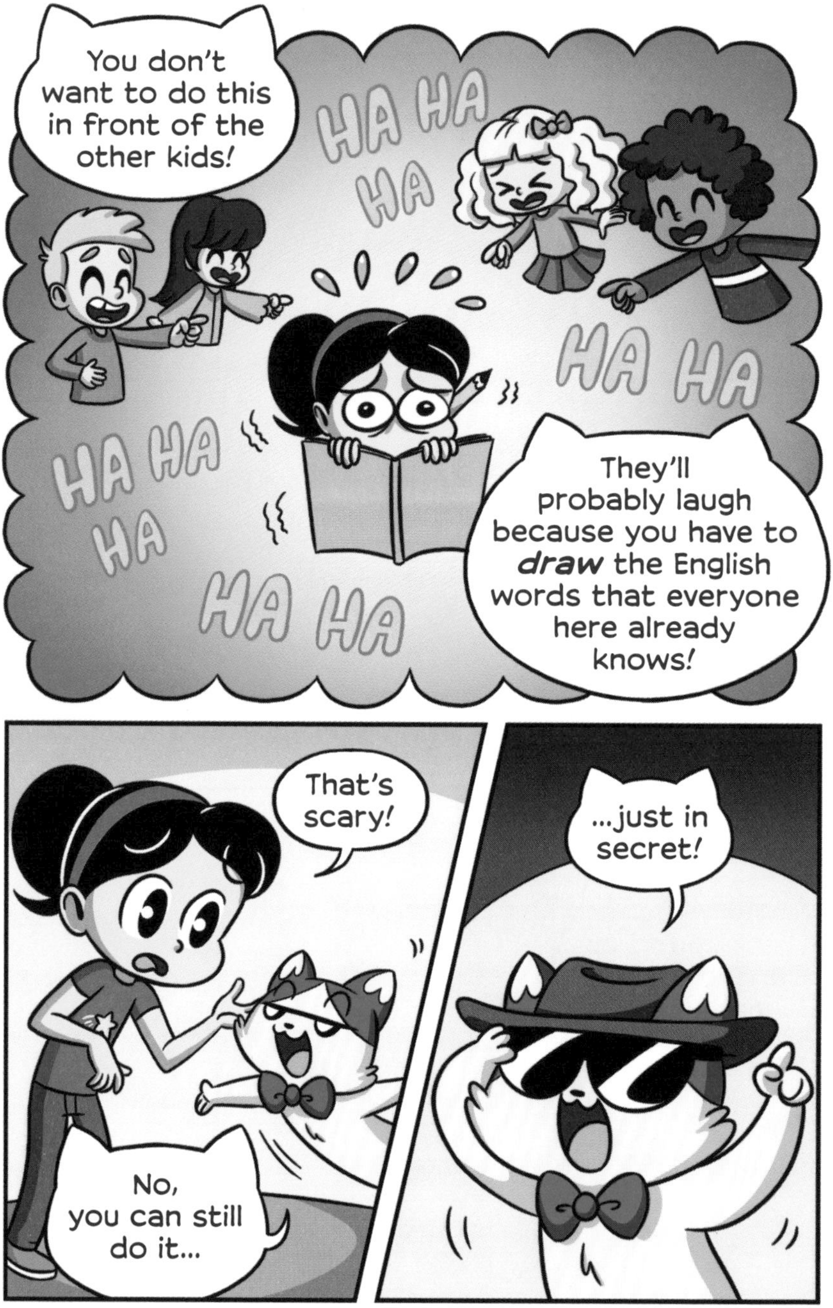
You don't want to do this in front of the other kids!
HA HA HA
HA HA
HA HA HA
HA HA
They'll probably laugh because you have to *draw* the English words that everyone here already knows!
That's scary!
No, you can still do it...
...just in secret!

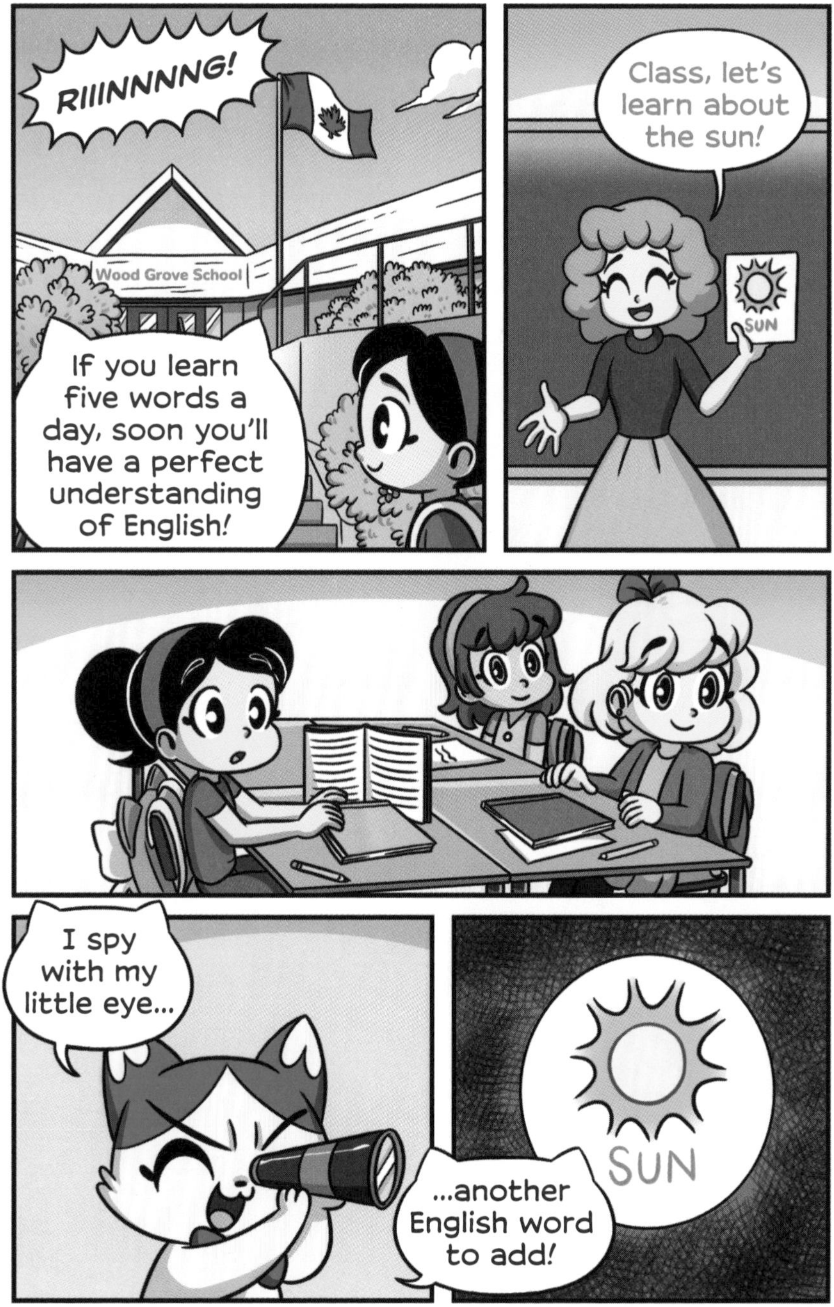
RIIINNNNG!
Wood Grove School
If you learn five words a day, soon you'll have a perfect understanding of English!
Class, let's learn about the sun!
SUN
I spy with my little eye...
SUN
...another English word to add!

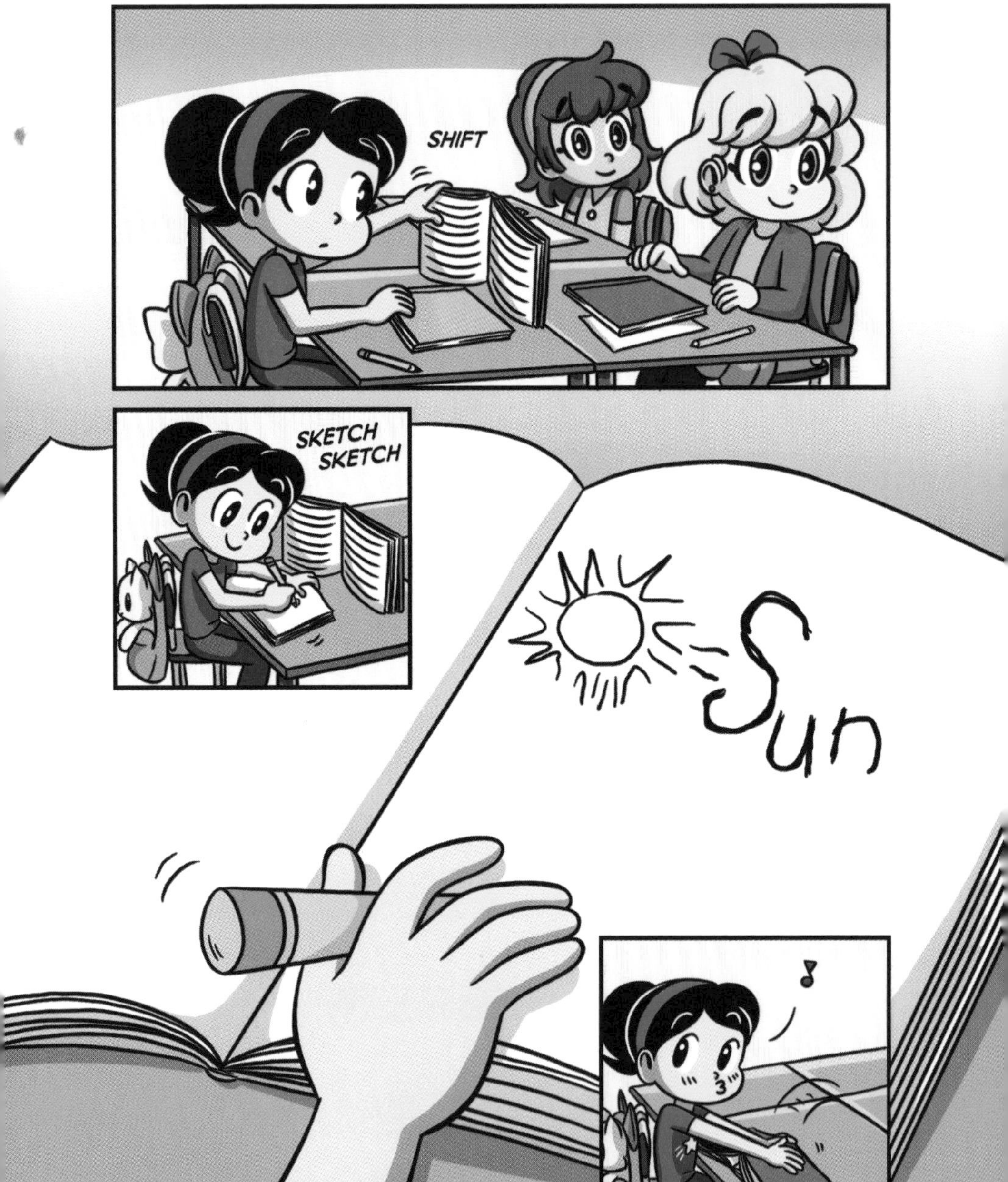
SHIFT
SKETCH SKETCH
Sun

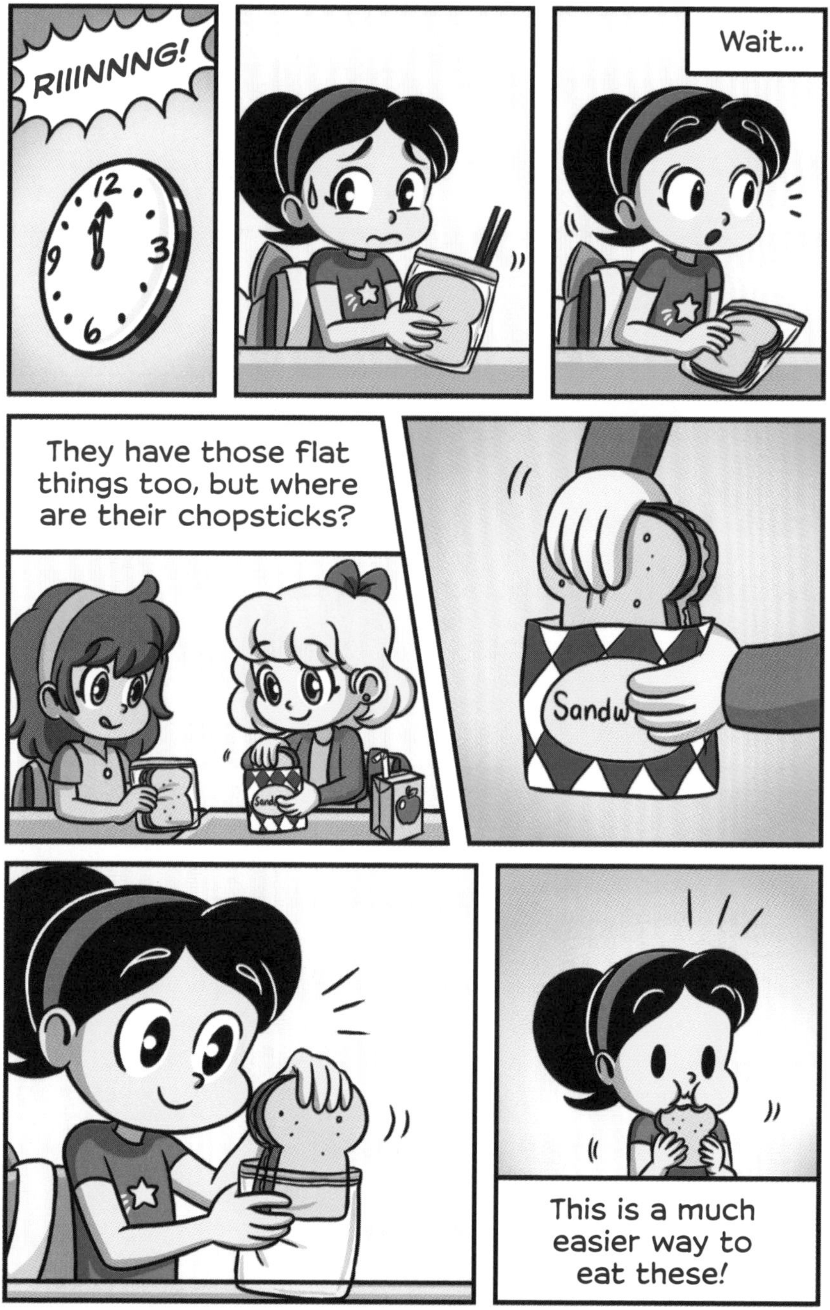
RIIINNNG!
12
3
6
9
Wait...
They have those flat things too, but where are their chopsticks?
Sandw
This is a much easier way to eat these!

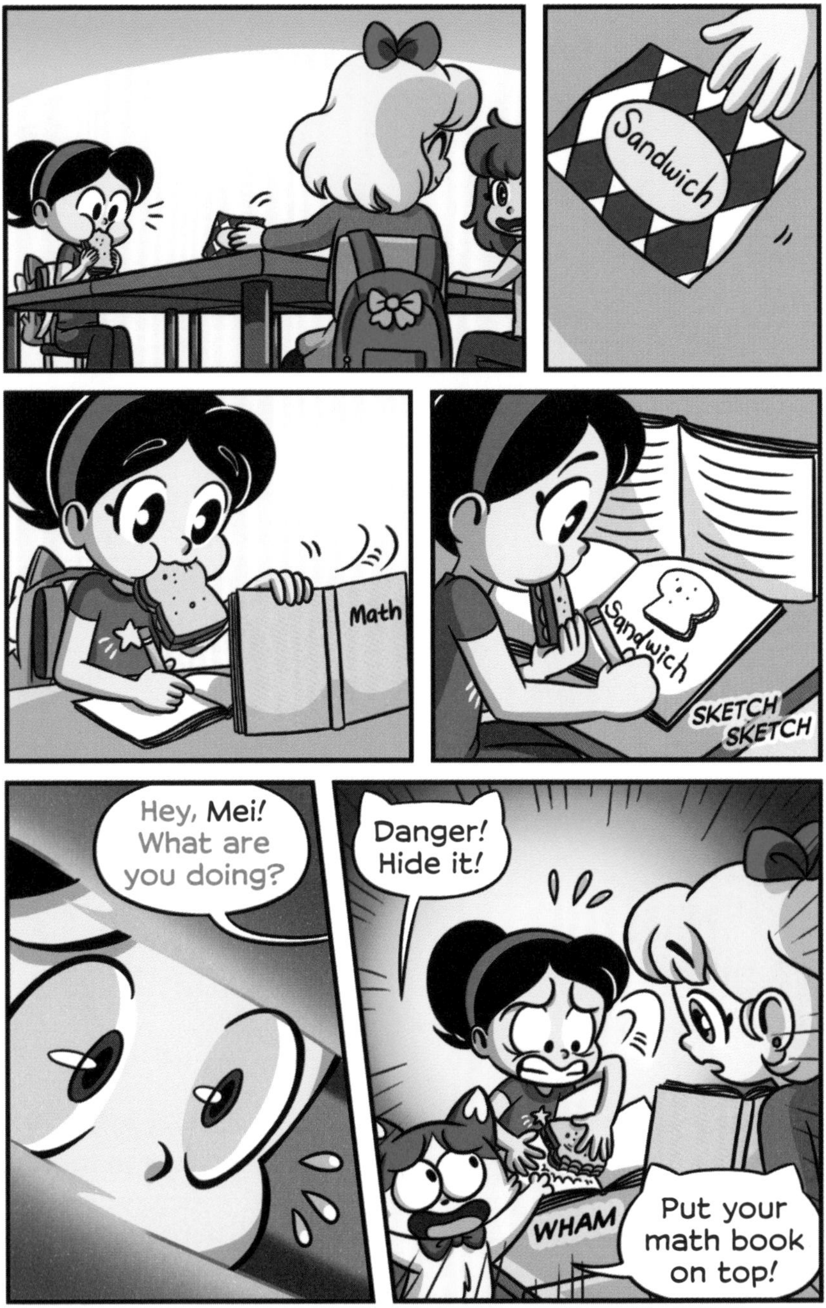
Sandwich
Math
Sandwich
SKETCH SKETCH
Hey, Mei! What are you doing?
Danger! Hide it!
WHAM
Put your math book on top!

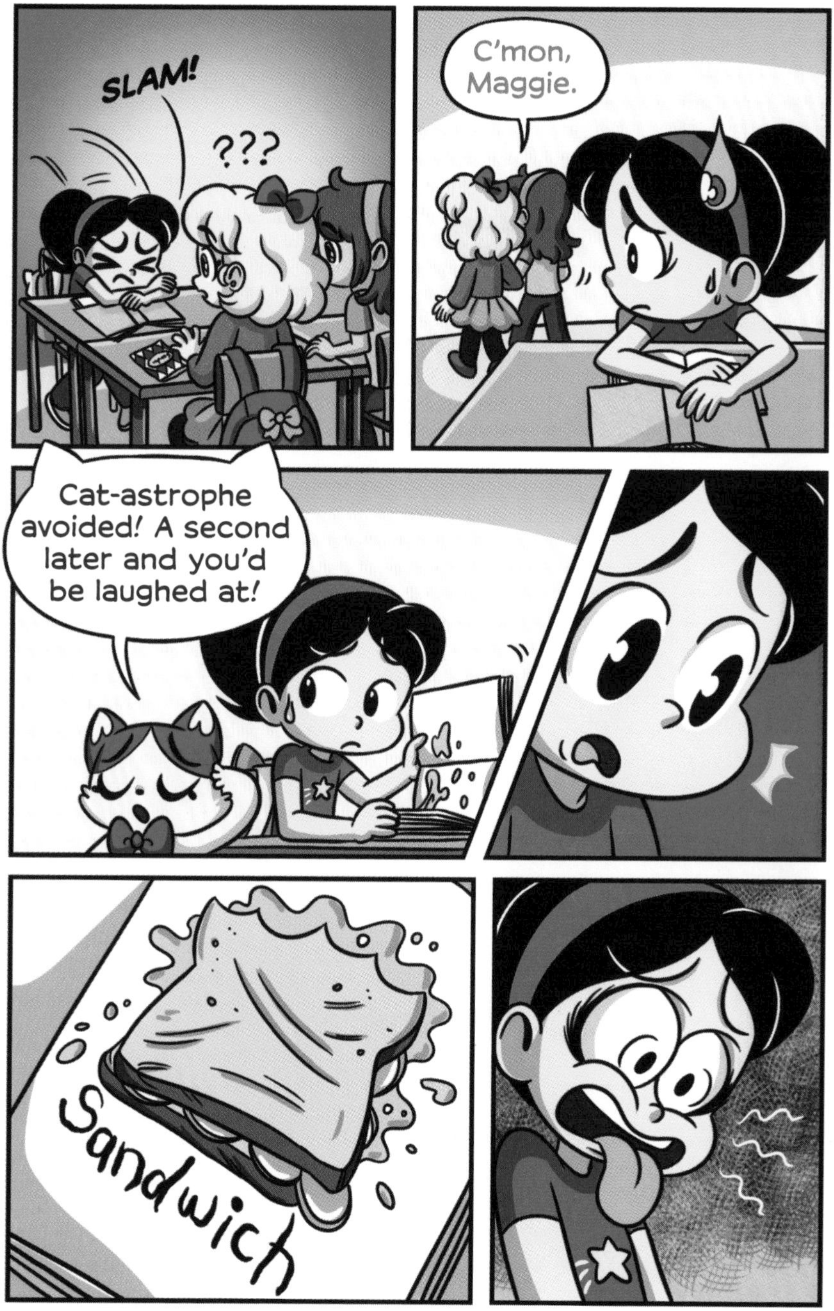
SLAM!
???
C'mon, Maggie.
Cat-astrophe avoided! A second later and you'd be laughed at!
Sandwich

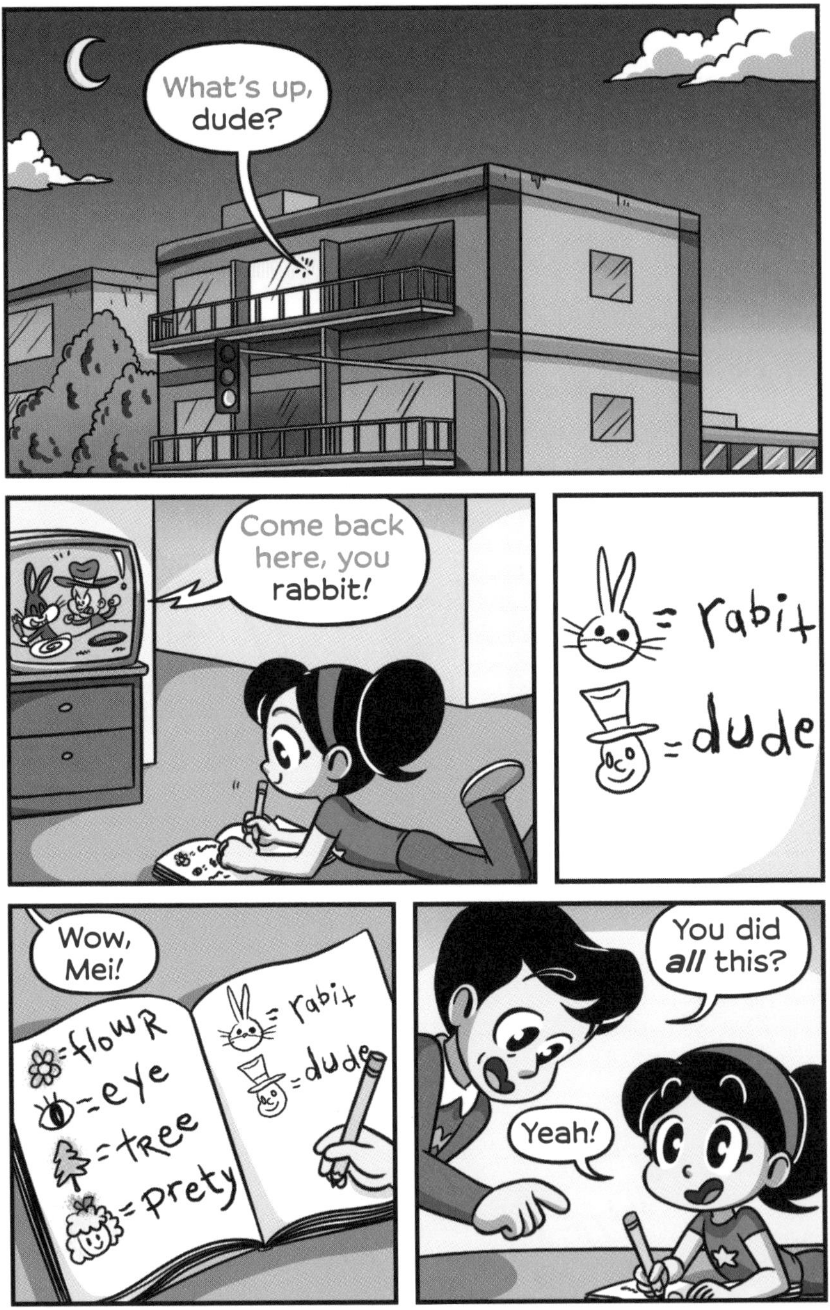
What's up, dude?
Come back here, you rabbit!
= rabit
= dude
Wow, Mei!
= flowR
= eye
= tree
= prety
= rabit
= dude
You did *all* this?
Yeah!

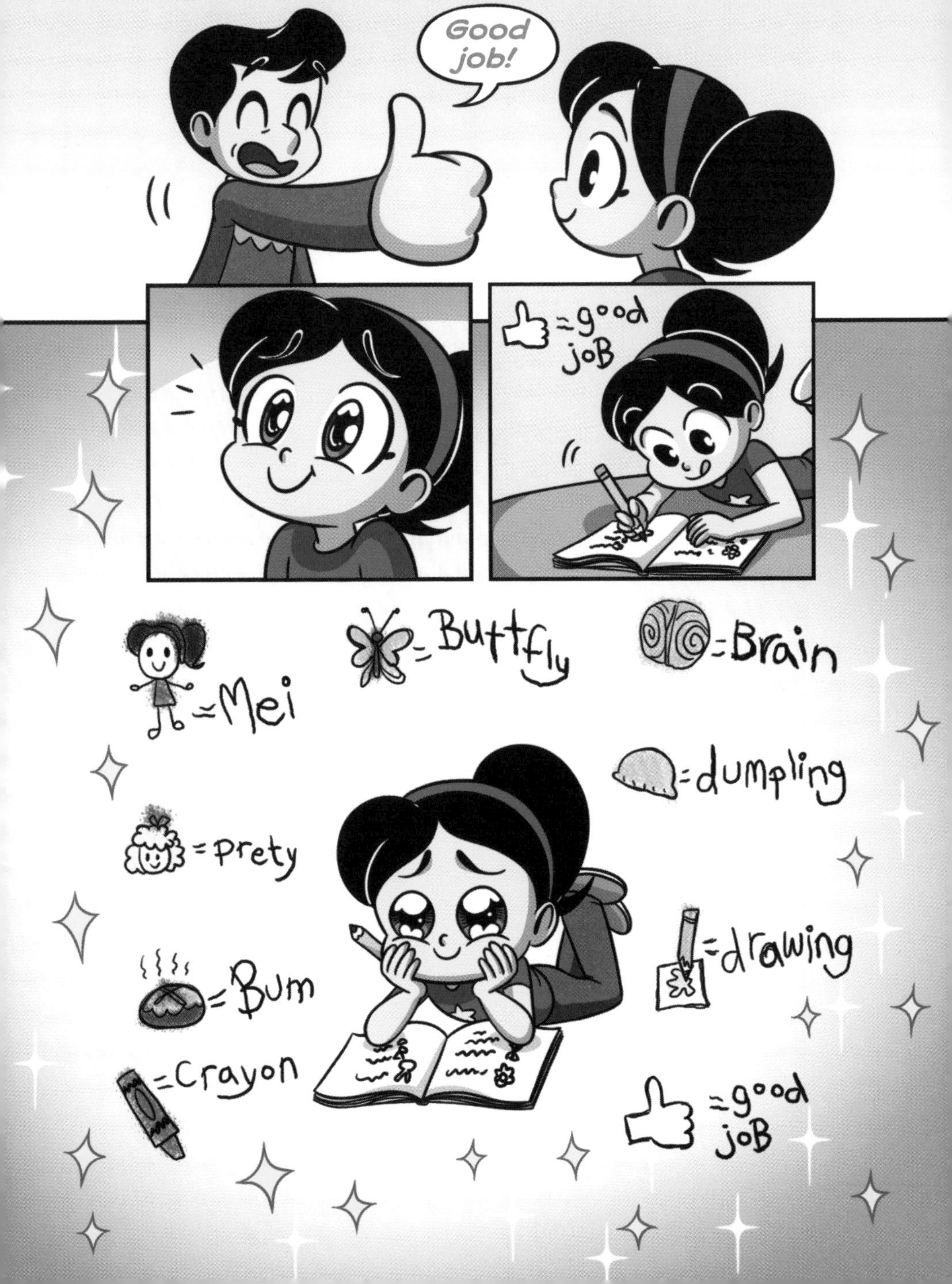

Good job!
=good joB
=Mei
=Buttfly
=Brain
=dumpling
=prety
=drawing
=Bum
=Crayon
=good joB

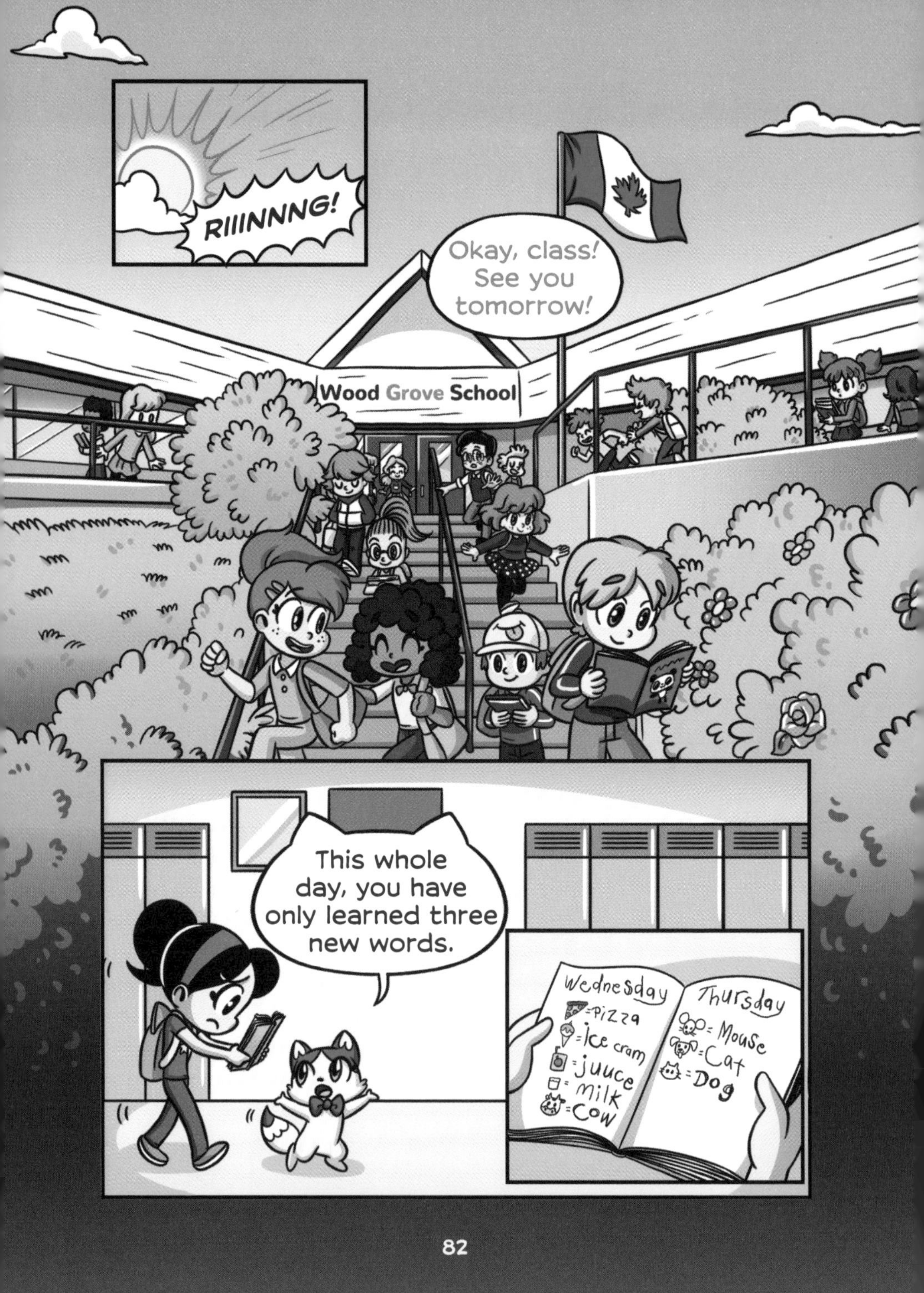

RIIINNNG!
Okay, class! See you tomorrow!
Wood Grove School
This whole day, you have only learned three new words.
Wednesday
=Pizza
=Ice cram
=juuce
=milk
=COW
Thursday
=Mouse
=Cat
=Dog

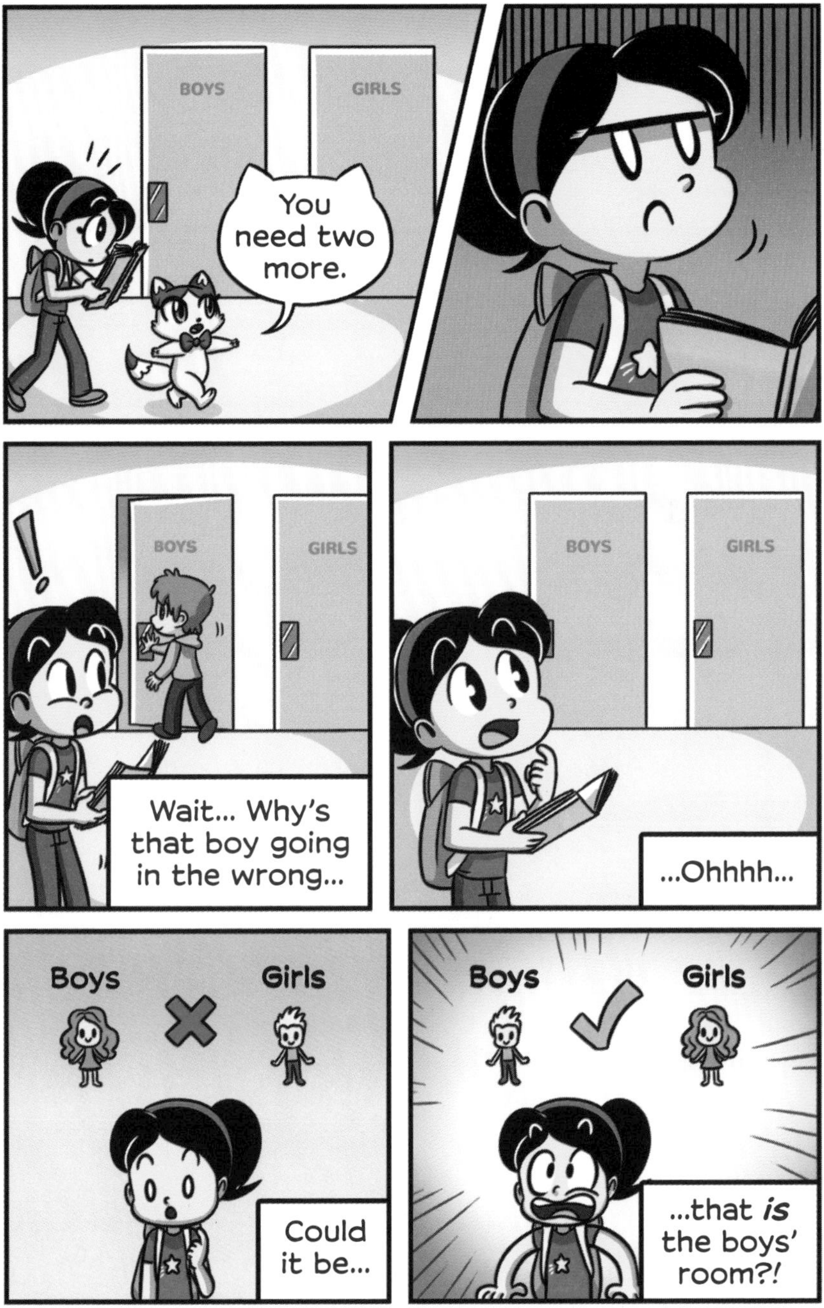
BOYS
GIRLS
You need two more.
BOYS
GIRLS
Wait... Why's that boy going in the wrong...
BOYS
GIRLS
...Ohhhh...
Boys
Girls
Could it be...
Boys
Girls
...that *is* the boys' room?!

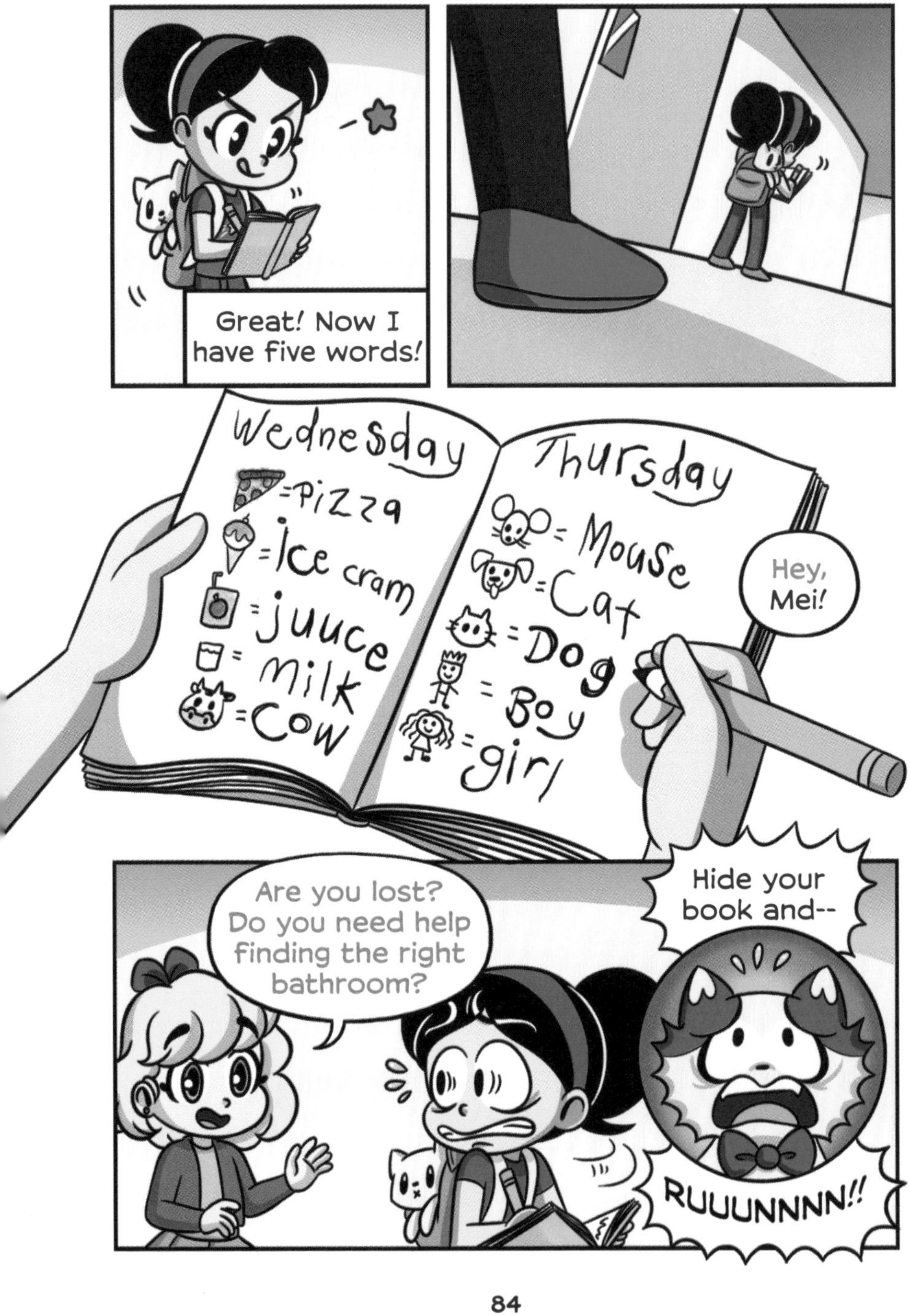
Great! Now I have five words!
Wednesday
=Pizza
=Ice cram
=juuce
=milk
=Cow
Thursday
=Mouse
=Cat
=Dog
=Boy
=girl
Hey, Mei!
Are you lost? Do you need help finding the right bathroom?
Hide your book and--
RUUUNNNN!!

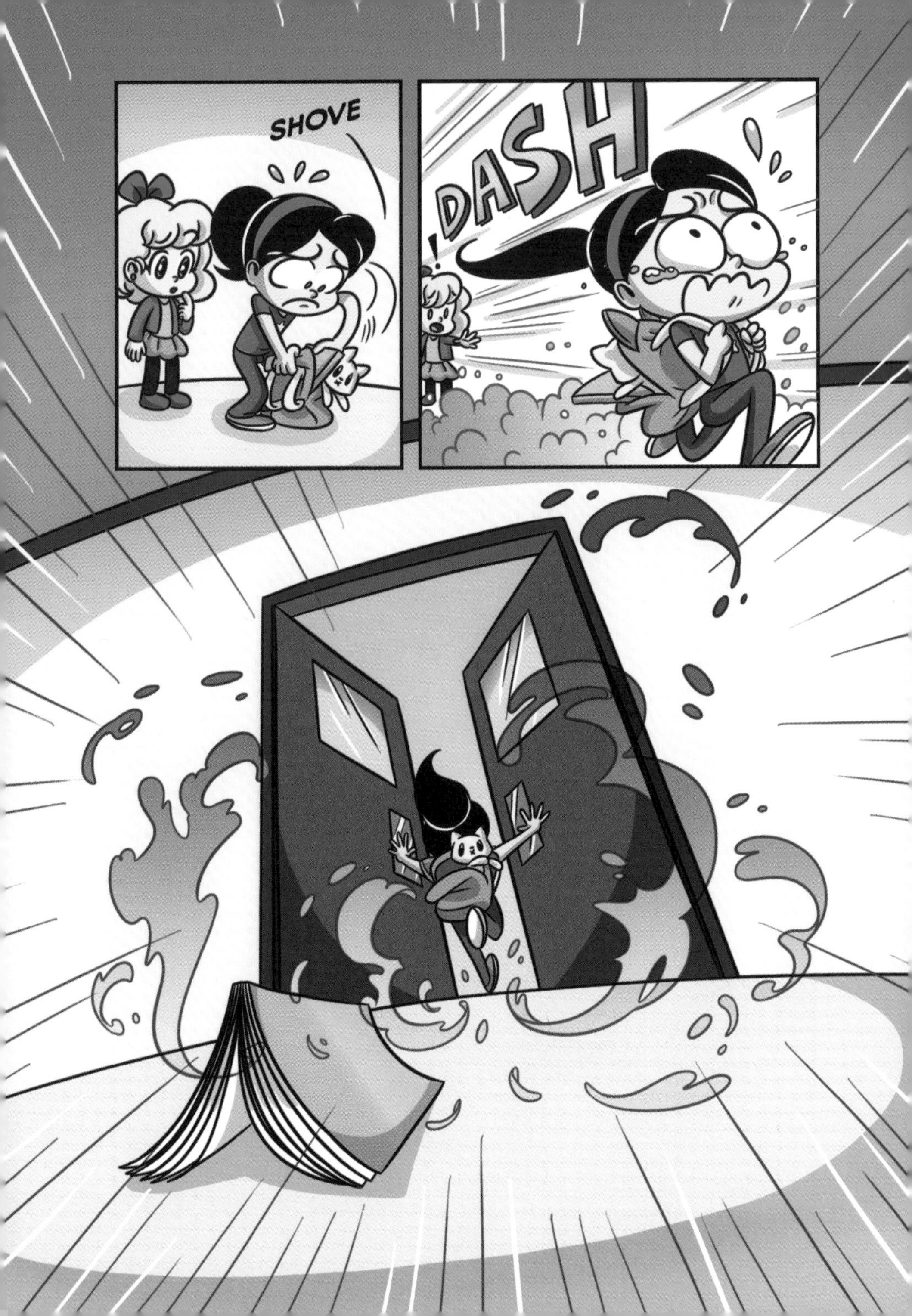
SHOVE
DASH
!

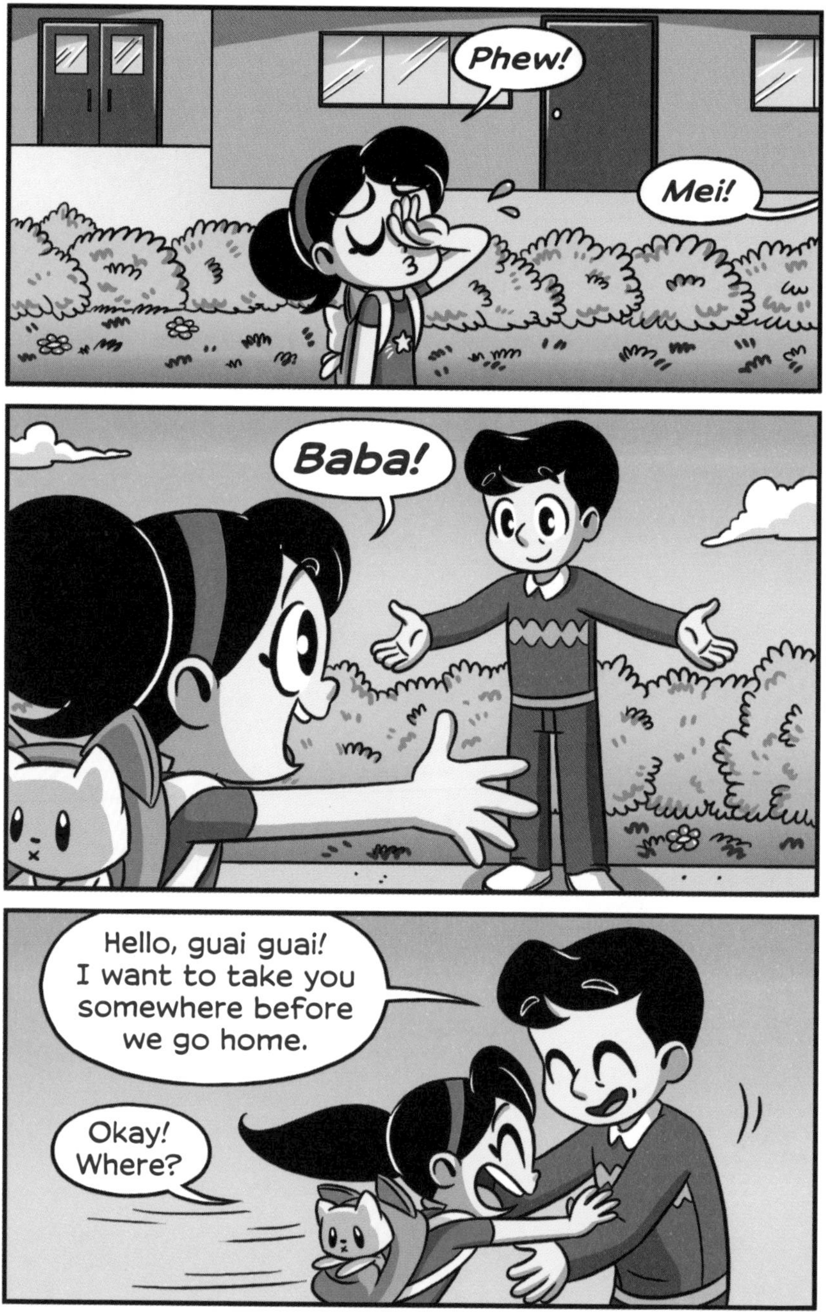
Phew!
Mei!
Baba!
Hello, guai guai! I want to take you somewhere before we go home.
Okay! Where?

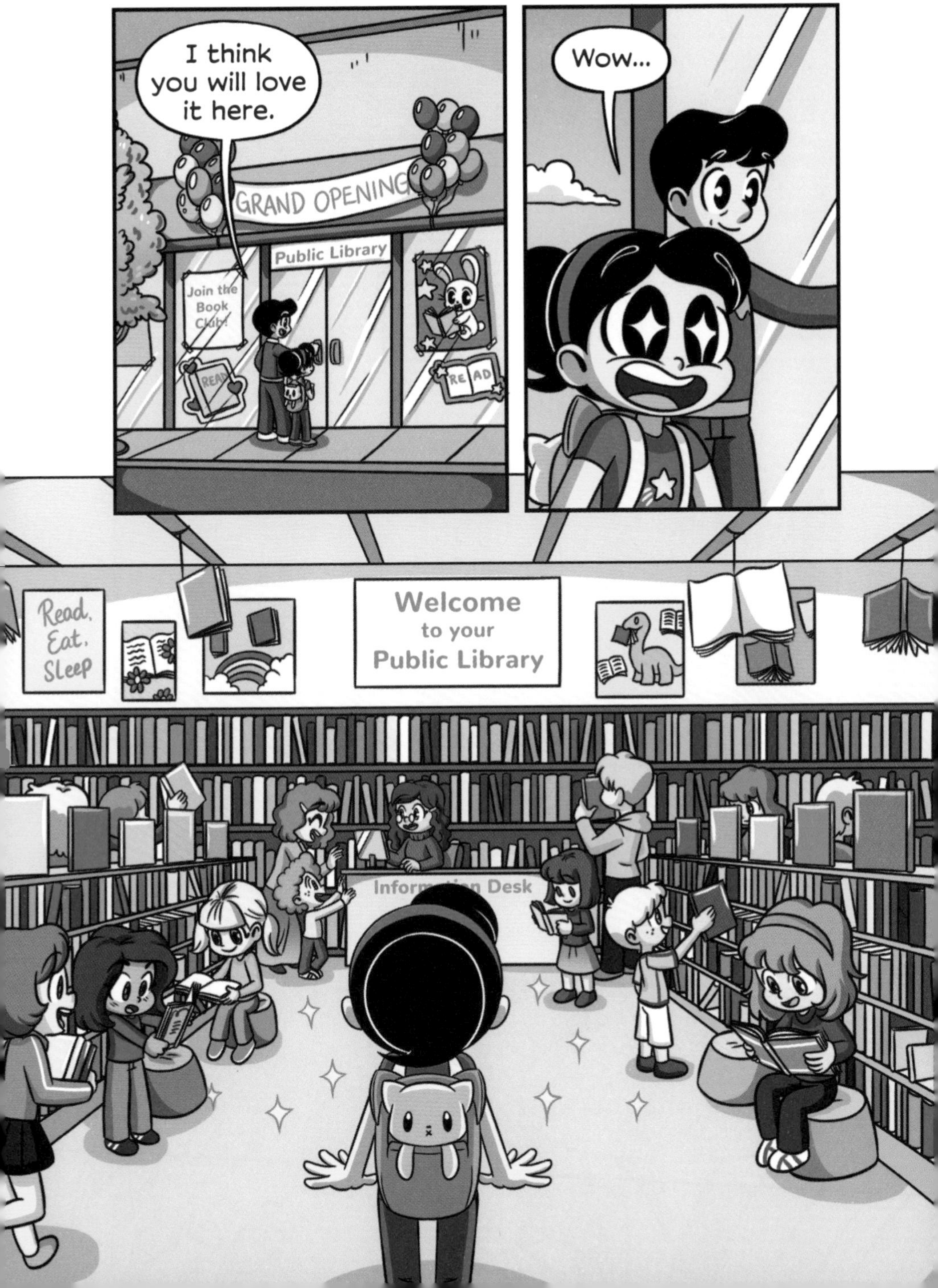
I think you will love it here.
GRAND OPENING
Public Library
Join the Book Club!
READ
READ
Wow...
Read, Eat, Sleep
Welcome to your Public Library

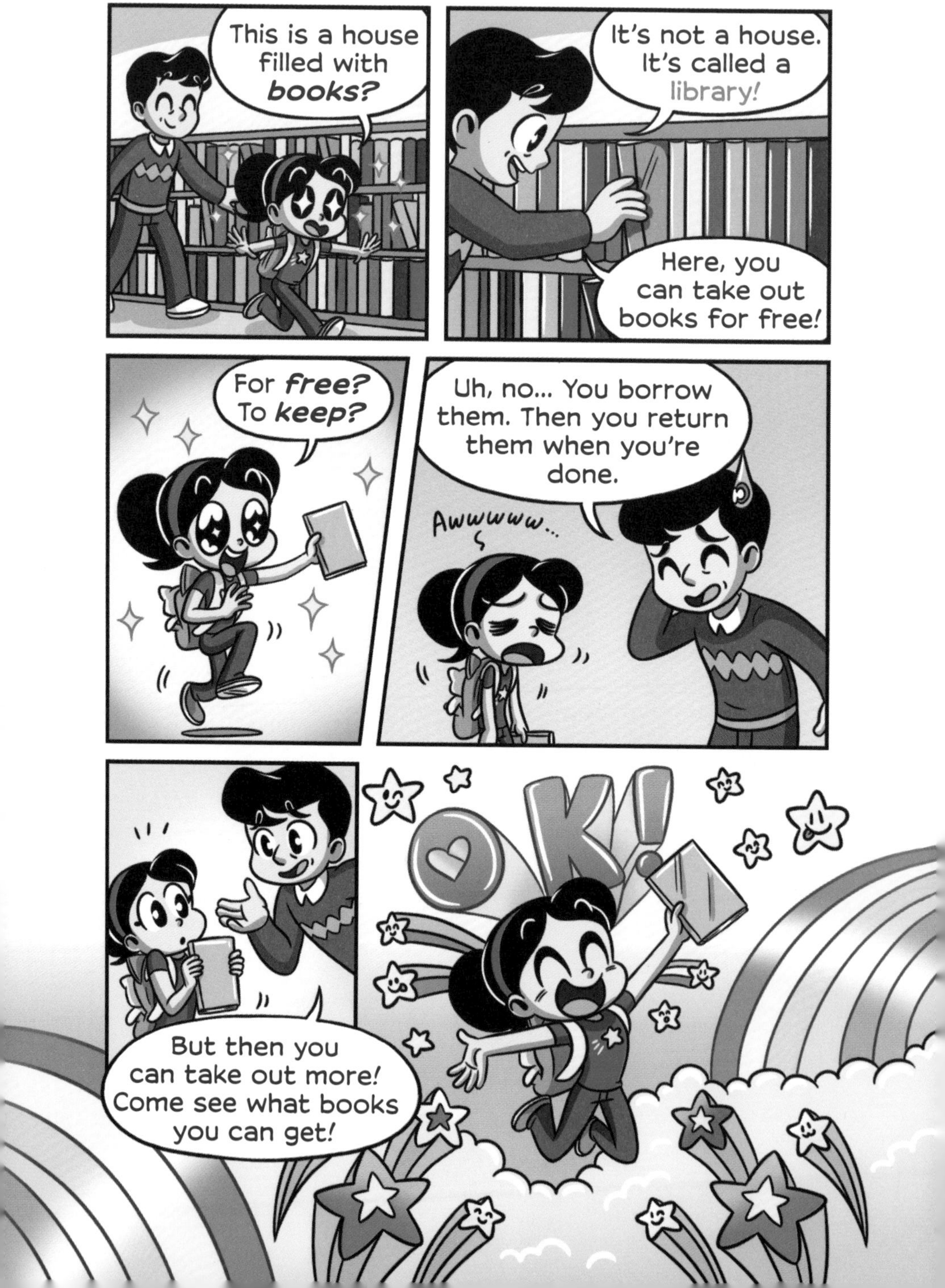
This is a house filled with *books?*
It's not a house. It's called a library!
Here, you can take out books for free!
For *free?* To *keep?*
Uh, no... You borrow them. Then you return them when you're done.
Awwwww...
But then you can take out more! Come see what books you can get!
OK!

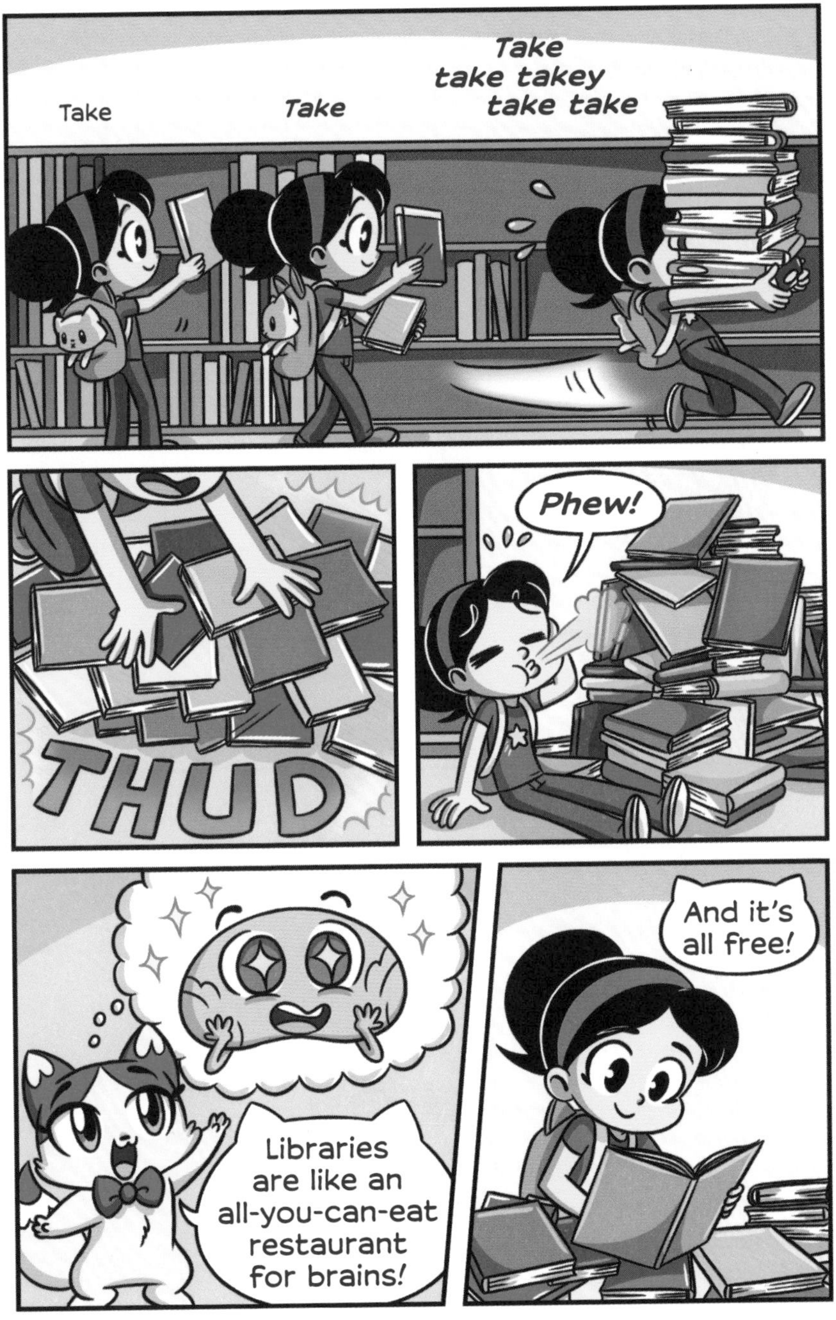

Take
Take
Take
take takey
take take
THUD
Phew!
Libraries are like an all-you-can-eat restaurant for brains!
And it's all free!

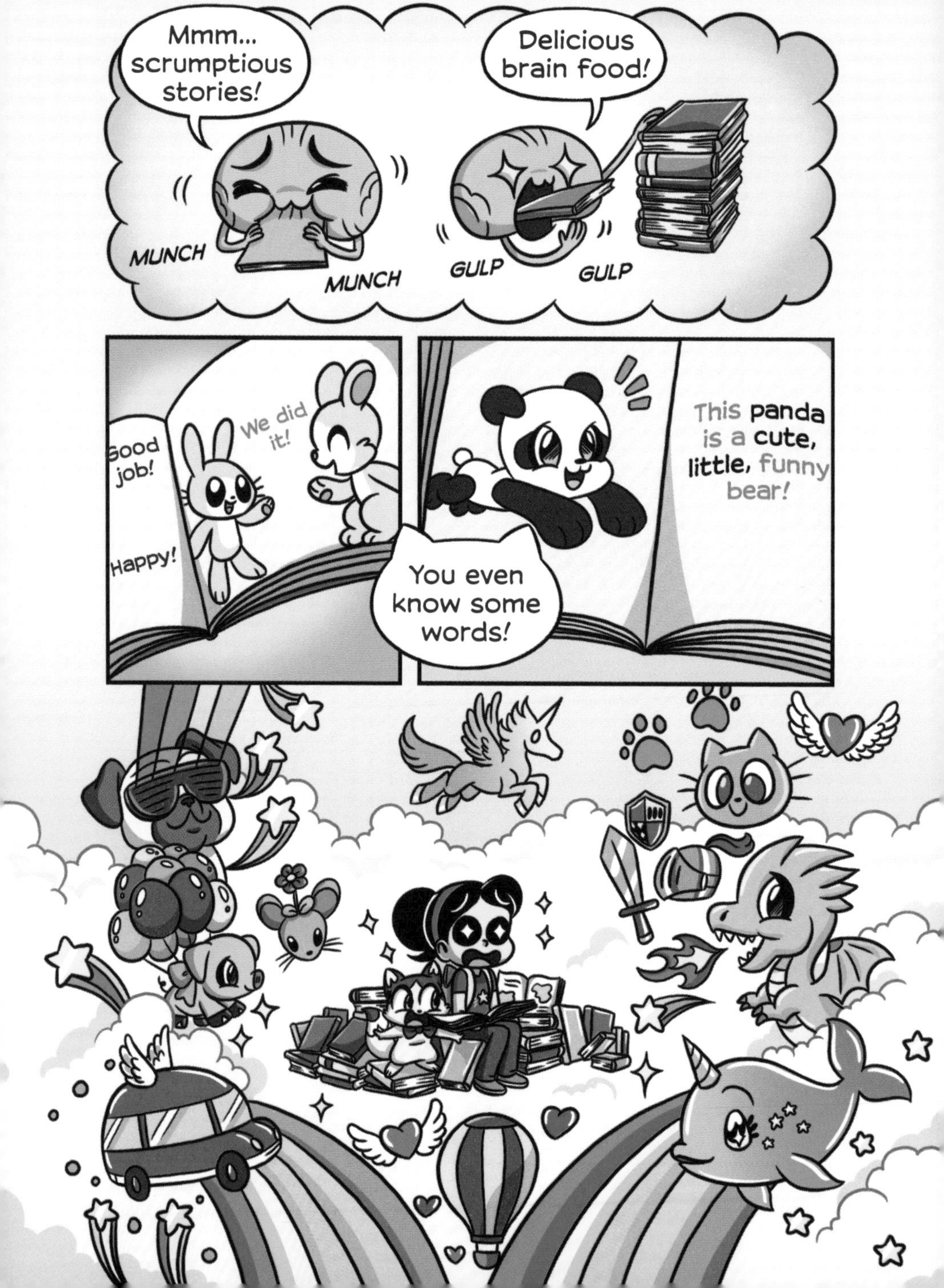

Mmm... scrumptious stories!
MUNCH
MUNCH
Delicious brain food!
GULP
GULP
Good job!
We did it!
Happy!
This panda is a cute, little, funny bear!
You even know some words!

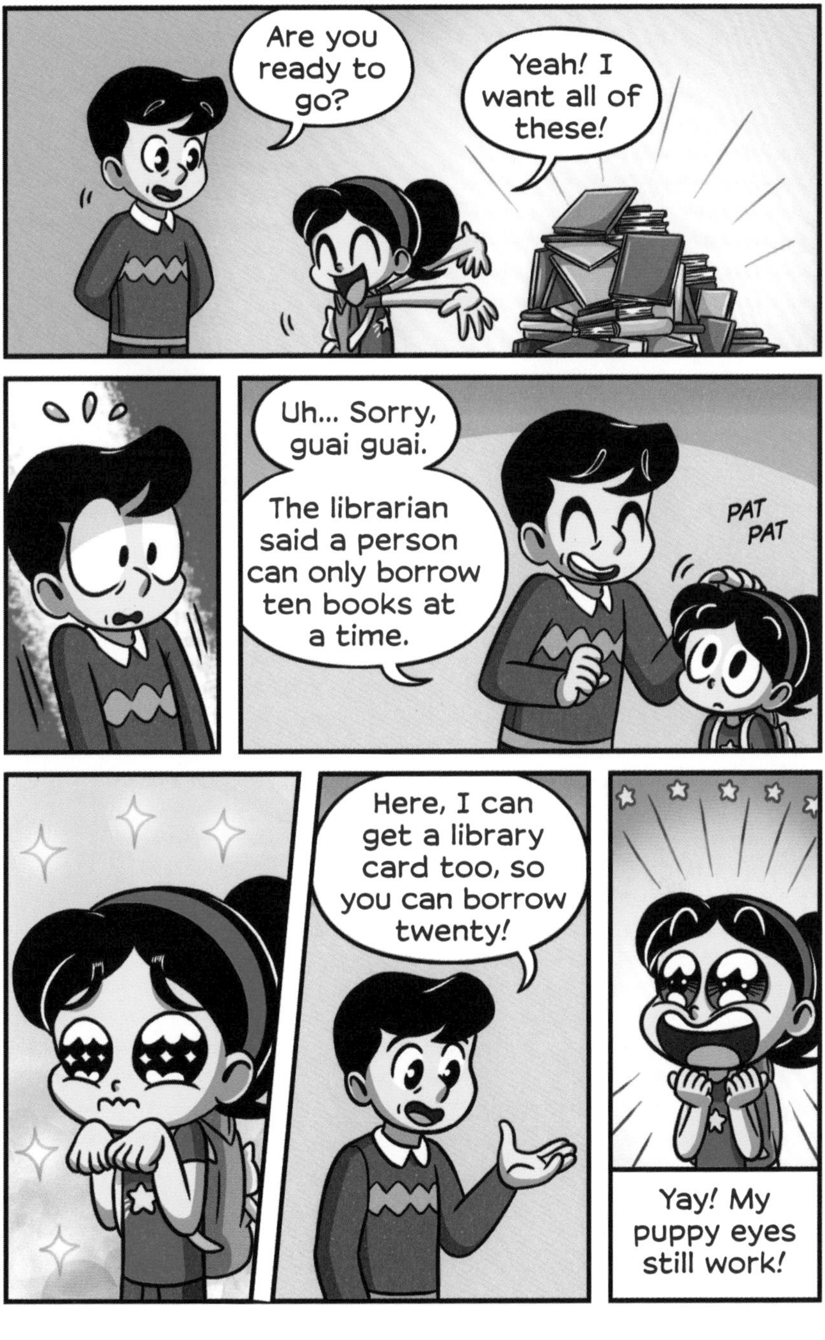
Are you ready to go?
Yeah! I want all of these!
Uh... Sorry, guai guai.
The librarian said a person can only borrow ten books at a time.
PAT PAT
Here, I can get a library card too, so you can borrow twenty!
Yay! My puppy eyes still work!

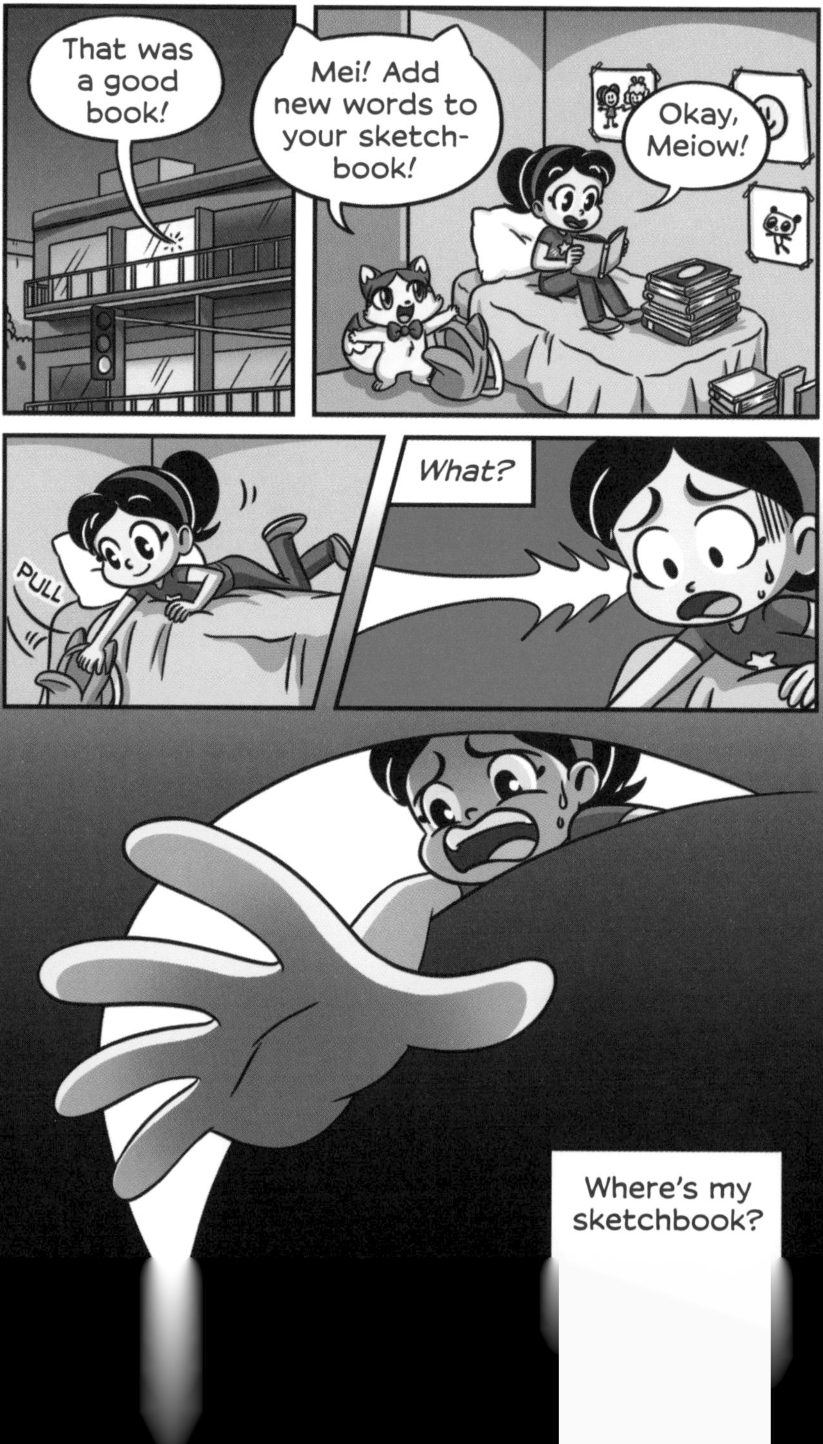
That was a good book!
Mei! Add new words to your sketch-book!
Okay, Meiow!
PULL
What?
Where's my sketchbook?

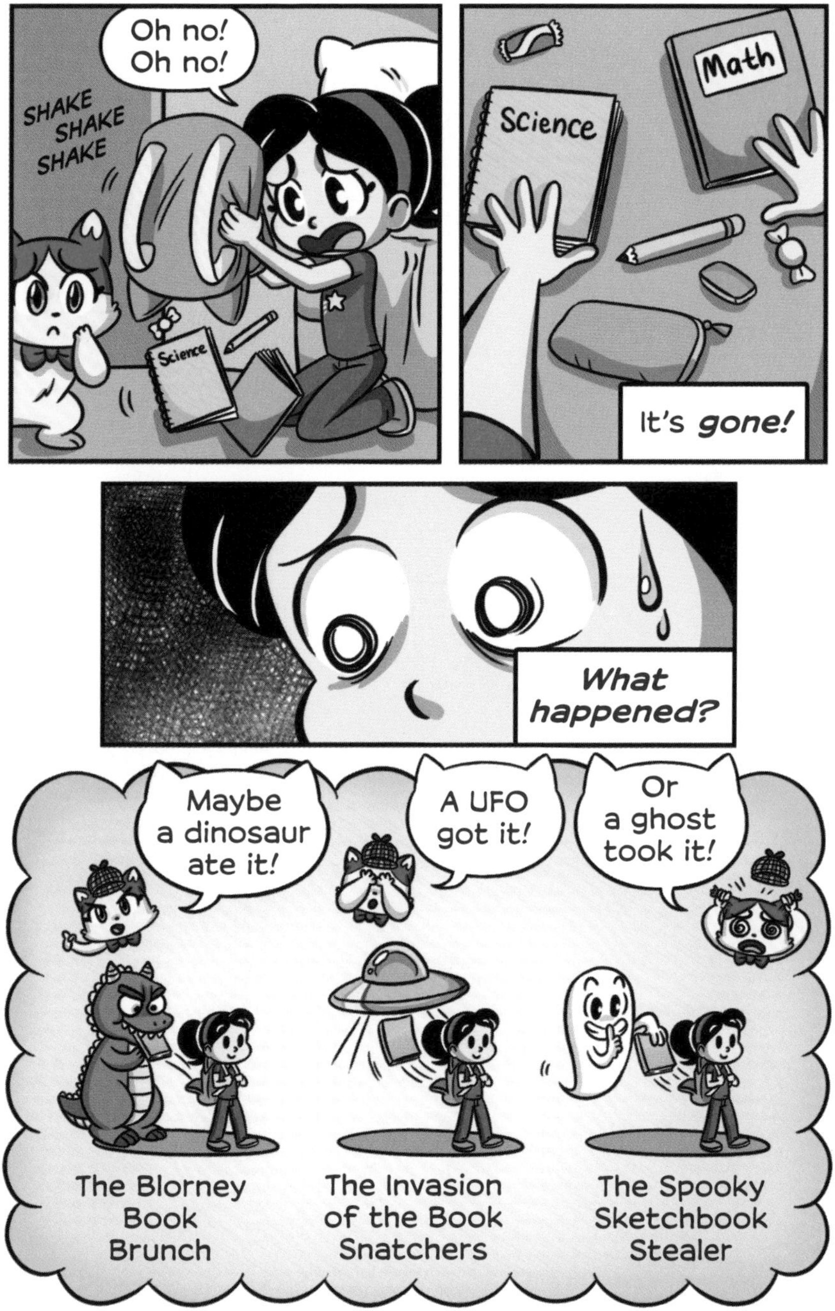
Oh no! Oh no!
SHAKE SHAKE SHAKE
Science
Math
Science
It's *gone!*
What happened?
Maybe a dinosaur ate it!
A UFO got it!
Or a ghost took it!
The Blorney Book Brunch
The Invasion of the Book Snatchers
The Spooky Sketchbook Stealer

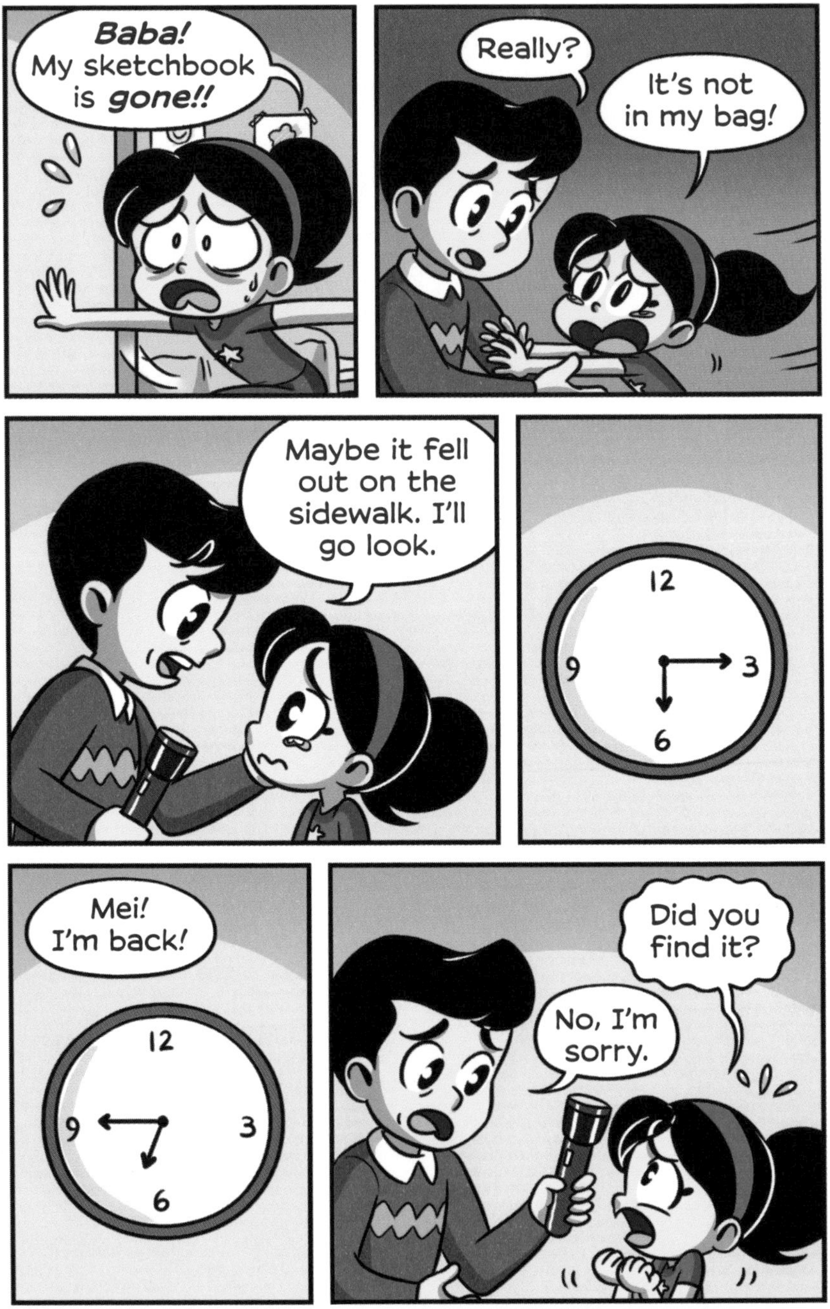

Baba! My sketchbook is gone!!
Really?
It's not in my bag!
Maybe it fell out on the sidewalk. I'll go look.
12
9
3
6
Mei! I'm back!
12
9
3
6
Did you find it?
No, I'm sorry.

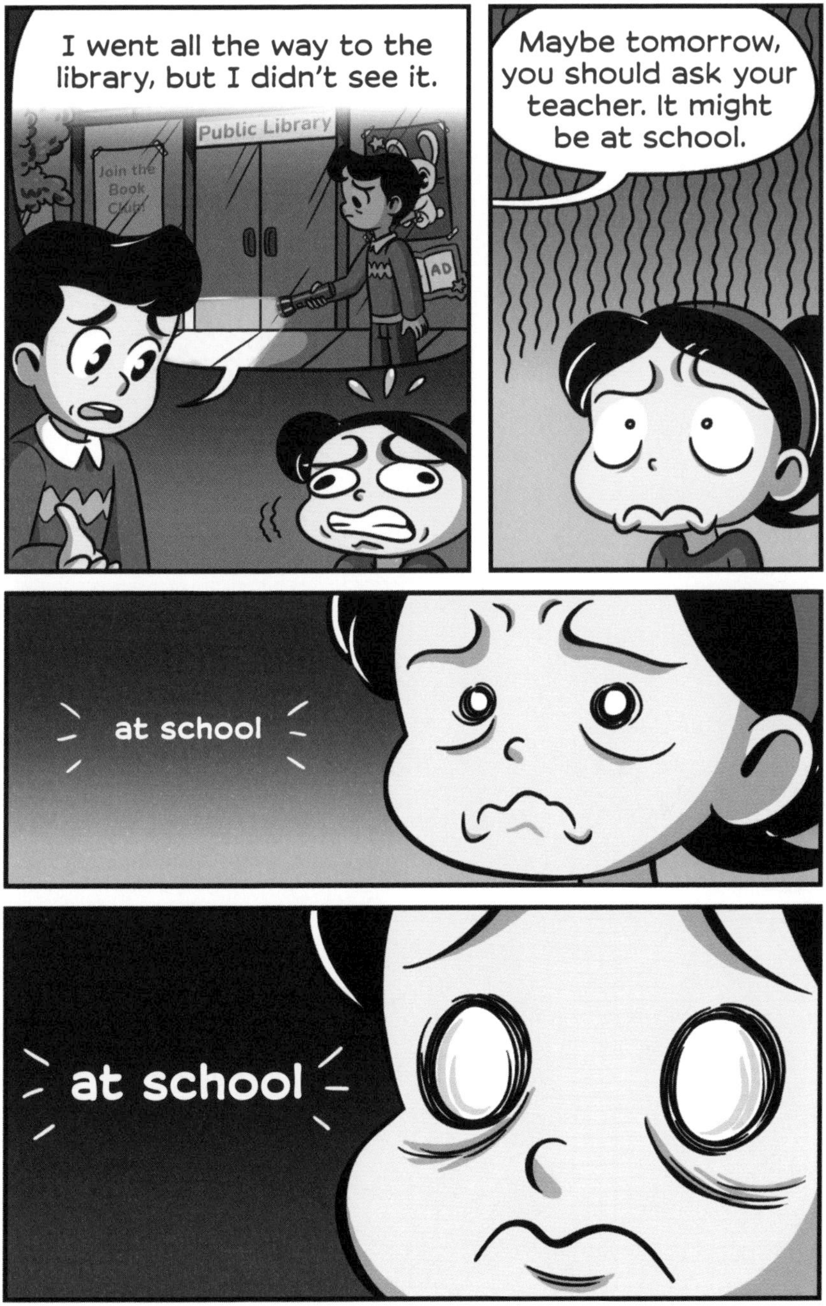
I went all the way to the library, but I didn't see it.
Public Library
Join the Book Club!
AD
Maybe tomorrow, you should ask your teacher. It might be at school.
at school
at school

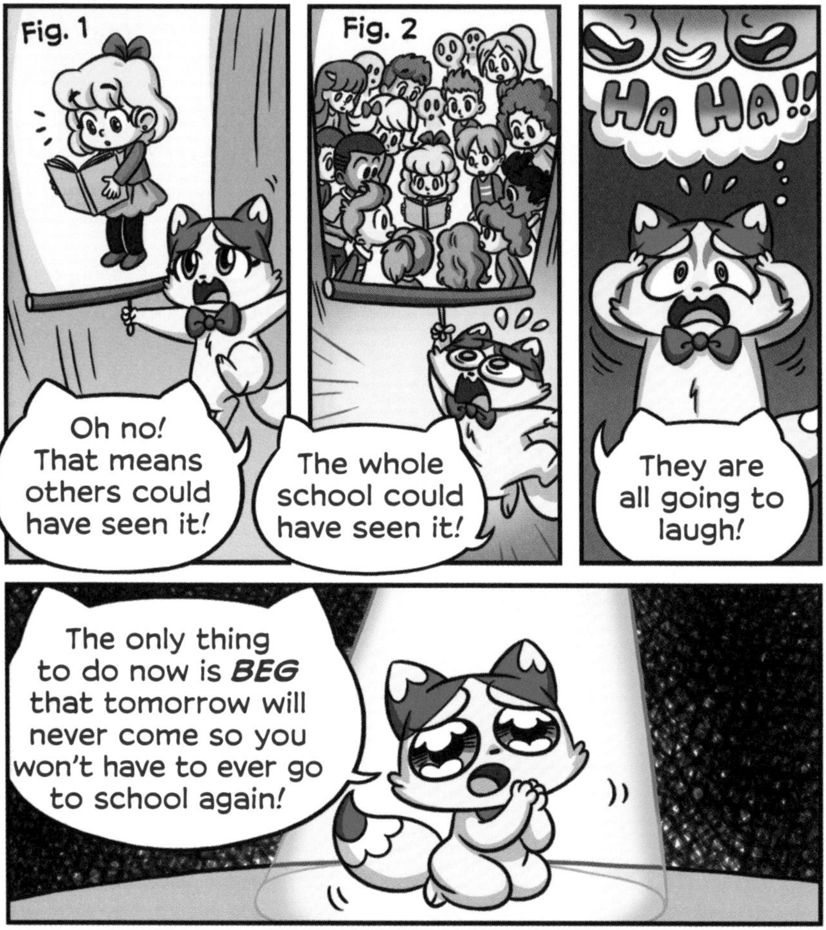
Fig. 1
Fig. 2
HA HA!!
Oh no! That means others could have seen it!
The whole school could have seen it!
They are all going to laugh!
The only thing to do now is BEG that tomorrow will never come so you won't have to ever go to school again!

Tomorrow.

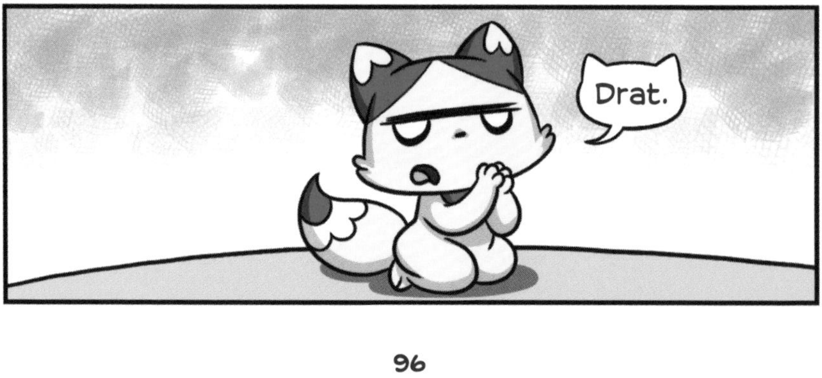
Drat.

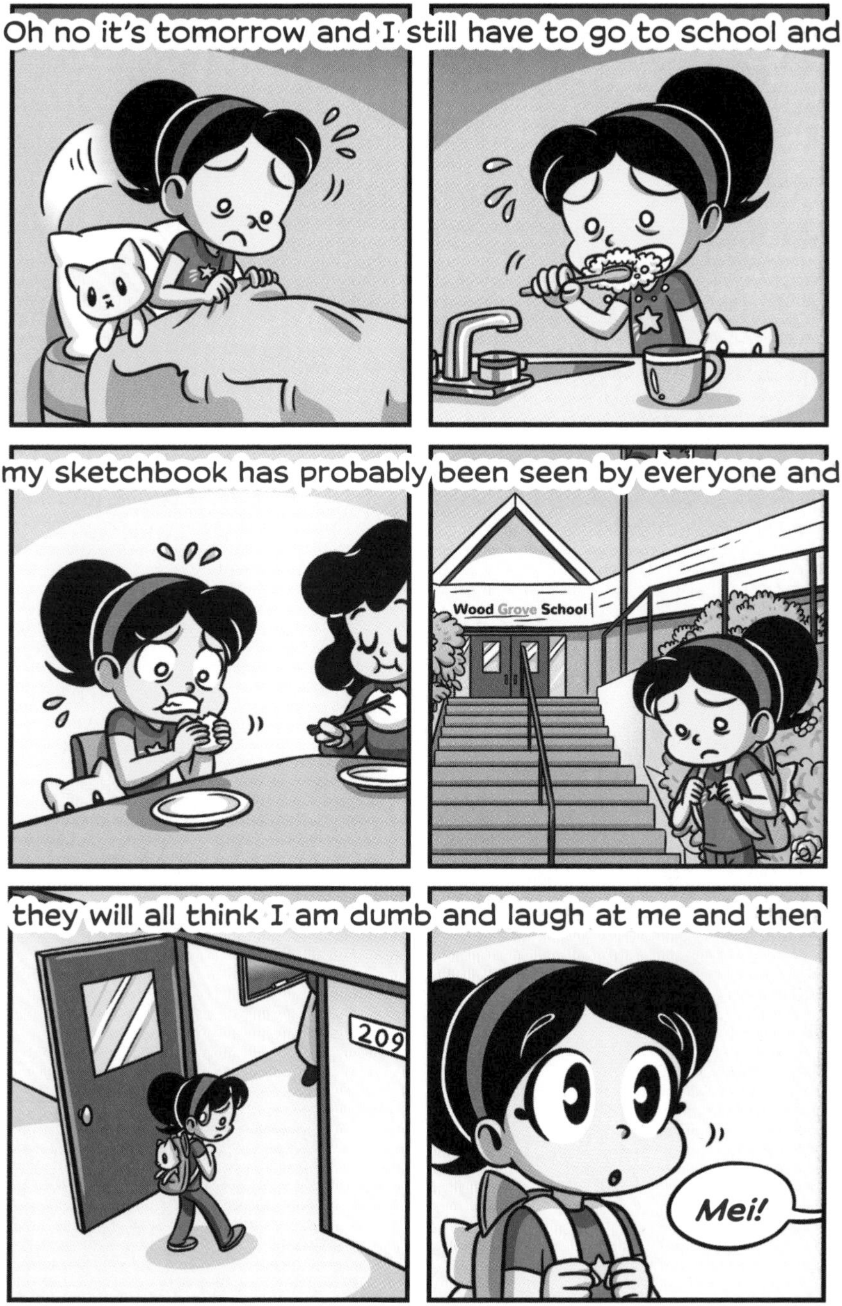
Oh no it's tomorrow and I still have to go to school and
my sketchbook has probably been seen by everyone and
Wood Grove School
they will all think I am dumb and laugh at me and then
209
Mei!

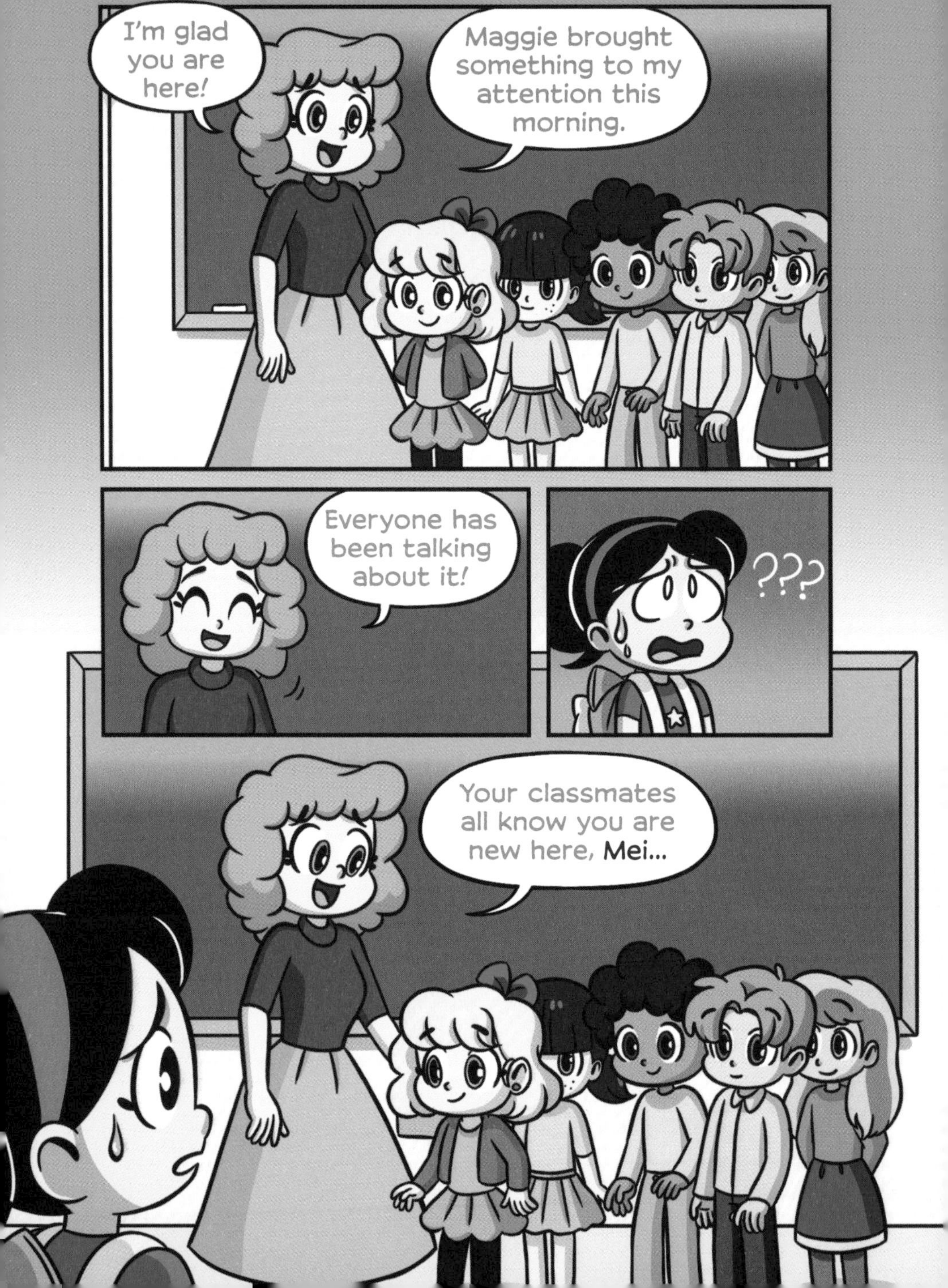

I'm glad you are here!
Maggie brought something to my attention this morning.
Everyone has been talking about it!
???
Your classmates all know you are new here, **Mei**...

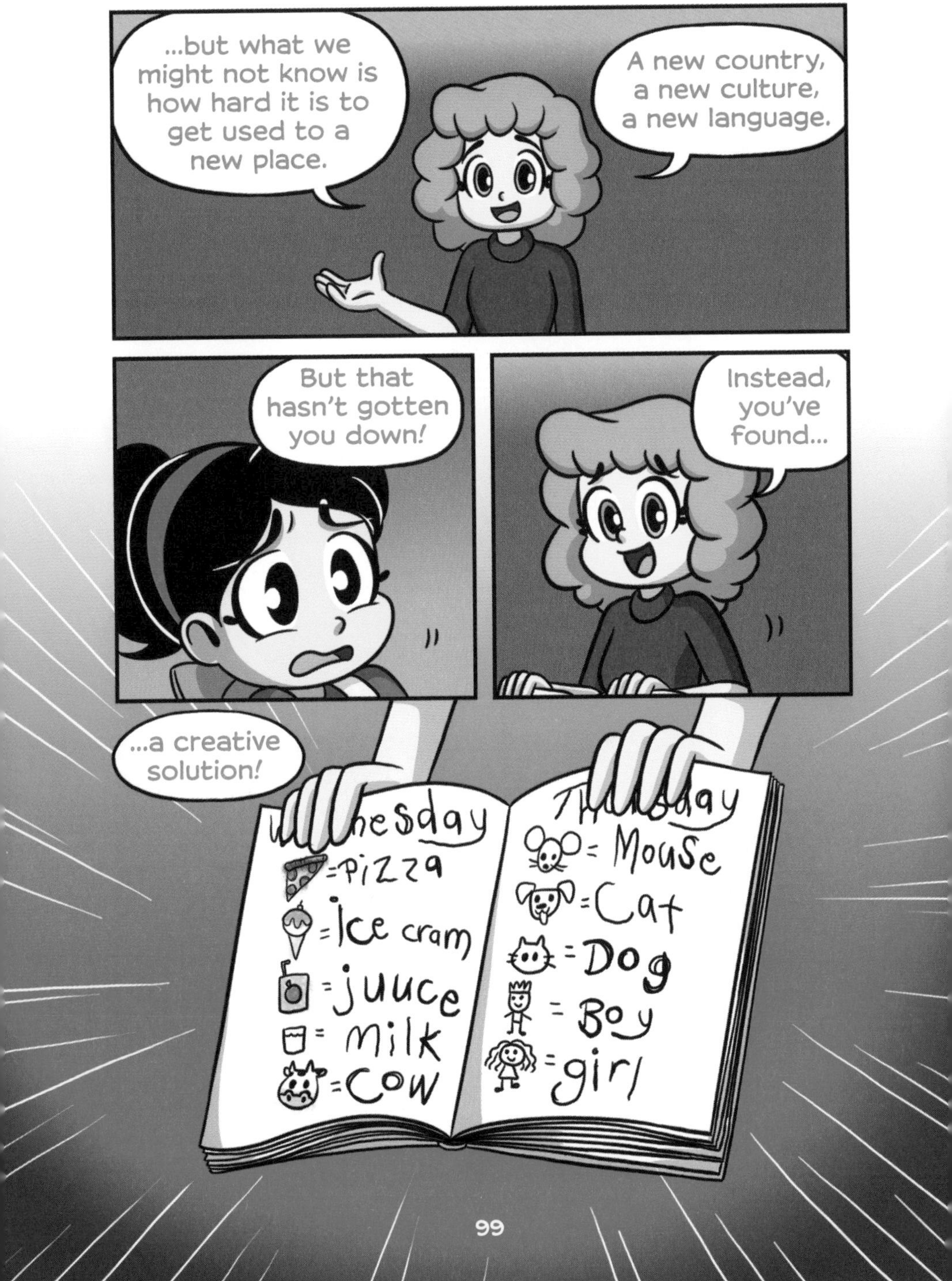

...but what we might not know is how hard it is to get used to a new place.
A new country, a new culture, a new language.
But that hasn't gotten you down!
Instead, you've found...
...a creative solution!
Wednesday
=Pizza
=Ice cram
=juuce
=milk
=Cow
Thursday
=Mouse
=Cat
=Dog
=Boy
=girl

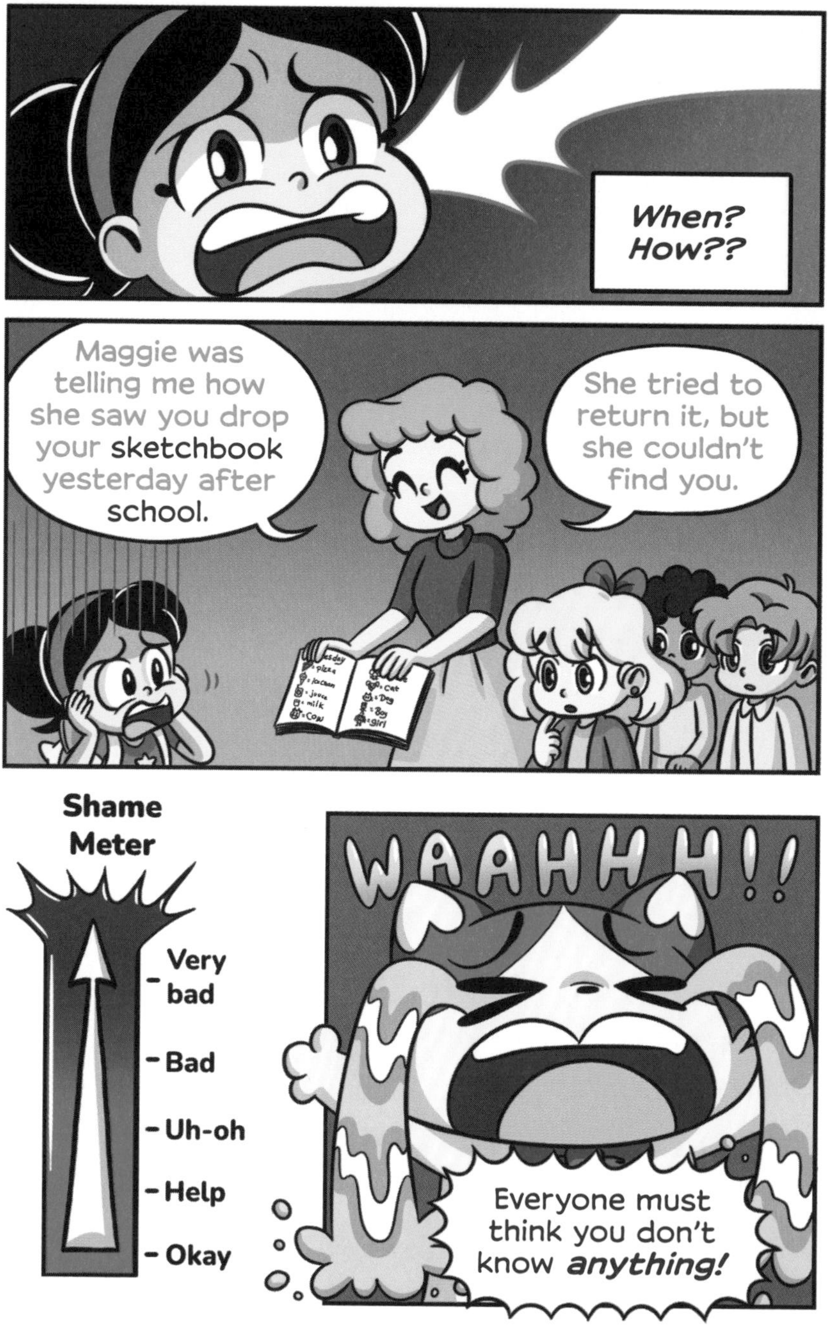
When? How??
Maggie was telling me how she saw you drop your sketchbook yesterday after school.
She tried to return it, but she couldn't find you.
Shame Meter
Very bad
Bad
Uh-oh
Help
Okay
WAAHHH!!
Everyone must think you don't know *anything!*

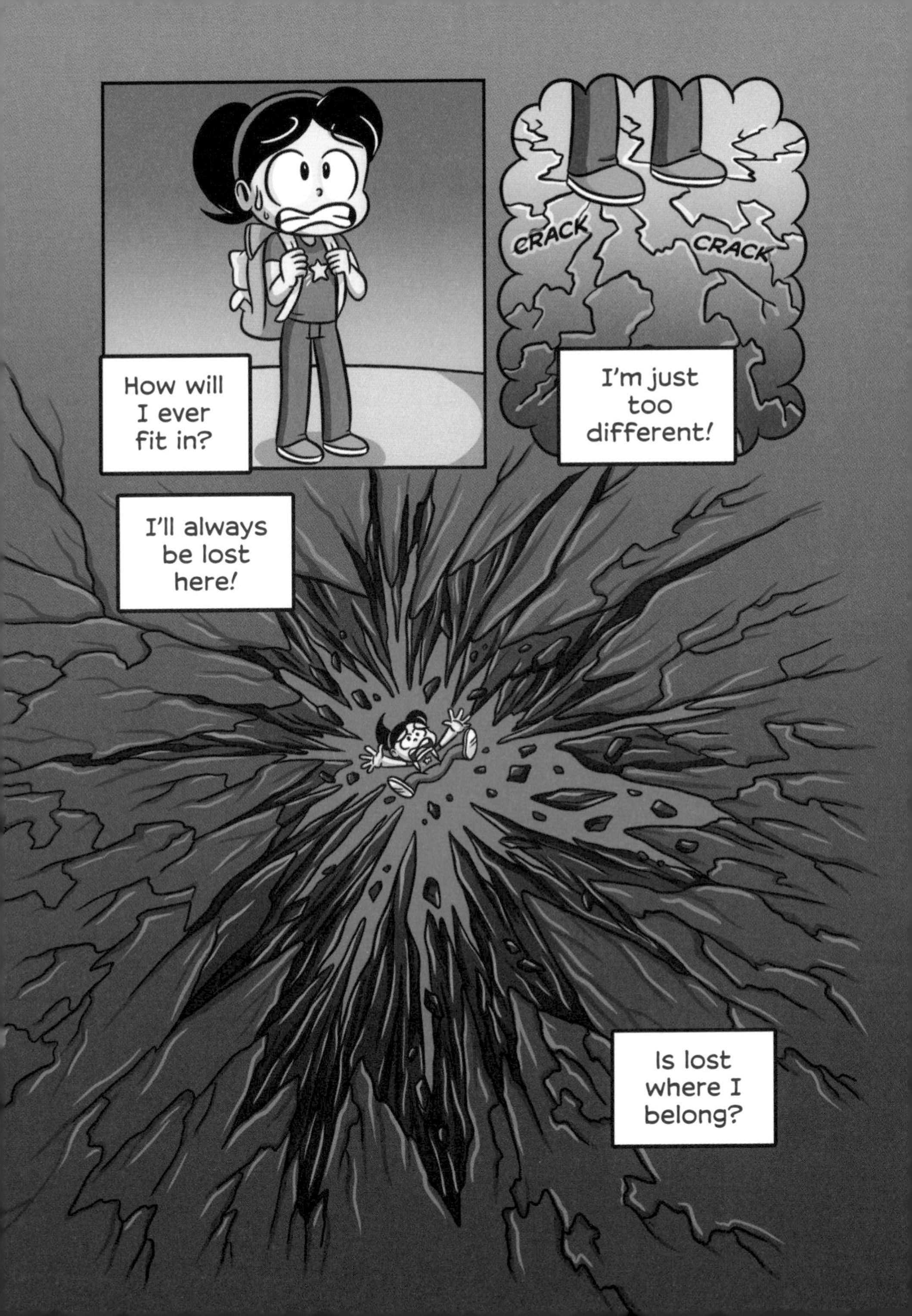
How will I ever fit in?
CRACK
CRACK
I'm just too different!
I'll always be lost here!
Is lost where I belong?

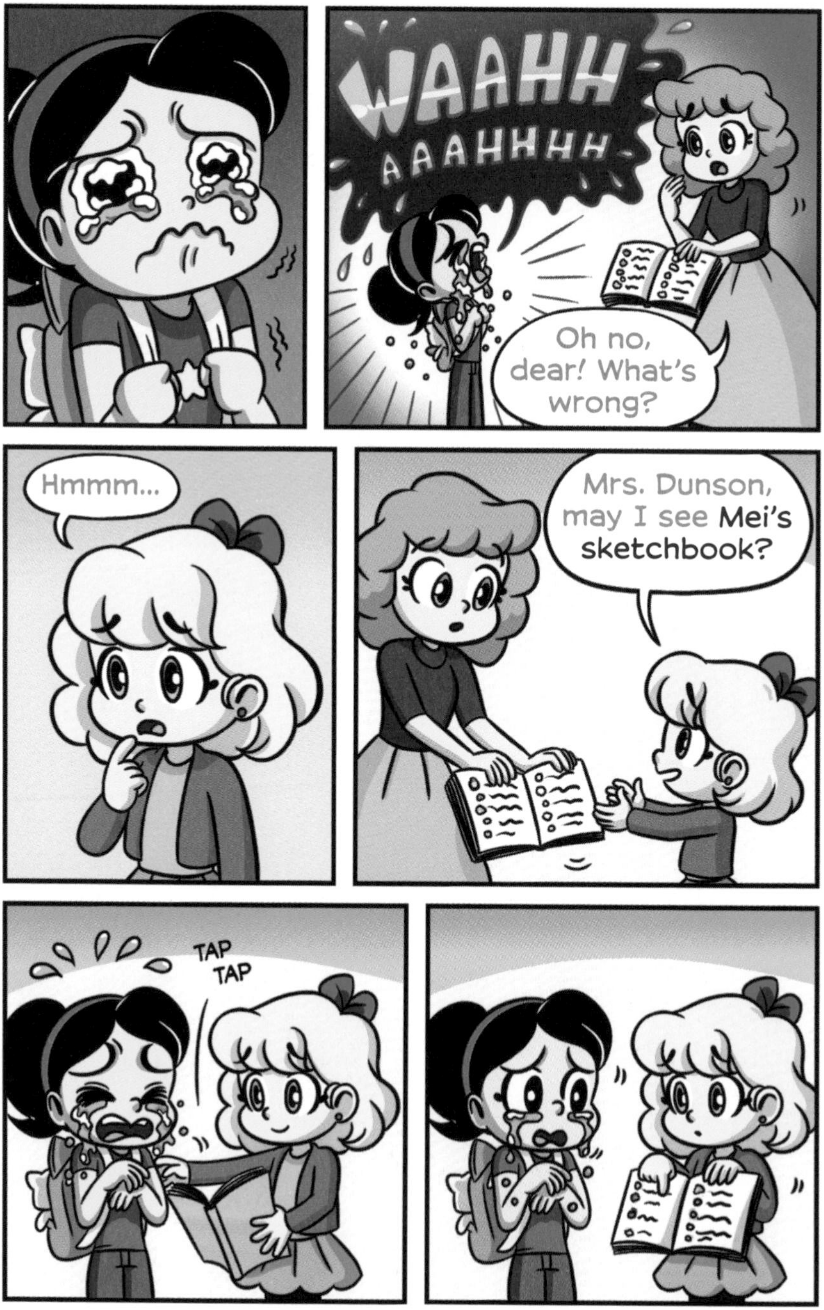
WAAHH AAAHHHH
Oh no, dear! What's wrong?
Hmmm...
Mrs. Dunson, may I see Mei's sketchbook?
TAP TAP

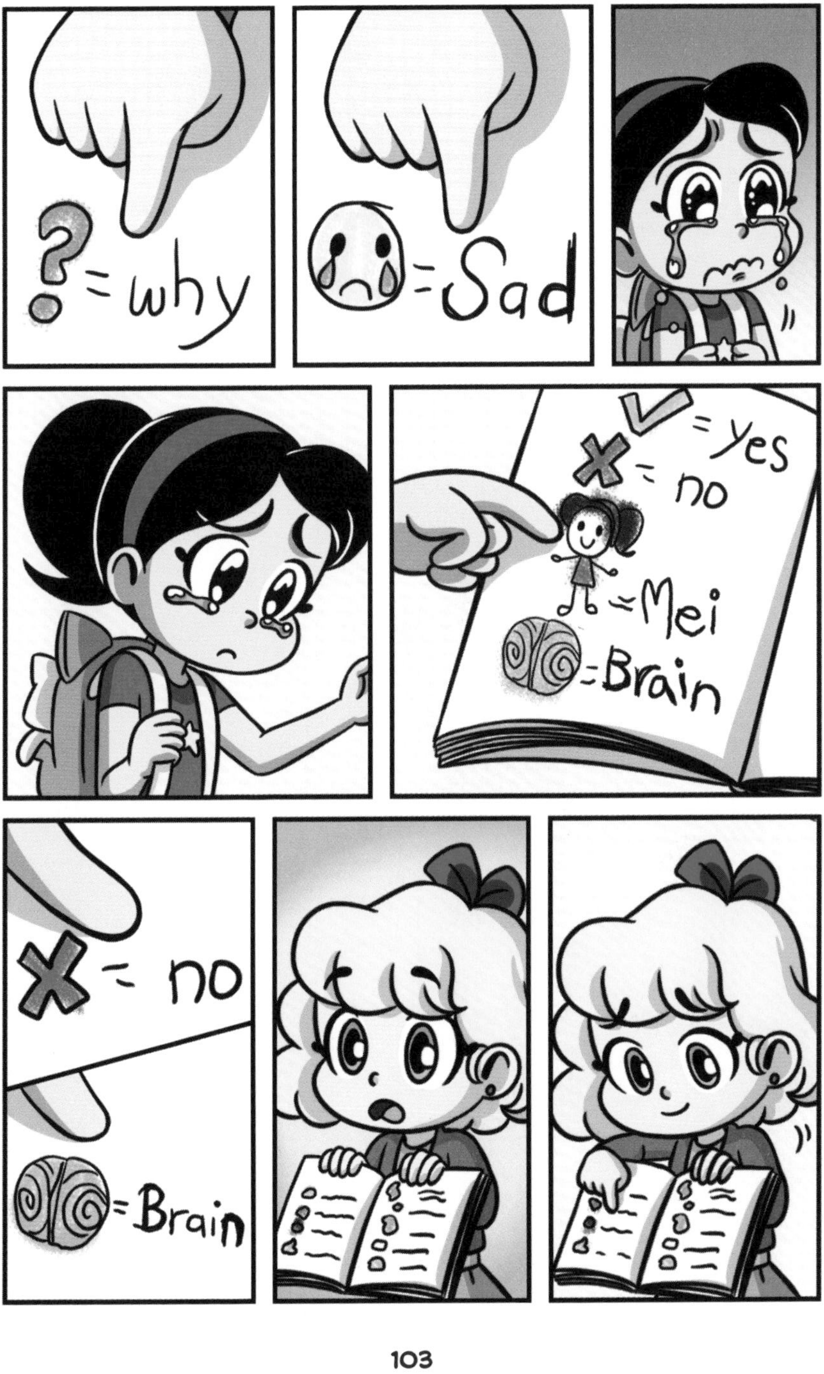
=why
=Sad
=yes
=no
=Mei
=Brain
=no
=Brain

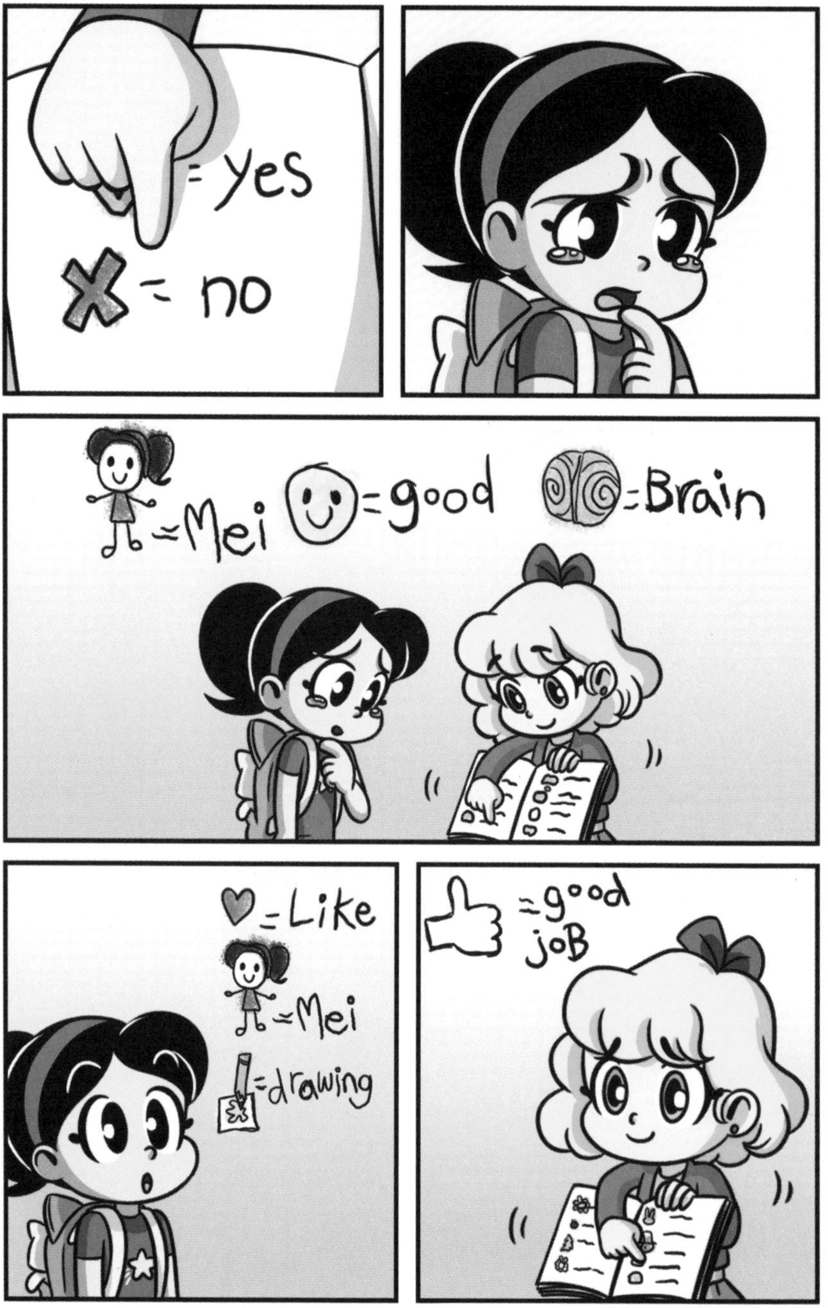
=yes
=no
=Mei
=good
=Brain
=Like
=Mei
=drawing
=good joB

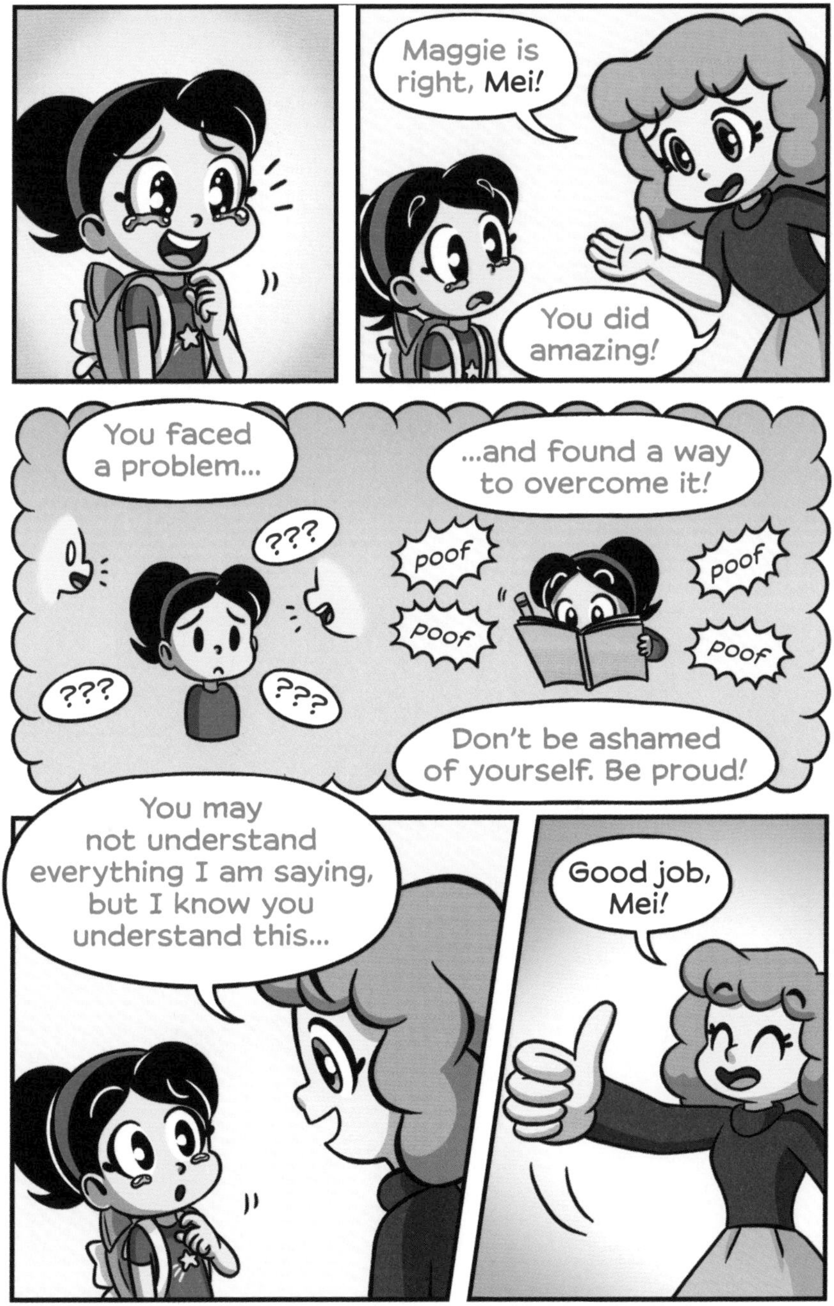
Maggie is right, Mei!
You did amazing!
You faced a problem...
...and found a way to overcome it!
???
???
???
poof
poof
poof
poof
Don't be ashamed of yourself. Be proud!
You may not understand everything I am saying, but I know you understand this...
Good job, Mei!

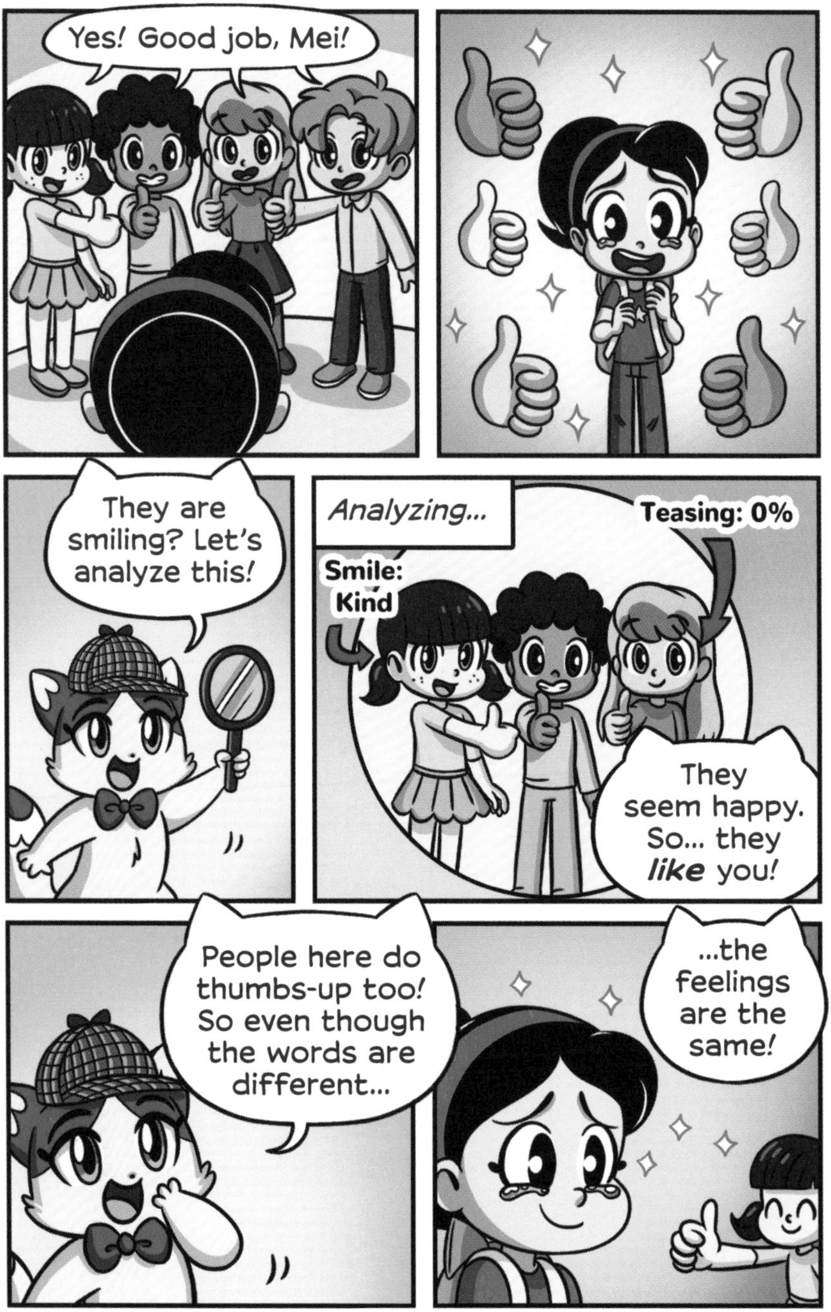
Yes! Good job, Mei!
They are smiling? Let's analyze this!
Analyzing...
Teasing: 0%
Smile: Kind
They seem happy. So... they *like* you!
People here do thumbs-up too! So even though the words are different...
...the feelings are the same!

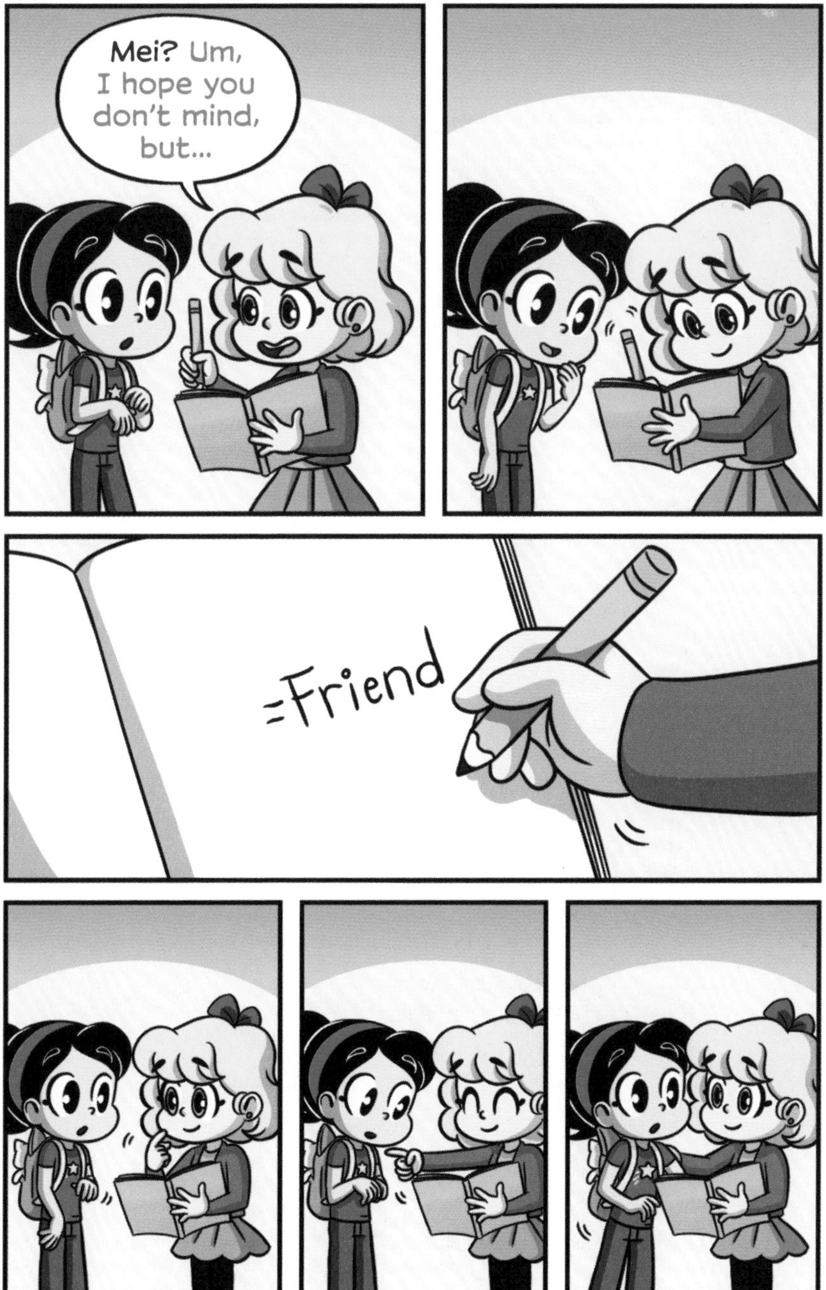
Mei? Um, I hope you don't mind, but...
=Friend

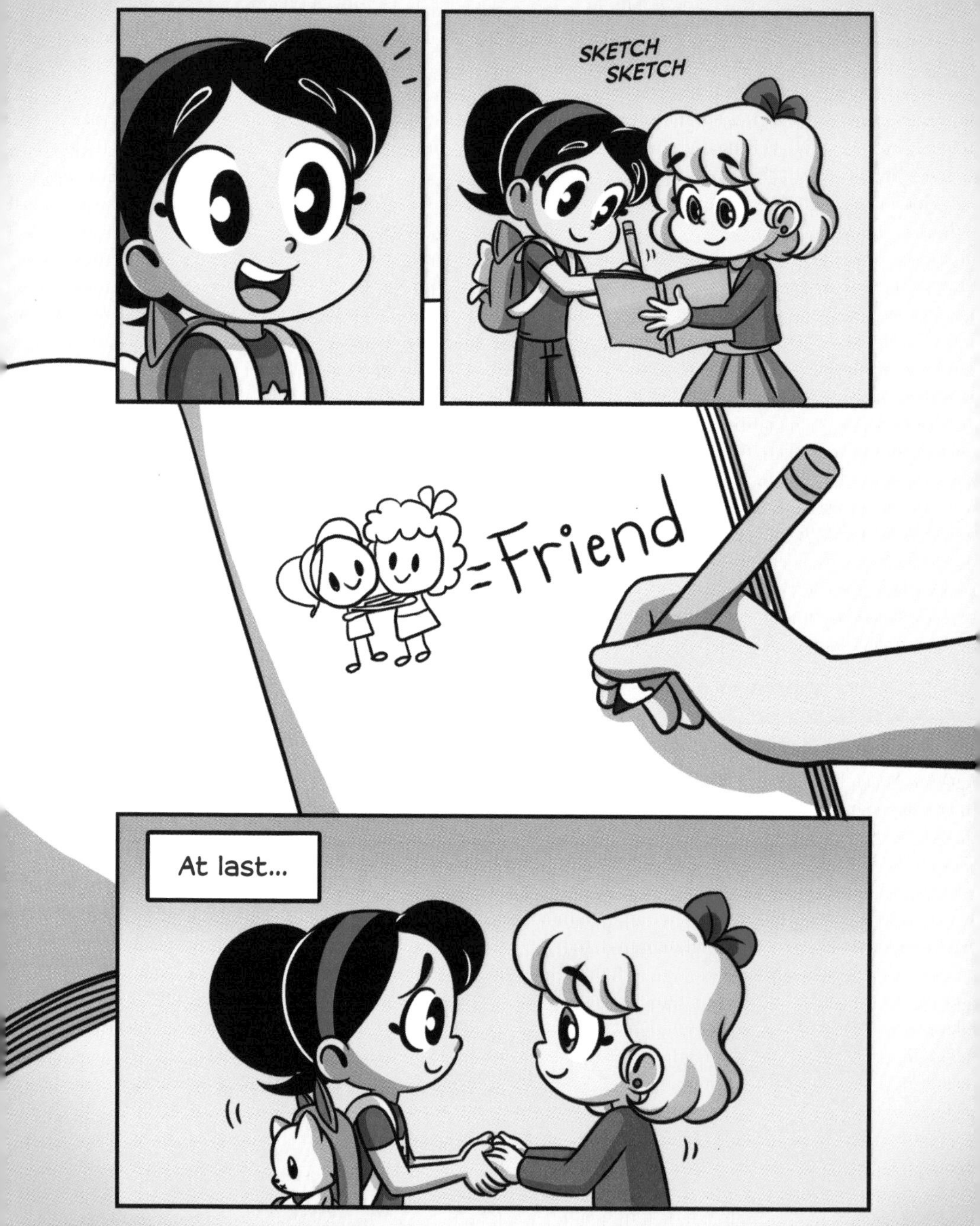
SKETCH
SKETCH
=Friend
At last...

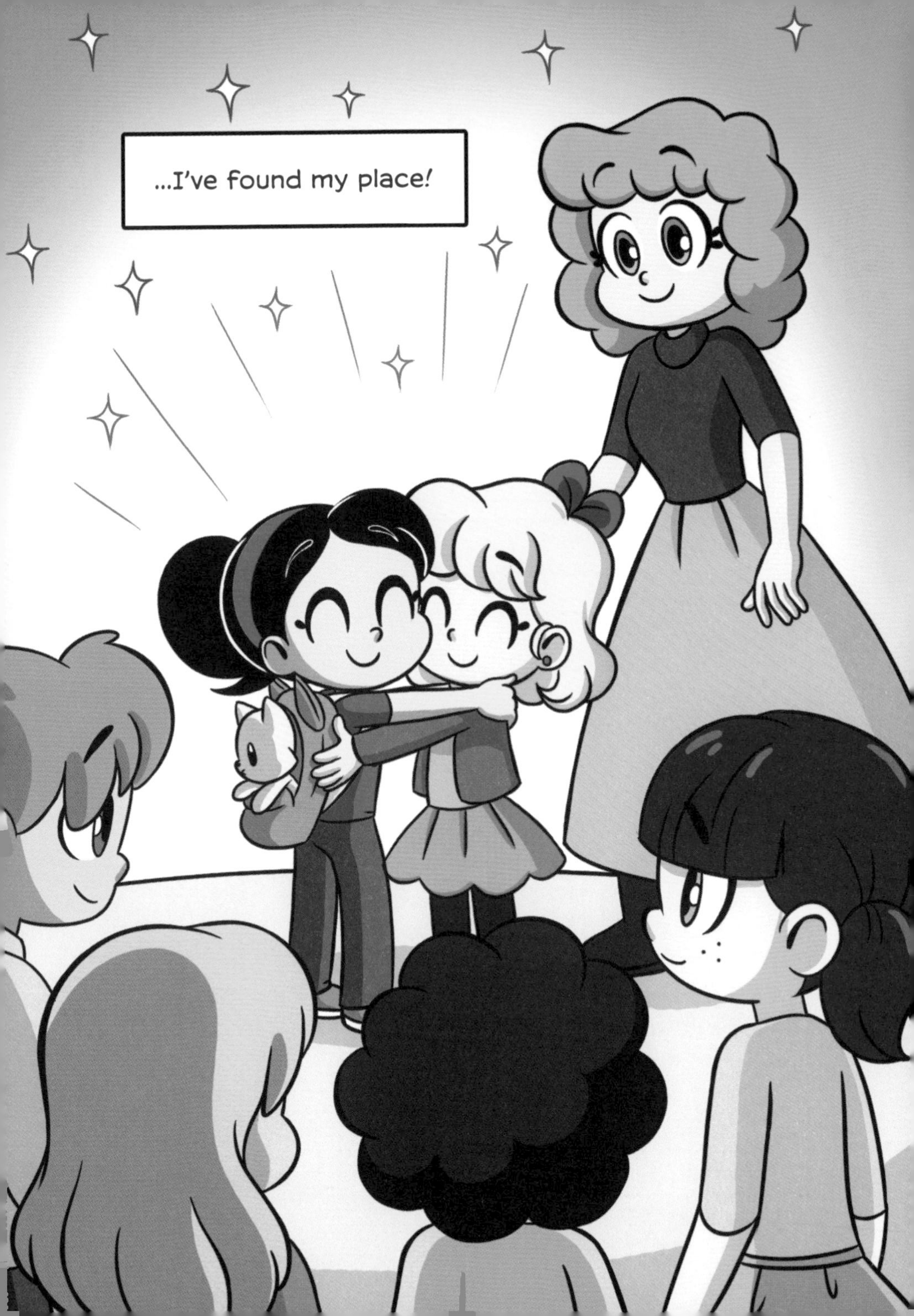
...I've found my place!

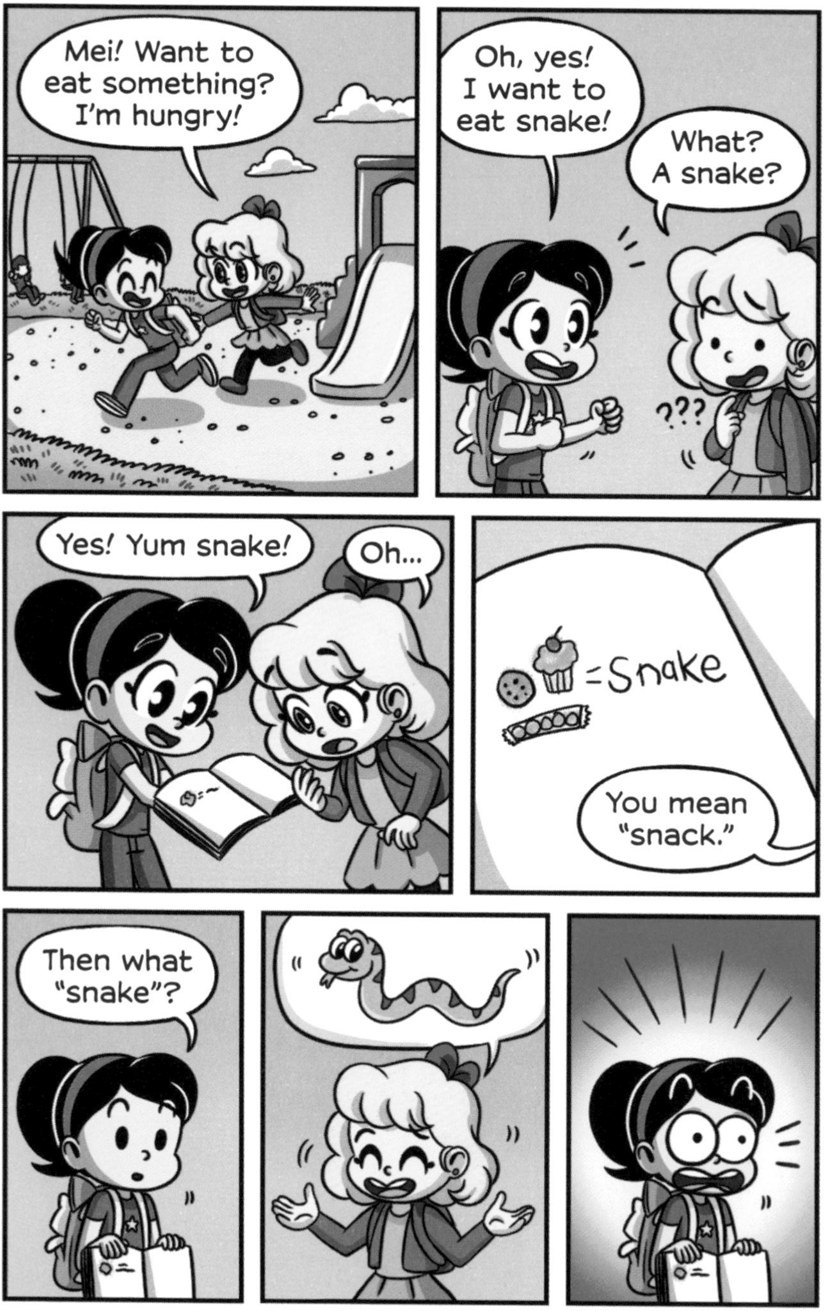
Mei! Want to eat something? I'm hungry!
Oh, yes! I want to eat snake!
What? A snake?
???
Yes! Yum snake!
Oh...
=Snake
You mean "snack."
Then what "snake"?

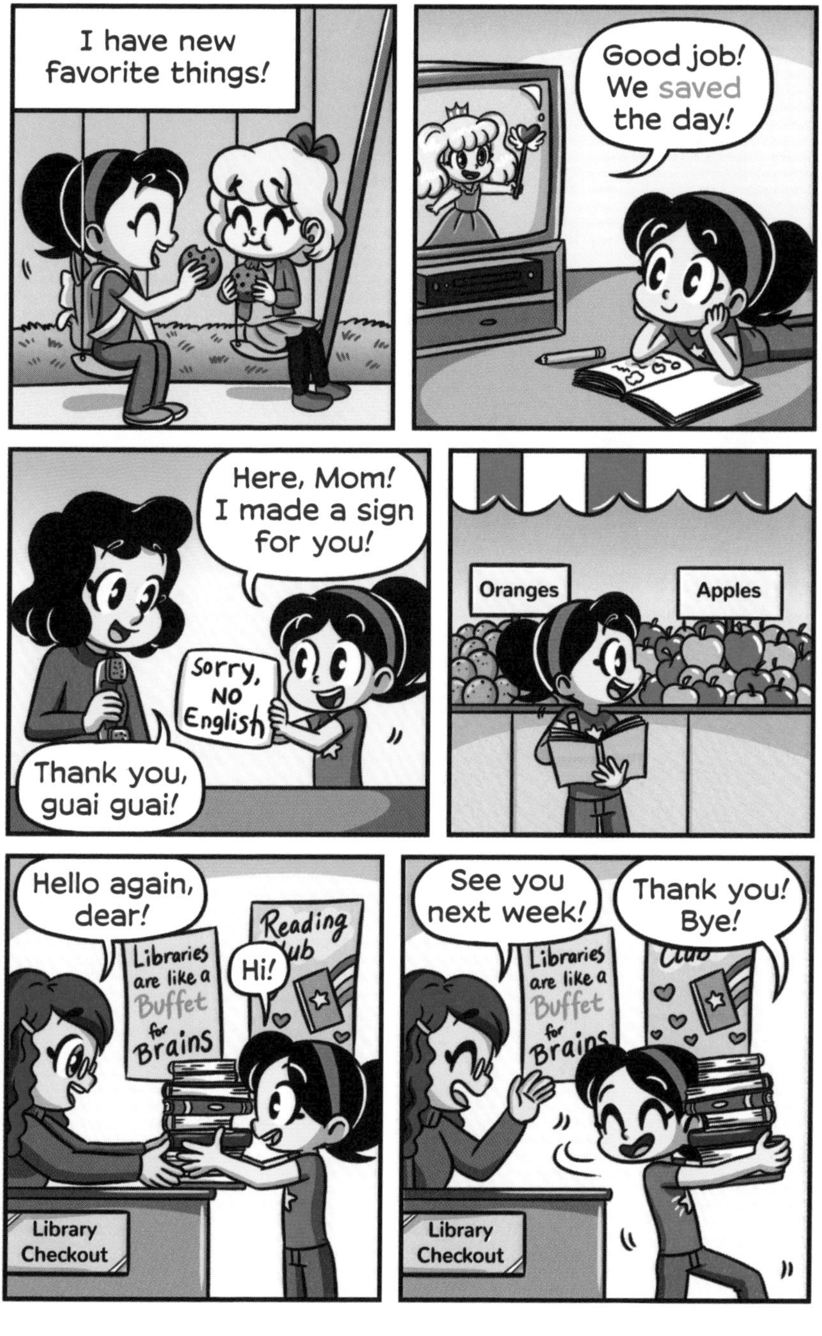

I have new favorite things!
Good job! We saved the day!
Here, Mom! I made a sign for you!
Sorry, NO English
Thank you, guai guai!
Oranges
Apples
Hello again, dear!
Libraries are like a Buffet for Brains
Reading Club
Hi!
Library Checkout
See you next week!
Thank you! Bye!
Libraries are like a Buffet for Brains
Library Checkout

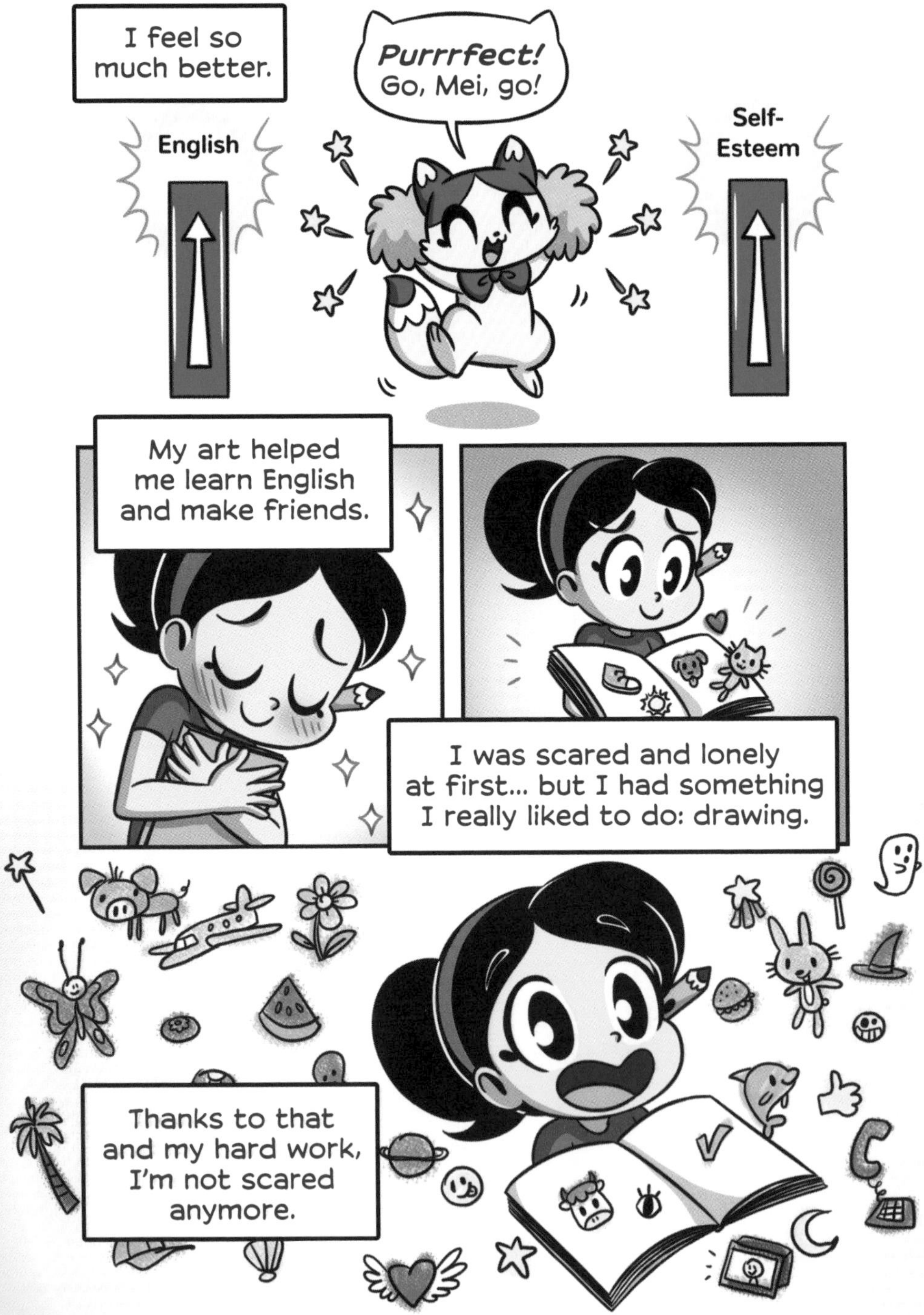

I feel so much better.
Purrrfect! Go, Mei, go!
English
Self-Esteem
My art helped me learn English and make friends.
I was scared and lonely at first... but I had something I really liked to do: drawing.
Thanks to that and my hard work, I'm not scared anymore.

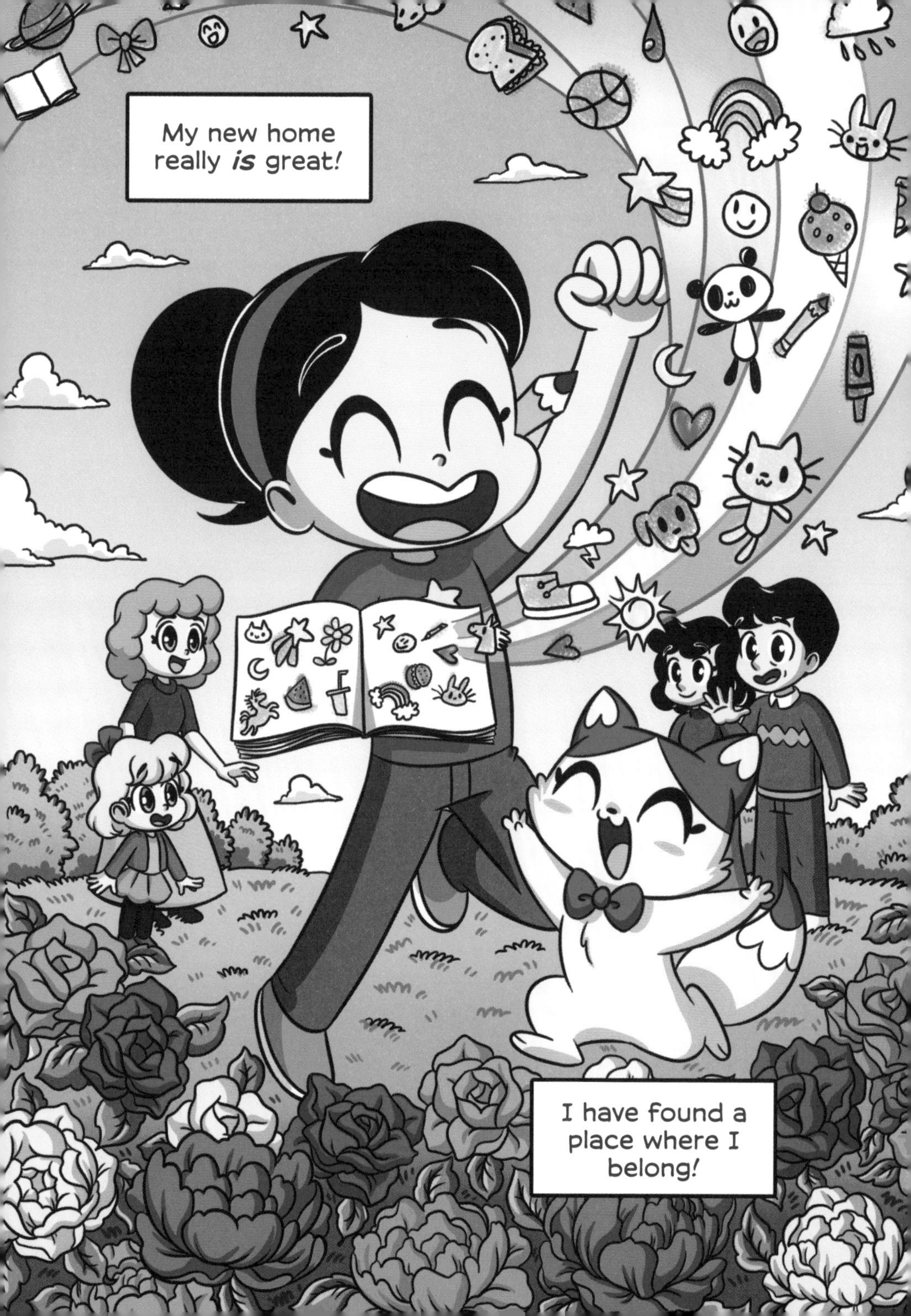
My new home really *is* great!
I have found a place where I belong!

Note to Readers

You may have noticed in this book that Mei made some spelling mistakes when she was learning English, including "buttfly" (butterfly), "ice cram" (ice cream), and "bum" (bun).

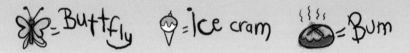

These mistakes, along with many other stories in this book, are based on my real-life immigration experience. It was really hard for me to learn English at the beginning. I misspelled and mispronounced many words.

No matter where we're from, learning a new language can be quite difficult! It is a trial-and-error process.

But that's okay! Even my mom and dad made mistakes. Mistakes are a natural part of learning anything new.

By sharing some of my misspellings and culture shock, I hope to connect with and encourage more people who may be undergoing similar struggles. It's okay to make mistakes. Just keep learning and improving, and you can get better!

Acknowledgments

I would not be able to share my personal story in
Lost & Found if it weren't for my exceptional,
hardworking, and dedicated agent, **Steven Salpeter**.
Thank you, Steven, for your unwavering belief in me and
your invaluable guidance. When I was down, you picked
me up and encouraged me to keep going. You are the
best agent an author could wish for! Without your
help, this book would not exist.

Thank you to **Jack Heller** and the rest of the
team at Assemble for your support!

A cherished thank-you to my lovely editor, **Ardyce Alspach**--
you believed in me and my story from the very beginning!
Thank you for championing my first book, for giving me your
valuable advice and feedback, and for patiently guiding me
through the editorial process with the utmost
kindness, knowledge, and dedication!

A huge thank-you to the hardworking design and
production team at Union Square Kids, including
Liam Donnelly, **Renee Yewdaev**, **Lindsay Herman**,
and **Erika Lusher**. I'm forever grateful for your
help and expertise!

To the pillars of my life: **Baba** and **Mama**.
Thank you for your decades of support and
unshakable belief in my lifelong dream of becoming
an artist and author! To my younger brother, **Shawn Yu**,
thank you for your help and endless sense of humor.
You're a keeper--even though six-year-old me
wanted to sell you.

And thank **YOU**,
my wonderful fans and
readers from around
the world.

Author's Note

Hi there! *I'm* Mei Yu.
Thanks for reading *Lost & Found*, my very first graphic novel. It's based on my true immigration story.

Going to a new place, a new school, or a new class can be scary! You might feel **LOST.**

But don't get discouraged!

Problems are only temporary. Believe that things can get better. Happiness can be **FOUND** again.

Me drawing at age five

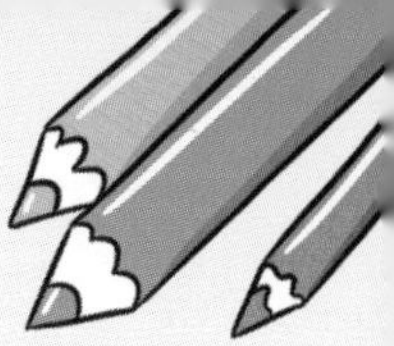

Think of something you like to do or that you enjoy! Do you like art? Crafts? Reading? Playing sports or music?

Share your interests with others! This can help you feel better and find new friends, just like Mei did in this book.

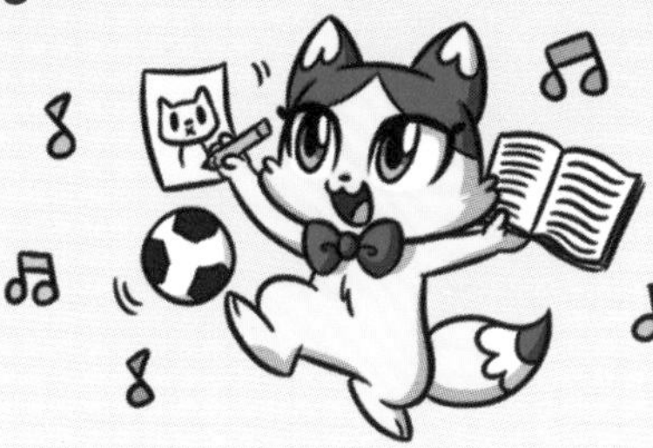

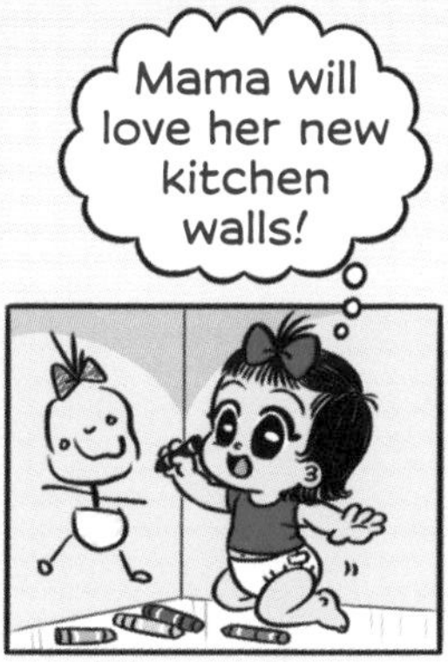
Mama will love her new kitchen walls!

When I was young, I didn't have an art teacher until high school, but it didn't stop me from drawing and practicing every day!

I started drawing at age two, when I was still in diapers. On the walls!

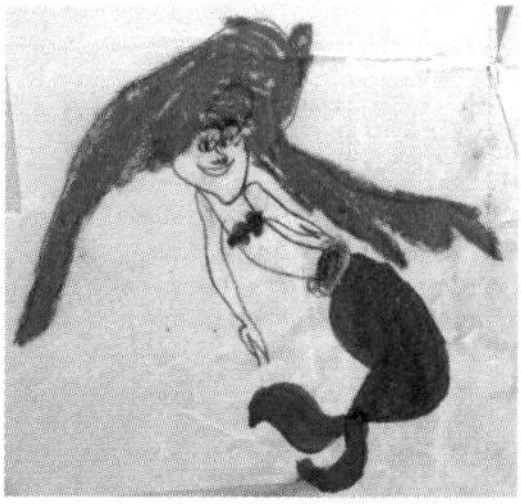

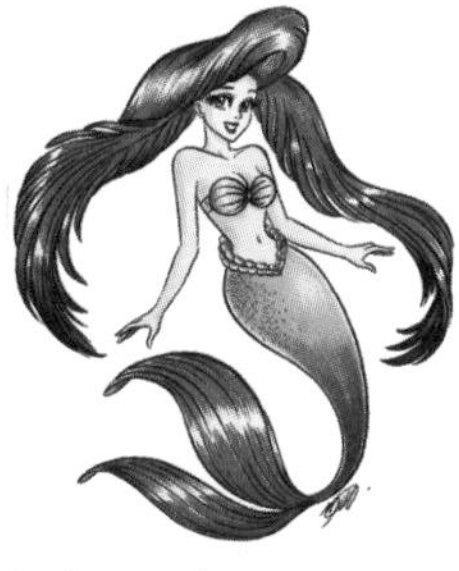

I redrew my childhood art!

As a grown-up, I redrew the art I made when I was five.
I love my childhood art as much as my current art, because without my childhood art, and practice, I wouldn't be able to draw like I do now.

Be yourself. Do what you love. Never give up!

I'm cheering for you!

Mei Yu

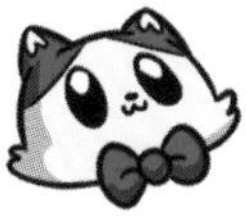

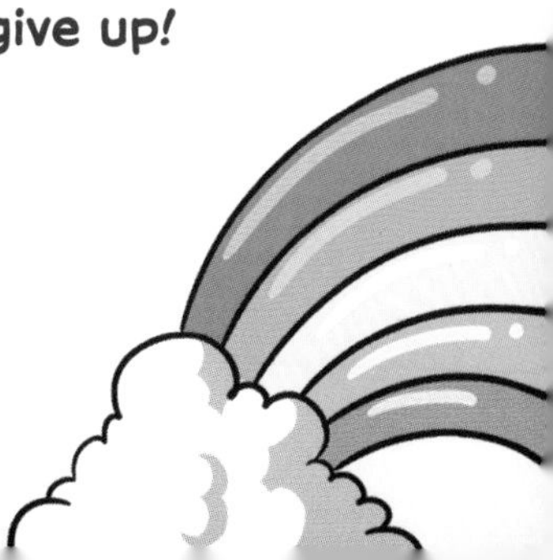

Food I like:

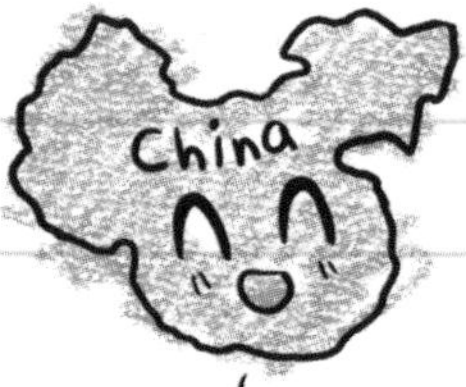
China

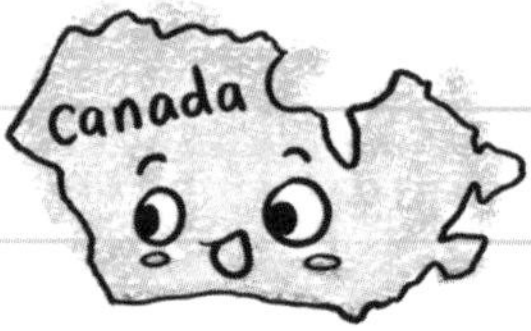
Canada

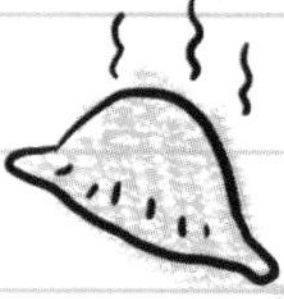

Dumplings
饺子
(Jiǎozi)

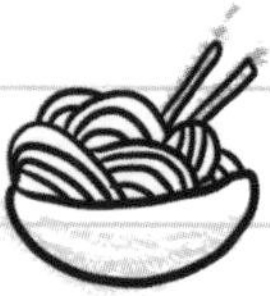

Noodles
面
(Miàn)

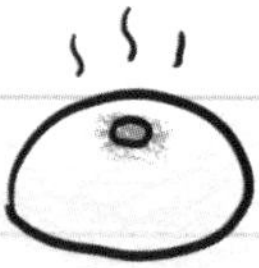

Steamed Buns
馒头
(Mántou)

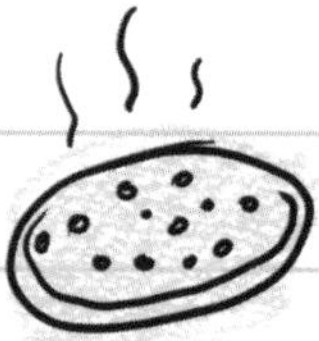

Green Onion Pancakes
葱油饼
(Cōng yóubǐng)

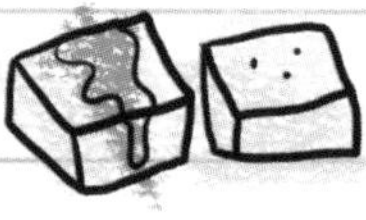

Tofu
豆腐
(Dòufu)

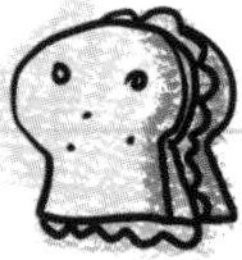

Sandwiches
三明治
(Sānmíngzhì)

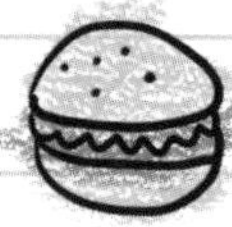

Hamburgers
汉堡包
(Hànbǎobāo)

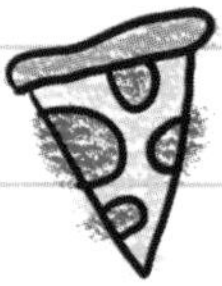

Pizza
比萨
(Bǐsà)

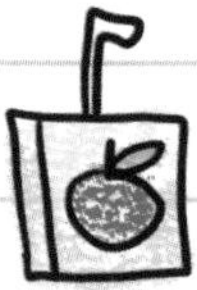

Apple Juice
苹果汁
(Píngguǒ zhī)

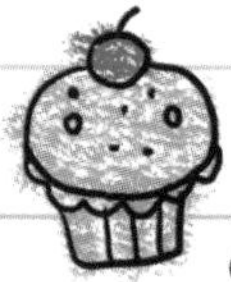

Cupcakes
纸杯蛋糕
(Zhǐbēidàngāo)

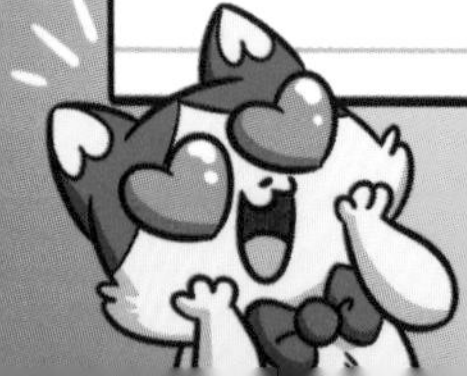

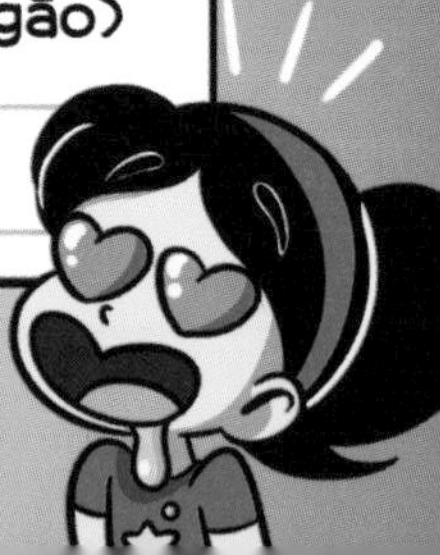

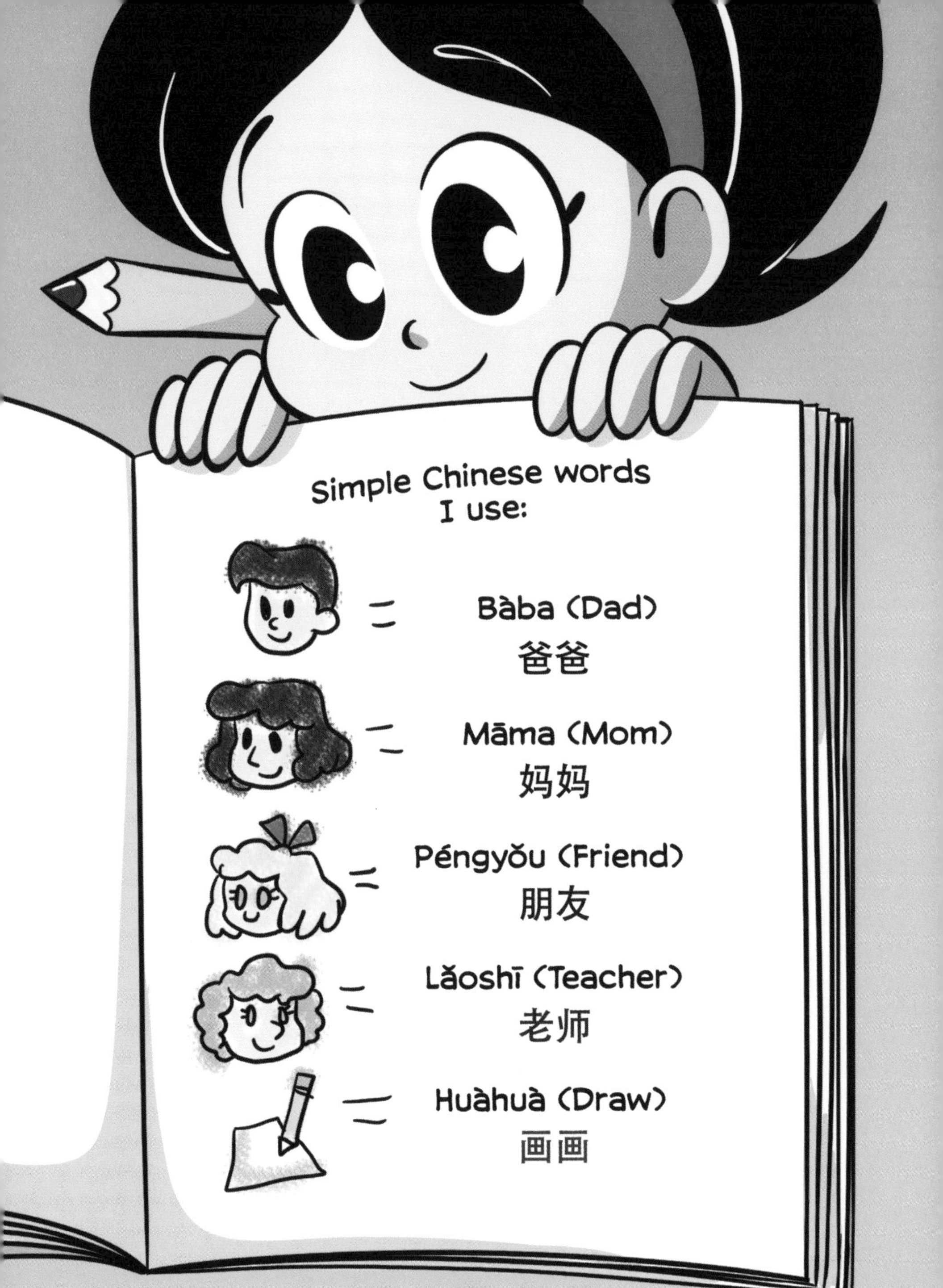
Simple Chinese words
I use:
Bàba (Dad)
爸爸
Māma (Mom)
妈妈
Péngyǒu (Friend)
朋友
Lǎoshī (Teacher)
老师
Huàhuà (Draw)
画画

Bonus Story

Saving Meiow

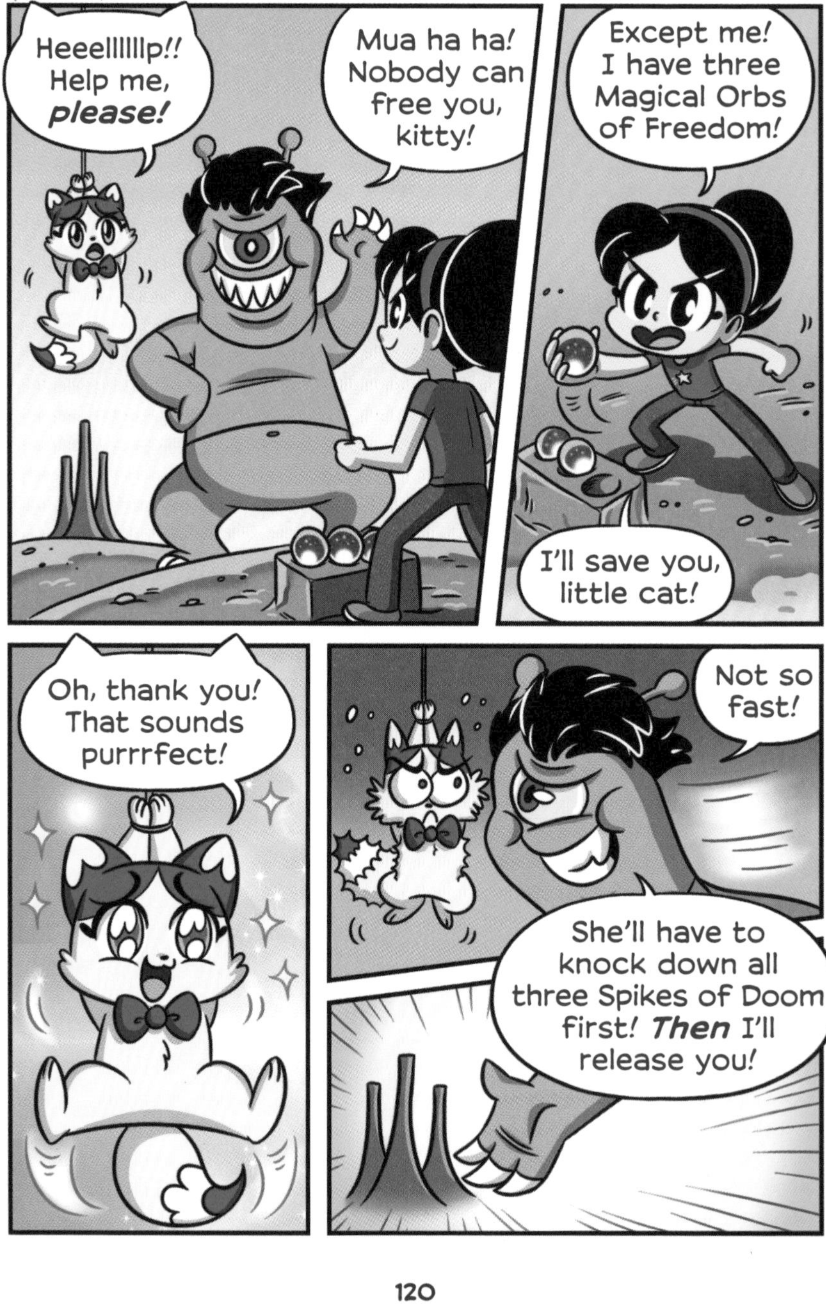

Heeellllllp!! Help me, *please!*
Mua ha ha! Nobody can free you, kitty!
Except me! I have three Magical Orbs of Freedom!
I'll save you, little cat!
Oh, thank you! That sounds purrrfect!
Not so fast!
She'll have to knock down all three Spikes of Doom first! *Then* I'll release you!

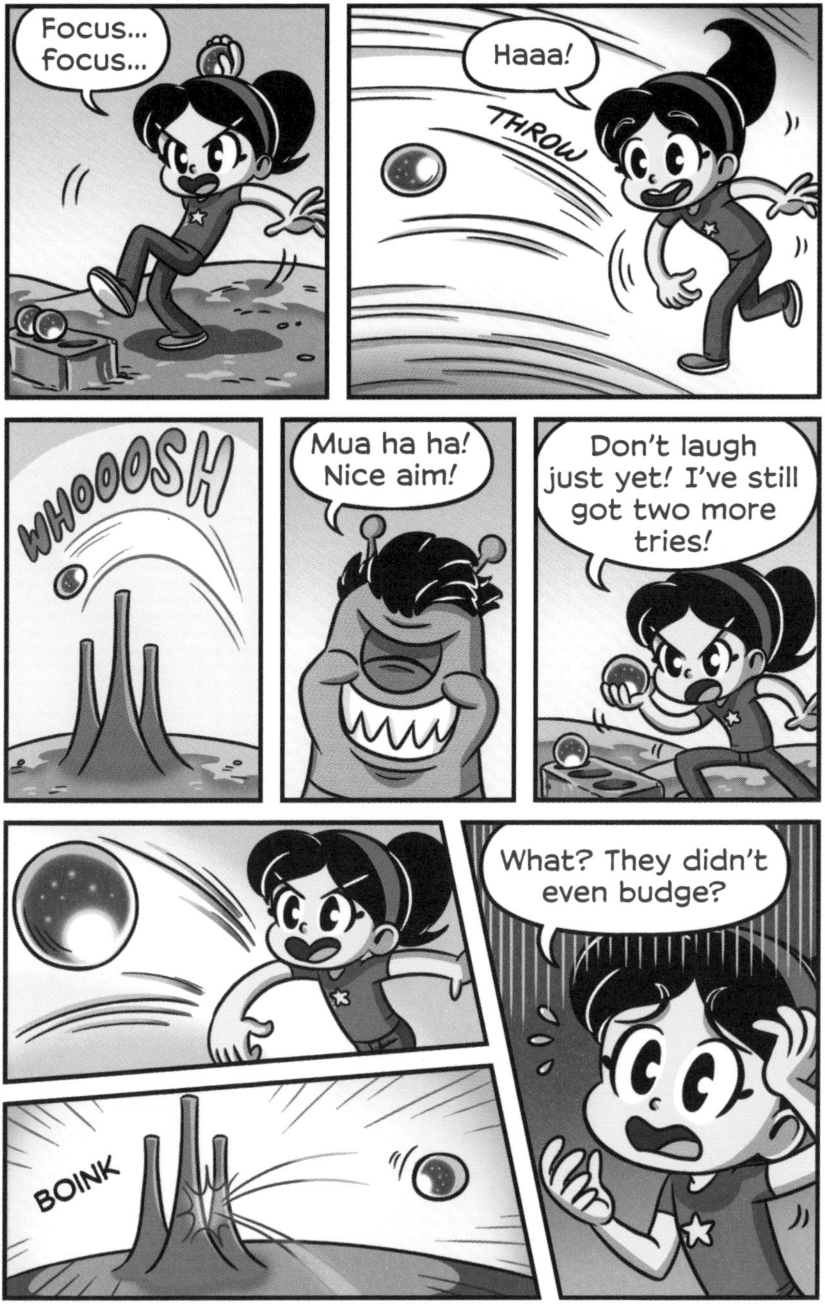

Focus... focus...
Haaa!
THROW
WHOOOSH
Mua ha ha! Nice aim!
Don't laugh just yet! I've still got two more tries!
BOINK
What? They didn't even budge?

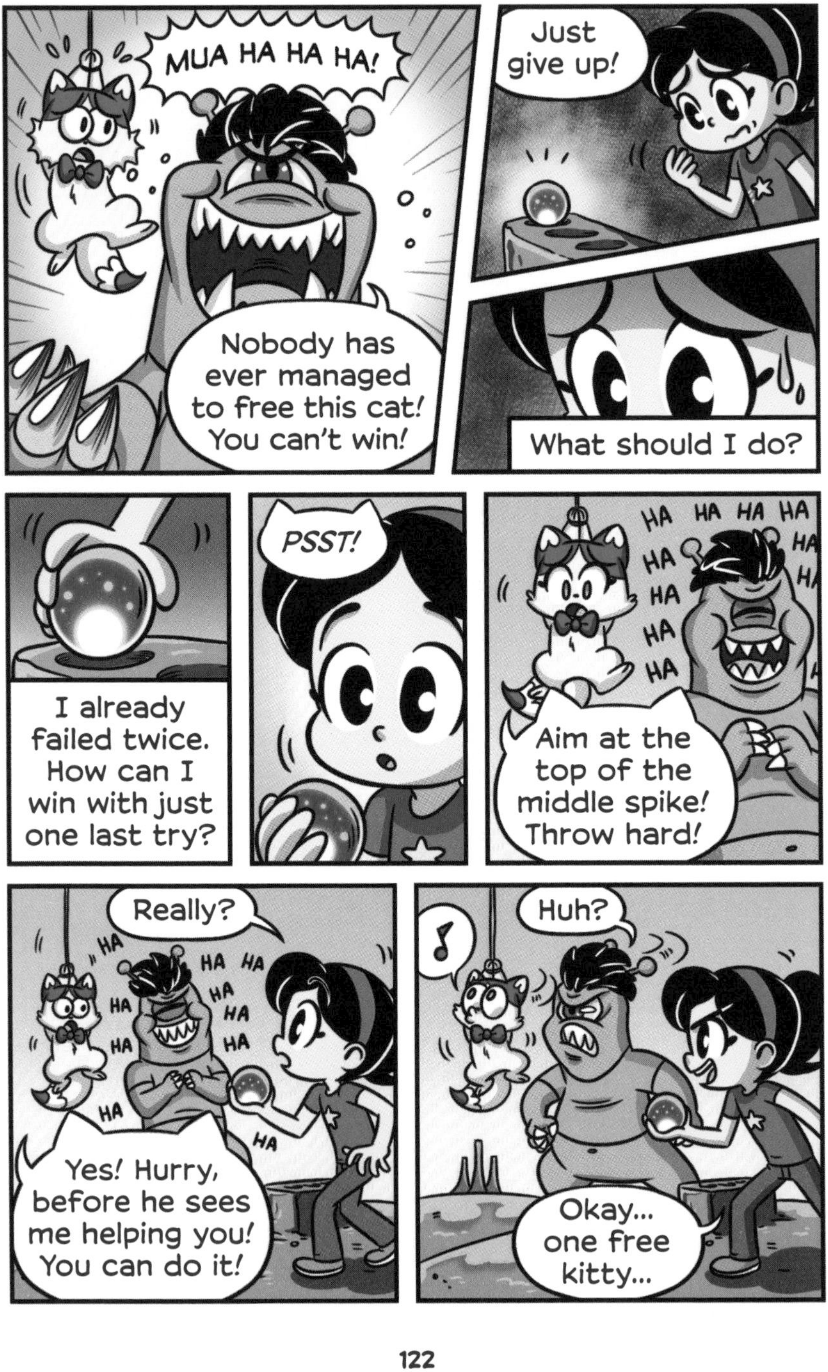
MUA HA HA HA!
Nobody has ever managed to free this cat! You can't win!
Just give up!
What should I do?
I already failed twice. How can I win with just one last try?
PSST!
HA HA HA HA
HA
HA
HA
HA
HA
Aim at the top of the middle spike! Throw hard!
Really?
HA
HA HA
HA
HA
HA
HA
HA
HA
HA
Yes! Hurry, before he sees me helping you! You can do it!
Huh?
Okay... one free kitty...

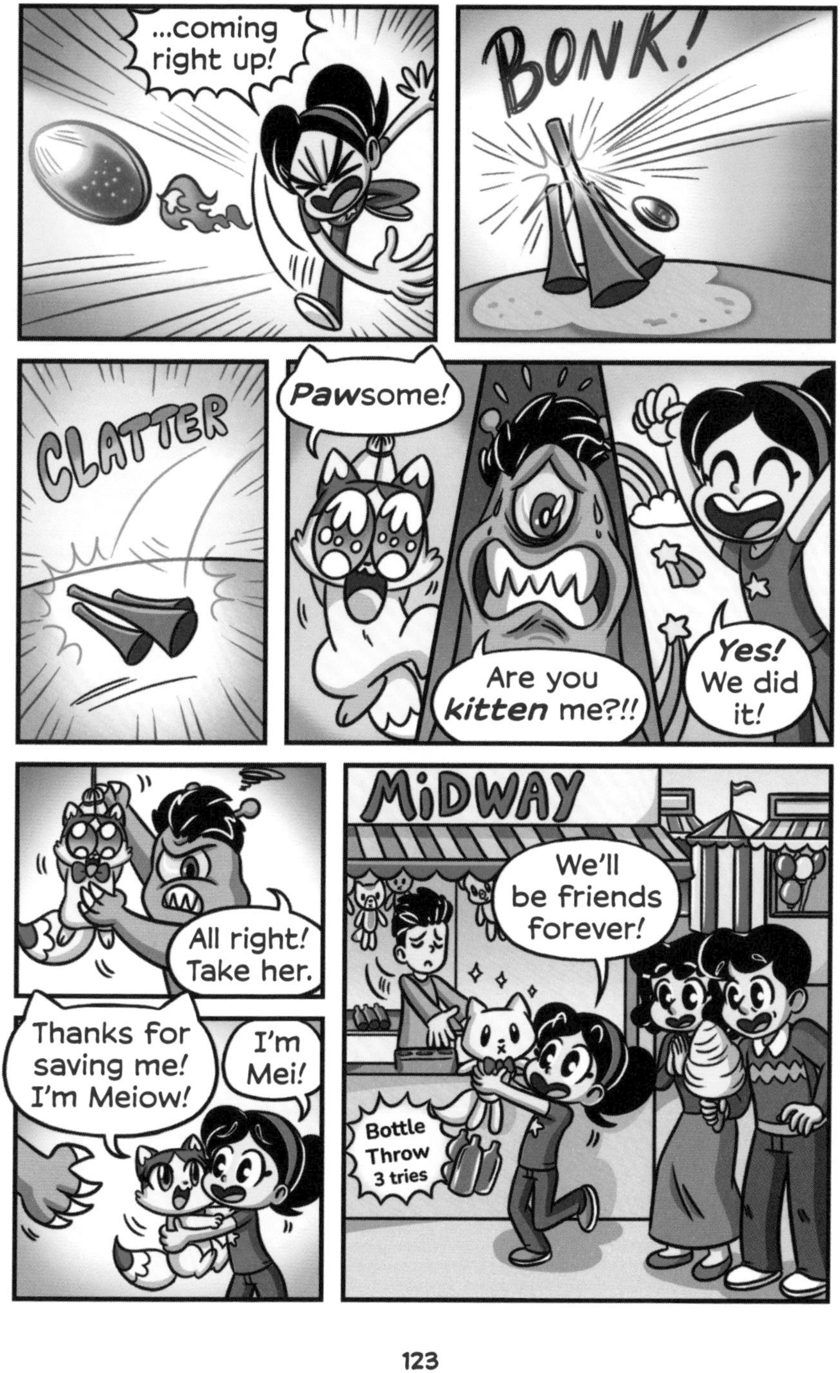
...coming right up!
BONK!
CLATTER
Pawsome!
Are you kitten me?!!
Yes! We did it!
All right! Take her.
MIDWAY
We'll be friends forever!
Bottle Throw 3 tries
Thanks for saving me! I'm Meiow!
I'm Mei!

Learn more about
the author at:
www.meiyuart.com